PEDAGOGY OPENED

Innovative Theory & Practice

Edited by Tiffani Tijerina

UNG
UNIVERSITY of
NORTH GEORGIA™
UNIVERSITY PRESS

Blue Ridge | Cumming | Dahlonega | Gainesville | Oconee

Equity Statement

As members of the *Pedagogy Opened: Innovative Theory and Practice* advisory board, we are committed to dismantling systems of supremacy, power, and privilege. By beginning with equity, we can enable action for stronger diversity, inclusion, and accessibility practices. As such, we recognize the systems, structures, policies, and practices that create barriers for marginalized populations. With this recognition, we attempt to generate transformational change through the adherence of the following values:

- Foster cultural humility and empower and respect different perspectives;
- Cultivate trust through transparency, empathy, and self-awareness;
- Stir curiosity to confront difficult problems, to be open to innovate, and to engage in creative solutions together.

In this series, we advocate for open pedagogy that centers the voices of students and educators who are historically disenfranchised and continue to be marginalized in higher education and the academic publication industry. To do this, we are committed to work toward diverse representation among our contributors and reviewers among all dimensions of diversity including racial and ethnic identities, Indigenous peoples, languages, geographic locations, ages, persons with disabilities, gender identities, sexual orientation, socioeconomic status, and lived experiences[1]. This work requires that we question biases, work to dismantle various forms of suppression, and educate ourselves through self-awareness and life-long learning. We hope that our efforts will empower our stakeholders to bring their whole, true, and authentic selves into their work.

Our goal is to produce a publication that not only includes but prioritizes the voices of those historically and currently marginalized by higher education, as well as celebrating the diversity of those voices. Through these values, intentional design, and relationship building, we aim to open and improve educational, economic, and social benefits across open education.

---

1 Thank you to the Open Education Conference for their list of dimensions of diversity found within their 2022 Call for Proposals.

PEDAGOGY OPENED

Innovative Theory & Practice

Edited by Tiffani Tijerina

Advisory Board:
Amy Eremionkhale, DePauw University
Heather Miceli, Roger Williams University
Lee Miller, Barton Community College
Judy Orton-Grissett, Georgia Southwestern State University
Elizabeth Robertson Hornsby, Southeastern Louisiana University
Veronica Vold, Open Oregon Educational Resources

Contributing Authors:
Daniela R. Amaya, University of California, Los Angeles
Michelle Barrett Ferrier, Media Innovation Collaboratory
Daniel J. Bartholomay, Texas A&M University – Corpus Christi
Lisa Bernd, Cleveland State University
Heather Caprette, Cleveland State University
Federica Goldoni, Georgia Gwinnett College
Geoffrey Graybeal, University of South Carolina
Elaine Kaye, James Madison University
Jeanne Law, Kennesaw State University
Bailey Otter, Texas A&M University – Corpus Christi
Caroline E. Parker, SRI International
Tamara Powell, Kennesaw State University
Shelley E. Rose, Cleveland State University
Krystal Thomas, SRI International
Kristina Watkins Mormino, Georgia Gwinnett College
Nicole Wilson, James Madison University

Copyright © 2024 by University of North Georgia Press

Pedagogy Opened: Innovative Theory and Practice is licensed under a Creative Commons Attribution 4.0 International License.

This license allows you to remix, tweak, and build upon this work as long as you credit this original source for the creation.

If you reuse this content elsewhere, in order to comply with the attribution requirements of the license please attribute the original source to the authors and the University of North Georgia Press.

Image Disclaimer: All images and figures in this book are believed to be (after a reasonable investigation) either public domain or carry a compatible Creative Commons license. If you are the copyright owner of images in this book and you have not authorized the use of your work under these terms, please contact the University of North Georgia Press at ungpress@ung.edu to have the content removed.

ISBN: 978-1-959203-09-4

Published by:
University of North Georgia Press
Dahlonega, Georgia

Cover Design:
Sidney Alexander, Kennesaw State University
CC BY 4.0 International

Book Design:
Corey Parson

For more information, please visit http://ung.edu/university-press
Or email ungpress@ung.edu

Table of Contents

Preface   vii
    Tiffani Tijerina, Texas Tech University and Kennesaw State University

Editor Acknowledgements   xv

Creating Learning Spaces for Social Justice Projects: Applying the Values of Critical Digital Pedagogy and Open Pedagogy   1
    Elaine Kaye, James Madison University
    Nicole Wilson, James Madison University

Open Pedagogy Assignments in Theatre and History Courses to Promote Constructionist Learning and Digital Skills   49
    Lisa Bernd, Cleveland State University
    Shelley E. Rose, Cleveland State University
    Heather Caprette, Cleveland State University

Culturally Sustaining Pedagogy & Open Educational Practices in K–8 Amidst High-Stakes Testing   79
    Daniela R. Amaya, University of California, Los Angeles
    Caroline E. Parker, SRI International
    Krystal Thomas, SRI International

Creating a Gender and Sexuality Inclusive OER World Language Course   97
    Federica Goldoni, Georgia Gwinnett College
    Kristina Watkins Mormino, Georgia Gwinnett College

A Hybrid Model of Media Entrepreneurship Using Open Pedagogy Principles   128
    Michelle Barrett Ferrier, Media Innovation Collaboratory
    Geoffrey Graybeal, University of South Carolina

Free is Good: Designing and Implementing a Composition 1 Template Course with Help from an Affordable Learning Georgia (ALG) Grant   156
    Jeanne Law, Kennesaw State University
    Tamara Powell, Kennesaw State University

Breaking the Textbook Barrier: Autoethnographic Reflections
on Open Educational Resources and Equity in Higher Education 184
    Daniel J. Bartholomay, Texas A&M University – Corpus Christi
    Bailey Otter, Texas A&M University – Corpus Christi

Practicing What We Preach: Doing Open Pedagogy in a Book
About Open Pedagogy   205
    Tiffani Tijerina, Texas Tech University and Kennesaw State University

Preface

Tiffani Tijerina, Texas Tech University and Kennesaw State University

When BJ and Corey at the University of North Georgia Press approached me in late 2021 seeking recommendations of someone with the expertise and interest in editing a monograph series on open pedagogy, my response was something along the lines of "um . . . yeah, me!" Though I have been working with open education in various capacities since 2015, I am fairly early in my career as a scholar, publishing my first peer reviewed works only in the last year. Despite my lack of publications, I felt confident in accepting this opportunity that I was fully capable of editing this series (and incredibly excited to do so), and that my status as an early career scholar in the field would be an asset to this publication and to open education in general. As you'll note in the papers we've collected in this first volume, it's incredibly important and valuable to amplify the voices of diverse and early career scholars, if only to hear perspectives and focuses beyond those we see cited repeatedly.

The advisory board for this series started with personal outreach to scholars and practitioners within my professional network whom I knew had experience in open pedagogy and instructional design of open education. I was fortunate to connect with four amazing board members, each with their own strengths. Our first task as a board was to develop an equity statement that reflected the values we wanted in this series. In developing the early drafts of our equity statement, the board recommended seeking two additional board members who could help us shape this series to publish diverse work and reach a diverse audience. After holding an open call, two additional board members joined us, bringing their own perspectives and expertise to the project. With the help of our two new members, we finalized our equity statement and also created a set of guidelines for submission review that focused on an equity lens.

Following our request for papers, each submission went through a multi-leveled peer review process. As editor of the series, I started with a round of "gatekeeping" in which I reviewed each submission to ensure they fit the series on a basic level, that they were anonymized, and that they met basic requirements of the series before continuing on to peer review. Our peer review team consisted of five members of the open education community selected via application. Each submission was reviewed by three double-blind peer reviewers—authors did not know who their reviewers were, and reviewers did not know who the authors were. At the end of that process, each of the reviewers gave us permission to publish their names in the acknowledgements of this first volume so that we could recognize and thank them for their essential contribution. At the end of the peer reviews, submissions and their reviews were then shared with the advisory board; board members read each submission and considered peer reviews before leaving their own thoughtful feedback and recommendations. We completed our review process with a live meeting in which we spent about two hours discussing each submission, its peer reviews, and its board feedback before making a decision on acceptance. Of the nine submissions we received, one was accepted immediately, six were accepted with revisions, and two were not accepted. Ultimately, all seven accepted papers were revised according to the feedback left by peer reviewers and board members.

The advisory board and I established an overarching "definition" of open pedagogy, recognizing that defining most categories of open education is rather hard to do. For the purposes of this series, we view open pedagogy as teaching and learning practices and environments that promote equity, collaboration, and innovation and invite students to create and share knowledge with future publics, often in association with the use of open educational resources (OER). And open pedagogy does not stand on its own in higher education pedagogy: "constructivist pedagogy, connected learning, and critical digital pedagogy are all recognizable pedagogical strands that overlap with Open Pedagogy" (DeRosa & Jhangiani, n.d.). Furthermore, open pedagogy is only one branch of an overarching "ecosystem of Open Education, Pedagogy, and Access" that the authors of our first paper, Kaye and Wilson, term with a general "Open" (p. 21). They echo Chtena's (2019) findings on the "social construction of openness" with their concluding question of "[h]ow might we change the ways we educate faculty about what it means to be Open that centers the common goals of Open initiatives rather than the discrete definitions that aren't even affirmed fully by our fields (Hyde & Hey, 2021)?" (p. 22).

This web of interconnected considerations in defining open pedagogy in mind, I'm thrilled to present this first volume of *Pedagogy Opened: Innovative Theory and Practice* in which we hope to synthesize the many branches and applications of open pedagogy and spark conversations that both deepen our existing knowledge and challenge us to branch further. To that end, this first volume includes seven thought-provoking discussions of research, theory, and practice within and connected to open pedagogy, each contributing a different set of ideas to spark further conversations.

In "Creating Learning Spaces for Social Justice Projects: Applying the Values of Critical Digital Pedagogy and Open Pedagogy," Elaine Kaye and Nicole Wilson start us off with a framework for social justice-centered open pedagogy that "can build community, require trust, and create spaces to share power in order to dismantle systems of oppression" (p. 21). Furthermore, their analysis of the common goals of open initiatives challenges faculty to engage in interdisciplinary work through open pedagogy, "reclaiming our praxis" from power differentials and disciplinary silos. Complimentary to this idea of "reclaiming our praxis," Lisa Bernd, Shelley E. Rose, and Heather Caprette share a series of open pedagogy assignments implemented in theater and history courses in "Open Pedagogy Assignments in Theatre and History Courses to Promote Constructionist Learning and Digital Skills." The results of those projects showed exciting opportunities to empower student voices and push back against government restrictions on curriculum because "[p]ublication of . . . students' voices supersedes restrictions on expressing and sharing valuable information about our nation's history . . . [and] provides a means of representation through participation for minority groups" (p. 53).

A few of our authors offer practical strategies for inclusive learning through open educational practices. In "Culturally Sustaining Pedagogy and Open Educational Practices in K-8 Amidst High-Stakes Testing," Daniela R. Amaya, Caroline E. Parker, and Krystal Thomas analyzed four K-8 OER programs dedicated to inclusivity to better understand how culturally sustaining pedagogy and open educational practices are being used in a K-8 context. They offer practical strategies for leveraging both for a more inclusive and equitable classroom that can be applied within and beyond K-8 education. Federica Goldoni and Kristina Watkins Mormino provide a captivating overview of gender and sexuality-inclusive language in modern language courses and the cultural issues that surround it in "Creating a Gender and Sexuality Inclusive OER World Language Course." They offer practical strategies for making world language courses more inclusive through the use of OER, including considerations for controversies in some of the target language cultures.

Open pedagogy offers opportunities for impact in non-western contexts, as Michelle Barrett Ferrier and Geoffrey Graybeal indicate in "A Hybrid Model of Media Entrepreneurship Using Open Pedagogy Principles." They developed an OER for media entrepreneurship via collaboration with a community of practice that led to programs for change in Ethiopia, supporting U.S. Embassy objectives through media innovation and digital literacy.

In "Free is Good: Designing and Implementing a Composition 1 Template Course with Help from an Affordable Learning Georgia (ALG) Grant," Jeanne Law and Tamara Powell shifted away from common focuses on student impact of OER use by creating a template Composition 1 course in response to ethical issues and institutional barriers for late-hires, part-timers, and limited-term faculty assigned to teach hybrid courses. Citing their department's hesitancy to create the template course, they state that "in an ideal world there would be no template courses, as all faculty would have the time, resources, support, and motivation to build their own" (p. 157). They provide the template course openly for use beyond their department and institution, as well.

And finally, Daniel J. Bartholomay and Bailey Otter close us out with "Breaking the Textbook Barrier: Autoethnographic Reflections on Open Educational Resources and Equity in Higher Education." They offer personal experiences with open education from the faculty perspective as well as the undergraduate student perspective. Unlike Goldoni and Mormino, who described concerns over fewer updates of OER materials in world language courses, Bartholomay and Otter found that OER are more up to date because they "are created by experts in the field who are passionate about sharing their knowledge with others" (p. 192). And echoing Bernd, Rose, and Caprette, they indicate that OER provide better representation for underserved communities and are "powerful tools for students with marginalized identities" (p. 196).

The advisory board and I are thrilled to finally present this first volume of *Pedagogy Opened: Innovative Theory and Practice*. Our hope is that this first volume will set the stage for a rich and diverse series of publications on open pedagogy and many other connected pedagogies and concepts.

References

Amaya, D. R., Parker, C. E., & Thomas, K. (2024). Culturally sustaining pedagogy and open educational practices in K-8 amidst high-stakes testing. In T. Tijerina (Ed.), *Pedagogy opened: Innovative theory and practice* (pp. 79-96). University of North Georgia Press. https://alg.manifoldapp.org/read/pedagogy-opened-v1-a3/

Bartholomay, D. J., & Otter, B. (2024). Breaking the textbook barrier: Autoethnographic reflections on open educational resources and equity in higher education. In T. Tijerina (Ed.), *Pedagogy opened: Innovative theory and practice* (pp. 184-205). University of North Georgia Press. https://alg.manifoldapp.org/read/pedagogy-opened-v1-a7/

Bernd, L., Rose, S. E., & Caprette, H. (2024). Open pedagogy assignments in theatre and history courses to promote constructionist learning and digital skills. In T. Tijerina (Ed.), *Pedagogy opened: Innovative theory and practice* (pp. 49-78). University of North Georgia Press. https://alg.manifoldapp.org/read/pedagogy-opened-v1-a2/

Chtena, N. (2019). The social construction of openness: Open textbooks and their interpretations. *The International Journal of Technology,*

Knowledge, and Society, 15(3). https://doi.org/10.18848/1832-3669/CGP/v15i03/23-40

DeRosa, R. & Jhangiani, R. (n.d.). Open pedagogy. *Open Pedagogy Notebook*. https://openpedagogy.org/open-pedagogy/

Ferrier, M. B., Graybeal, G. (2024). A hybrid model of media entrepreneurship using open pedagogy principles. In T. Tijerina (Ed.), *Pedagogy opened: Innovative theory and practice* (pp. 128-155). University of North Georgia Press. https://alg.manifoldapp.org/read/pedagogy-opened-v1-a5/

Goldoni, F. & Mormino K. W. (2024). Creating a gender and sexuality inclusive OER world language course. In T. Tijerina (Ed.), *Pedagogy opened: Innovative theory and practice* (pp. 97-127). University of North Georgia Press. https://alg.manifoldapp.org/read/pedagogy-opened-v1-a4/

Kaye, E. & Wilson, N. (2024). Creating learning spaces for social justice projects: Applying the values of Critical Digital Pedagogy and Open Pedagogy. In T. Tijerina (Ed.), *Pedagogy opened: Innovative theory and practice* (pp. 1-48). University of North Georgia Press. https://alg.manifoldapp.org/read/pedagogy-opened-v1-a1/

Law, J., & Powell, T. (2024). Free is good: Designing and implementing a Composition 1 template course with help from an Affordable Learning Georgia grant. In T. Tijerina (Ed.), *Pedagogy opened: innovative theory and practice* (pp. 156-183). University of North Georgia Press. https://alg.manifoldapp.org/read/pedagogy-opened-v1-a6/

Editor Bio
Tiffani Tijerina, Texas Tech University and Kennesaw State University

Tiffani Tijerina is a PhD candidate in the Technical Communication and Rhetoric program at Texas Tech University (TTU), where she is studying OER with the support of an Open Education Research Fellowship from the Open Education Group. She has previously served as program manager for Affordable Learning Georgia (ALG) and on the steering committee for the Open Education Conference, and she is currently an instructor at Kennesaw State University and TTU. Since 2015, she has worked on and led numerous Affordable Materials Grant projects through ALG's offerings, including producing, adopting, and sustaining OER. She is the author of several publications, including *Open Technical Communication* (http://open-tc.com/)(2020, 2016), "Perspectives from a Departmental Adoption of an Open Technical Communication Textbook" (https://programmaticperspectives.cptsc.org/index.php/jpp/article/view/40) (2023), "Fostering Student Agency Through Ungrading: Project- and Portfolio-Based Methods and Case Studies" (https://doi.org/10.13001/joerhe.v2i1.7847) (2023), and "'But who really pays when it's free?': Debunking Publisher Claims About OER in Writing Courses" (https://cdq.sigdoc.org/wp-content/uploads/2023/12/CDQ-11.4.pdf) (2023). She is the editor for this edited collection, *Pedagogy Opened: Innovative Theory and Practice*.

Editor Acknowledgements

This rich volume of scholarship and practice would not have been possible without the help and support of a several people and groups along the way.

To my advisory board, Amy Eremionkhale, Elizabeth Robertson Hornsby, Heather Miceli, Lee Miller, Judy Orton Grissett, and Veronica Vold, thank you for your expertise and guidance in shaping *Pedagogy Opened* into an emerging peer-reviewed series centered on openness, ethics, justice, and diversity in our pedagogy. Your time is incredibly valuable, and I'm thankful that you have been equally as excited as I have been to share that time for such an important project.

Thank you, in particular, to Lee Miller, for donating your time and expertise to the advisory board in our first year of project development. We were sad to lose your voice and perspective as you moved on to bigger things this past year, but we're very excited for you in your new goals.

Thank you to our peer reviewers, Clément Aubert, Tremika Cleary, Becky Cottrell, Catherine Payne, and Kristen Totleben, for your valuable input and thorough feedback on author submissions, which contributed to the completion of seven strong and thought-provoking manuscripts. *All peer reviewers consented to their names being published within the volume to recognize their time and work.*

Thank you to Leslie Hankey for working with us to implement an open pedagogy project in your visual design courses. Through our work with you, we are thrilled to be able to publish the design work of 25 undergraduate students in this volume, including that of our cover page.

Thank you to Sidney Alexander for your beautiful design work that we're excited to have as our cover art and for your openness to feedback and revision as we worked to help you finalize your design.

Thank you to the students of IAD 3150: Visual Design I at Kennesaw State University for your interest and enthusiasm to help us design our cover page. We're so excited to share your amazing work with the world openly—to see all of your designs, check out the "Practicing What We Preach: Implementing Open Pedagogy in a Book About Open Pedagogy" section at the end of the book.

Thank you to the many open education community listservs and social media tags we used to distribute our calls for advisory board members, papers, and peer reviewers over the last two years. Without these valuable communication avenues in our community, it is unlikely that we would have received the diversity of submissions we hoped for in this first volume.

Thank you to Affordable Learning Georgia for providing access to OpenALG for open and accessible sharing of this volume.

And finally, thank you to BJ Robinson and Corey Parson at the University of North Georgia Press for your confidence in me as a scholar and expert in instructional design and open educational resources to lead this project, my first edited collection.

Creating Learning Spaces for Social Justice Projects: Applying the Values of Critical Digital Pedagogy and Open Pedagogy

Elaine Kaye, James Madison University
Nicole Wilson, James Madison University

Abstract:

This chapter operationalizes the values of Critical Digital Pedagogy (Morris & Stommel, 2018; Stommel, Friend, & Morris, 2020a) and Open Pedagogy by sharing the stories from two projects that center social justice: the *Emotional Oral Histories* and *Teaching Hard Histories for Racial Healing* projects. Through these reflections with collaborators, we share how a values-based framework was applied to various layers of open pedagogy work, such as creating space for interdisciplinary faculty, staff, and student teams; supporting faculty decisions for teaching and learning; and supporting student engagement in open pedagogy. By applying this values-based framework to Open Pedagogy projects, advocates for Open can widen the entrance to Open Education as another avenue for seeking social justice in learning spaces. One key lesson from our experiences and the narratives shared in this chapter is how a values-based framework can cut across the disciplinary silos that make up our current systems to support work that is interdisciplinary and directly addresses other types of power differentials. Our work is an invitation to faculty and students to think beyond OER and textbook adoption and see how their own pedagogical and educational goals—including creating more equitable learning spaces—can be realized through Open Pedagogy. In this co-created chapter, we are amplifying student and faculty voices in the evolving understanding of the role of Open Pedagogy in social justice work.

Key words: equitable learning spaces, open pedagogy, critical digital pedagogy, values, social justice

Suggested citation: Kaye, E., & Wilson, N. (2024). Creating learning spaces for social justice projects: Applying the values of Critical Digital Pedagogy and Open Pedagogy. In T. Tijerina (Ed.), *Pedagogy opened: Innovative theory and practice* (pp. 1-48). University of North Georgia Press. https://alg.manifoldapp.org/read/pedagogy-opened-v1-a1/.

Introducing the Framework

The connection between Open Education and Open Pedagogical practices and social justice is a topic that's continuing to evolve (Bali et al., 2020; Lambert, 2018; Hodgkinson-Williams & Trotter, 2018; Roberts-Crews, 2022). Open practices are often discussed as being "transformative, ameliorative, neutral or even negative" (Bali et al., 2020, p. 3) in combating injustice. Lambert (2018) developed a definition of social justice, as follows: "A process and also a goal to achieve a fairer society which involves actions guided by the principles of redistributive justice, recognitive justice or representational justice" (p. 227). As instructional designers in higher education, as well as scholars, practitioners, teachers, and activists, we must continue to critically analyze and apply social justice as a process and a goal (Lambert, 2018); creating spaces that can hold that tension while making design choices is one aim of our framework. Through our project design process, we strive to transform the oppressive and marginalized ways of being that currently exist in social and political institutions, specifically as they intersect with higher education. The movement toward critically analyzing Open Education and Open Pedagogy as an endeavor for social justice is in clear alignment with Critical Digital Pedagogy (CDP), which inherently values social justice work. We have developed a framework that centers social justice while applying the values of Critical Digital Pedagogy and Open Pedagogy to decision-making throughout our experiences of the two projects presented in this chapter. Applying the framework (Image 1) to the various layers of Open Pedagogy work includes creating space for interdisciplinary faculty, staff, and student teams; supporting faculty decisions for teaching and learning; and guiding student engagement in open pedagogy. The three overlapping circles in the framework are representative of the co-creators and their experiences that are necessary for designing and developing Open Pedagogy projects that center social justice. In order for these three experiences to function together requires a humanized pedagogy that critically acknowledges, honors, and deconstructs power which invites students to develop a committed involvement to re-create knowledge (Freire et al., 2018).

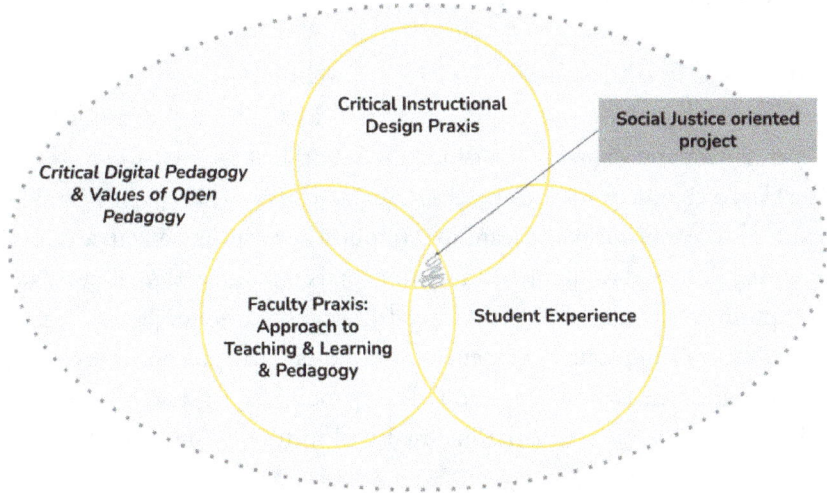

Figure 1: A values-based framework for Open Pedagogy

About the Authors

This narrative has been co-created with project collaborators, but the two primary authors are instructional designers at James Madison University. CDP has contributed to our development through necessary personal reflection and work, centering an ethic of care, and modeling our values in all we do so that we can focus on building authentic relationships with faculty and students (Kaye & Wilson, 2022). In these interdisciplinary projects, our roles include project coordination, design work, implementation, assessment, facilitation, and outreach efforts. The instructional designers had previously worked with the faculty from these projects, building trust and relationships over several semesters. Because of the ethos with which we approach our work, faculty trusted us to co-develop the projects with them where we could implement our values-based framework. Faculty and students could also take the next step of trusting the authors to be good stewards of their stories (Brown, 2021), thus deepening the conversation around Open Pedagogy.

The stories and experiences from the following project teams (e.g., faculty and students) were selected to highlight how our values-based framework has been implemented, but specifically these projects are exemplars of how faculty and instructional designers can build trust.

Emotional Oral Histories

The authors have supported Dr. Kristen McCleary in her pedagogical development and digital scholarship. The Emotional Oral Histories project is a class assignment for a General Education course. This course examines issues in recent history as a means to introduce, develop, and enhance critical thinking skills and to supplement writing, oral communication, library, and computing skills objectives for General Education. The project is a major component of the course. Students move through the process of preparing for, conducting, transcribing, and sharing publicly on a website (Social Change Interviews, 2023) the finalized oral histories. For more detail on the project see the [Open Ed conference presentation](https://youtu.be/habFdzPj08) (Kaye, Wilson, et al., 2021).

Teaching Hard Histories for Racial Healing

The authors are part of a multi-disciplinary and multi-institutional project team focusing on developing open-curricular and pedagogical materials for secondary education that use the research and scholarship on the history of lynchings in Virginia (JMU COE Curriculum Development Team, 2021). Our team includes College of Education and Justice Studies faculty, Libraries faculty and staff, and graduate students (De Fazio et al., 2021; Kaye, Cancienne, et al., 2021). The foundation for the lesson plans comes from the digital scholarship project, Racial Terror: Lynching in

Virginia, and work of Dr. Gianluca DeFazio and his students over the past few years.

Trust and Praxis

As educators, activists, and learners, we must create and engage in communities of trust that are built on an ethic of care because at the heart of CDP is "a way we treat one another" (Stommel, Friend, & Morris, 2020b, p.2). Through our personal and professional growth, the authors have developed a community of trust. Charles Feltman defines trust as "choosing to risk making something you value vulnerable to another person's actions" (Brown, 2021b). Trust is strengthened through behaviors like reliable collaboration, extending generosity toward each other, making space for and engaging in difficult conversations, and a commitment to self-reflection and curiosity (Brown, 2023). Pearce et al. (2022) highlight the importance of bringing care into the classroom when doing the work of Open Pedagogy. We create spaces where care is modeled and experienced. The role of praxis as part of CDP is one of the most powerful spaces of activist teaching (hooks, 1994).

Defining CDP and the Open Values

Stemming from Critical Pedagogy, specifically the work of Paulo Freire, CDP is a growing approach to education; it is a social justice movement and a "method of... humanization" that's desperately needed in all levels of our education systems (Morris & Stommel, 2018, ch. 1). CDP leverages the questions and perspectives of critical theory to de-center the role of technology in teaching and learning, and re-center our humanity (Morris & Stommel, 2018; Stommel, Friend, & Morris, 2020a). Diverse voices build a shared understanding of CDP through the reflection and practice of its core tenets. One key distinction between CDP and other approaches to education is the insistence that teaching is political—we cannot separate education and politics. From its historical roots in Critical Pedagogy, CDP and those that ascribe to this work "hold values that are anti-racist, anti-patriarchal, anti-capitalist, anti-fundamentalist" (Rorabaugh, 2020, p. 15). CDP upholds the following values: "centers its practice on community and collaboration; requires invention to reimagine the ways that communication and collaboration happen across cultural and political boundaries; [. . .] cannot be defined by a single voice; [. . .] have use and application outside traditional institutions of education; [. . .] open and networked educational environments [. . .] must create dialogues in which both students and teachers participate as full agents" (Morris & Stommel, 2018, ch. 1).

One key lesson from our experiences and the narratives shared in this chapter is how a values-based framework can cut across the disciplinary silos that make up our current systems to support work that is interdisciplinary and directly addresses other types of power differentials. When people (e.g., faculty, students, and community members) see themselves represented and have a shared goal of creating knowledge that's more accessible and inclusive, we can move towards creating a more socially just world. Audrey Watters (2020) writes, "The web promised openness. Open access. Open knowledge. Collaboration. Distribution. Instead what we have today is a mass of information silos and content farms. What we have today, if we're honest with ourselves, are old hierarchies hard coded into new ones" (p. 27). CDP provides a guide to question the technologies we use in the process of open pedagogy and to seek better ways of dismantling and re-imagining these old hierarchies, rather than centering digital tools as a savior for teaching and learning.

As our project teams learn, reflect, and refine our processes (Kaye & Wilson, 2022) and outcomes, all of our work is underpinned by the values stated in the 5 Rs for Open Pedagogy: respect, reciprocity, risk, reach, and resist. Jhangiani (2019) defines the 5 Rs and invites us to use, remix, and be in conversation about how these values can move our work forward. Below you will see a few examples of how the 5Rs show up in our spaces of praxis as well as the connections we make with the values of CDP and how we use the values to name our choices and behaviors.

We experience and center **respect** for all voices, which is required to uphold the value of CDP that states that it "...cannot be defined by a single voice" (Rorabaugh, 2020 p. 15) and take great care to focus on how the stories and experiences of interviewees and people of the past are honored. We analyze the role of respect in the classroom and what this means for labor-intensive processes. Finally, being intentional and leveraging the values of respect make space for authentic and valuable collaboration.

Reciprocity is only achieved through vulnerability from those involved (Brown, 2010). The *Teaching Hard Histories for Racial Healing* project is created upon the value of reciprocity. For example, scholarship and teaching practices directly inform each other when openly published lesson plans, which use primary sources and digital scholarship, engage current and future educators to rethink and redesign curriculum—which can then be shared back out. Creating teaching spaces that center reciprocity is deeply connected with the work of CDP which requires building spaces of praxis that question power structures and seek to dismantle oppressive systems, in and outside of the classroom. In our project teams, we intentionally and collaboratively articulate the narratives about each project while considering the needs of each team member in terms of promotion, tenure, and annual evaluation processes.

We consciously understand and grapple with the **risks** involved for all—the risk for students publishing openly, the risk for interviewees, and the risk of our teams engaging in social justice work—while also acknowledging the privileges and responsibilities we hold as a group. The value of risk is closely tied to the CDP tenant that teaching is inherently political—it is the politicized nature of education that makes this work "risky". When the values of Open and CDP are used as a framework for social justice projects, we can also see when the decisions to create open materials or engage with open projects become political. We often discuss and assess the risk for faculty and teachers who implement these pedagogical practices—recognizing that some departments and systems don't value digital projects or Open Pedagogy and instead prefer more traditional forms of teaching and scholarship. We also acknowledge the risk involved for the interviewees and emphasize their agency and choice in the process of determining what information is public and how it is presented.

When students are publishing openly, the work **reaches** beyond the semester and the classroom. Future student-scholars can use and add to this work, current teachers can implement and adapt lessons, and faculty can incorporate content into other courses, and these resources are open to all. Gathering and sharing stories openly that are not available via traditional informational materials is aligned with the CDP value of "having use and application outside of traditional institutions of education" and "re-imagining the ways in which communication and collaboration happen across cultural and political boundaries" (Morris & Stommel, 2018).

Inherent in our being and work is a focus on **resisting** the structures and tenets of white supremacy culture (Okun, 2022) and other systems of oppression. The value of resistance clearly overlaps with the values of CDP (Rorabaugh, 2020). Specifically, we approach our spaces with a "method of humanization" (Morris & Stommel, 2018). Also, as mentioned earlier, we are specifically focused on resisting the hierarchical structures inherent in higher education and empowering students.

The following image is a representation of the values of CDP and Open Pedagogy that guide the work of social justice projects, like the *Emotional Oral Histories* and *Teaching Hard Histories for Racial Healing* projects. By sharing these values and framework with faculty and students, we can design learning spaces, make project management decisions, choose curriculum, construct pedagogical practices, and formulate assessments that are grounded in liberatory practices (Freire et. al., 2018; hooks, 1994).

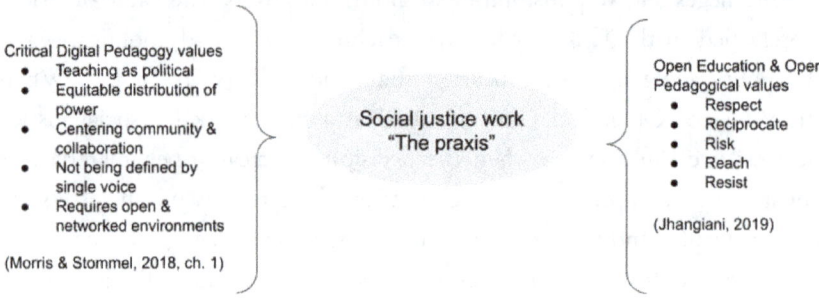

Figure 2: Applying the Values of CDP and Open as "The Praxis" for Social Justice Work

The Process of Co-creating our Narrative

Above, we have described the values that influence our work—the approach to collecting, reflecting on, and sharing out the stories of our collaborators was based on the same values. For example, the designers selected possible publication venues that allow for the acknowledgement of contribution from faculty and students as authors to clearly elevate the voices of faculty and students. The purpose of gathering narratives from our collaborators is not to create an original research study but rather to tell the story of these projects in a way that is equitable, inclusive, and demonstrates "good story stewardship" (Brown, 2021a, p. 265). When reviewing the written responses, the authors went line-by-line and through a lens of respect to bring in as much of each narrative as possible to highlight how the values from our framework are experienced by both faculty and students in the implementation of an Open Pedagogy project. We have organized the shared experiences into themes to support readers as they engage with these reflections in order to engage in a more inclusive dialogue about Open Pedagogy. Our goal in doing this work is to amplify student and faculty voices. To gather our stories for the chapter, we created tailored and open-ended reflection questions for all stakeholders to respond to in writing if they were interested in contributing. Finally, this process also included conversations about how the authors could use the reflections provided.

Contributor Responses

The co-constructed findings section is organized around the themes from the questions we asked. The authors have selected contributors' quotes that highlight their experiences and support connections to the values of CDP and Open Pedagogy. Readers can engage with full responses, and we encourage you to do so. It's important to note that not all collaborators chose to contribute a response.

Faculty and Students' Evolving Perceptions of Open

As instructional designers, we have grappled with what Open means for our work. Being part of an academic library, we have observed and participated in the trends around the field of Open. The field of information sciences has made progress in labeling and defining the various aspects of Open: open access, open publishing, open educational resources, open pedagogy, and open educational practices (Lambert, 2018). While these definitions have provided a foundation and moved open efforts forward, at what point do the discrete distinctions become a barrier to making Open for everyone? In their responses, it's clear that faculty and students view and label open as a more singular goal by often referring to this larger idea as "Open". This indicates how they value access, publishing, and pedagogy as all work toward a common goal. Through the implementation of these projects, faculty indicate a clear and expansive growth in terms of how they understand—and label—Open. It's important to acknowledge that the reflection and vulnerability needed to accomplish this growth doesn't happen serendipitously. By grounding the projects in the values of CDP and Open Pedagogy, we can hold space for transformative experiences. These faculty reflections exemplify this:

> Prior to engaging in this project, I had very little understanding of Open Educational Practices. My familiarity with Open was largely as a consumer. For example, I had accessed some resources on Open to support a book talk. My evolution of understanding regarding Open Educational Practices, therefore, was quite substantial during this project. I have learned why Open is important, discussed this importance with my students, learned about copyright, and engaged in the process of creating, editing, and uploading items to Open.

> I had not heard of open educational practices. However, now that I have worked with this team *Teaching Hard Histories for Racial Healing* project I have an in-depth understanding of what it means for educational materials to be Open.

Students also indicated growth through their work on these projects noting confusion early in the process about what Open is. This confusion eventually evolved into valuing the creation and use of Open materials, which demonstrates the Open value of reciprocity, as seen in the following student responses:

> Before this class, I understood Open Educational Practices as a flipped classroom structure where students do most of the instruction for themselves and their peers. Now, I see Open Ed as a way for a professor and students to each contribute work and ideas and for students to find inspiration from other students' work. I consider a "world view of open" to be a way to understand and value others' work, ideas and efforts.

> The Open Educational Projects we completed were incredibly valuable to my overall learning experience. They provided academic benefits through an inherently collaborative and flexible structure while also fostering deeper communication and interactions with my peers and their ideas.

> I did not know a lot about Open Educational Practices before this class. This is a topic that I otherwise would not have had any exposure to in other classes.

> I had never heard of Open Educational Practices or Open Educational Resources before this project. This project has opened my eyes to a new way to accept, teach, and share resources and information.

Faculty broadly defined an Open worldview through their experiences. In the exploration of the Open worldview, they considered how Open practices, grounded in CDP's value of open and networked environments, can disrupt current information systems.

> It has been a long process for me to let go of the 'banking system' of education model. I have had to let go of the control that a textbook promises for shaping a class. I have found connections in unexpected places by looking at history from the margins.

> These materials, now provided on Open, are no longer behind a paywall but are now accessible to all who search, engage, reflect, and use the materials. This idea of a "window" into various places and spaces that might not have been accessible without Open, is how I would define a "world view of open" - one that offers consumers a place to access educational resources and materials that may not have been previously accessible as well as a place where consumers are now able to view (as well as engage with) new ideas, texts, strategies, etc. Also, once your "world view" is opened, due to Open, then you become not only a consumer, but also a producer or creator of educational materials.

It's clear that faculty and student experiences are transformative, and they recognize Open as a process and a goal.

Open is a Space for Co-creating and Listening

One of the key characteristics identified as being incredibly valuable to faculty and students was the way in which Open makes space to hear from many voices and reach more people. Through the following reflections, we see those values of CDP and Open Pedagogy surface.

> (student) I think that a "world view of open" means experiencing and learning from various types of sources that allow students to broaden their perspectives. This project allowed me to learn and hear from others' perspectives about events that were occurring or had occurred, in the world. This allowed me to develop a better understanding of what was going on in the world and how it was impacting people.

> (faculty) They are accessible in that they provide a space and place for educators to go to and engage with a community of Open authors, resources, materials, and institutions that may not have been easily available, if not due to Open.

Faculty and students both commented on the lack of diverse voices found in textbooks and the current curriculum. We see the role this work has in changing the curriculum to be more inclusive:

> (faculty) By collecting the interviews on a public website, students create an alternative textbook to contemporary 'history.' This exercise helps them to deconstruct the textbooks of their past by seeing all of the small changes and events that were left out of their past history texts. It, thus, asks them to reimagine or re-envision the ways in which the educational system has prioritized the memorization of facts over other more nuanced historical analysis.

> (student) By choosing to make my oral history project public for anyone to see, it gives people an opportunity to learn about eras of history or

topics from different and more personal, emotional perspectives unlike what one might find in a textbook.

As we build these spaces of praxis grounded in values of CDP and Open, we must consider the risk and emotional labor needed to ensure that our materials and resources do not replicate and perpetuate harm (Bali et al., 2020; Pearce et al., 2022). In the reflections from faculty and students, the role of risk and the "weight" of social justice work is evident:

> The Open process wasn't easy or natural for me. *Part of it is me constantly questioning, "is this ready to be shared with the world?" I worry. I worry it isn't ready, for the precise reasons I mentioned above. I want to create curriculum that is centered on equity, social justice, and challenges the status quo. I want to center historically marginalized and oppressed voices and do so in humanizing and beautiful ways. Does our work do this? I don't know.* I think we are trying, and I think that is where we are headed, but we have to be okay with it being "open" while still involved in the process. It isn't/won't be perfect and perhaps that is the point. We are engaging in a community of consumers and producers in the Open space, and things will likely shift and change, that is the purpose of Open after all, right?

Faculty and students share the importance of learning from multiple voices and experiences, including how they have learned to value "reaching" back out and contributing:

> (faculty) As an educator, "world view of open" means this grassroots endeavor gives students and the world writ large access to curriculum materials and resources without having to pay for them. As a result, all learners worldwide have access to educational curriculum and resources, which lessens the monetary value of receiving a high-quality education, and thus supports equality and educational opportunity globally.

> (student) My lesson plan dealt with providing a voice to those that cannot tell their stories, and I think that if I left my name off, it would feel like I was deliberately choosing not to share my voice and ideas with

others. This information isn't something to hide from or run from. It's something that we need to discuss and use to educate the masses.

(faculty) My English methods students are not just writing lesson plans for the instructor. They are writing lesson plans for teachers across America and around the world. As beginning teachers, they now have OER Commons that allows them to change, update, and add to their lessons as they decide what works best for their high school students. The open worldview that curriculum can be used, revised, and remixed may produce globally differentiated lessons, materials, and resources.

(student) These types of open sources have allowed me to hear from authors with different backgrounds, and I find their voices invaluable to my work regarding social justice.

Challenges

Finally, faculty and students reflect on the incredible value of engaging in and doing research as well as using each other's work as part of the learning process. Through these reflections, and in the literature (Pearce et al., 2022), it is clear that there are challenges in building spaces to co-create knowledge for faculty and students. One faculty member notes that

> I also realize how embedded that ideology is in our students and part of the challenge of teaching in a collaborative way that contributes to Open Educational Practices is to convince the students that they can be co-creators in the classroom, that this is worthy of their time.

We see similar challenges show up for students through the following reflections:

> I was definitely nervous that I wasn't going to be able to produce anything worthwhile. Having my work published was a really strange feeling–I felt like it wasn't detailed enough and that no one would understand what I was trying to say. I know that that isn't the case, but it was still nerve racking.

I am not exactly comfortable saying that I am a "co-creator" because the resources I used for my projects already existed, and I gathered them to share with the world.

Even though I completed the oral history interview and the other requirements of the assignment, I wouldn't consider myself a co-creator of knowledge for this Open Educational Project. I view my role as someone who elevated and shared my interviewee's knowledge with others more than a contributor to their knowledge.

I would not necessarily use the word co-creator because the information I used in my projects was already available and had been compiled by other people. I worked more as an organizer and put the research together in my project.

I think I would consider myself a co-creator of knowledge. I didn't create any information from either discipline that people couldn't have already found on their own–I just put some of it together.

Simultaneously we see other students voicing their perspectives by affirming their role in co-creating knowledge.

For this assignment in particular, sharing content openly allowed for other students and myself to recognize insights that may not have been easily discoverable from other forms of research—much of the knowledge shared came from anecdotes and/or personal experience with a historical moment. In a sense, I would describe myself and my peers as co-creators of knowledge—by sharing our content with one another, we were able to draw conclusions and develop new insights based on how we each synthesized our previous contributions.

In this instance, I would describe myself as a co-creator of knowledge because I did the work to create a cohesive interview with supplemented secondary research and helped a story be shared.

Exploring how the values of CDP and Open can be applied to build spaces where multiple voices are included, listened to, and valued is a powerful tool for learning and dismantling oppressive systems. The more we talk with students and engage them in the process of creating knowledge, the more we are doing the work of "transformative justice" (Bali et al., 2020).

Reclaiming our Praxis through CDP and Open

bell hooks (1994) claims that "Again and again Freire has had to remind readers that he never spoke of conscientization as an end itself, but always as it is joined by meaningful praxis" (p.47)—and praxis is "action and reflection upon the world in order to change it" (p. 14). Through reflection on their teaching and the implementation of our framework, faculty have the space and tools to reclaim their praxis. When prompted to explore their own praxis, we see how each discipline requires making different decisions, grappling with various theories and practices, and grounding work in theory while also focusing on application and reflection. One theme that arises is the need for support and encouragement for faculty to be transparent in their choices around Open while using language that is relevant and important in their own field. The following reflections provide a window into faculty experiences:

> Praxis is the relationship between theory and practice. Freire (2018) defined praxis as the process of action and reflection to transform the curriculum. Like Freire, reconceptualist curriculum theorist, Pinar (2019), applied the notion of praxis to teachers by asking them to read theoretical curricular perspectives and then, based on the principles of the theory, asked teachers to construct curricular lesson plans, materials, and resources. This example is one way of engaging in praxis to reconceptualize and transform the curriculum for students.

> The idea that curriculum must be reconceptualized for schools to succeed and for students to learn is not a new concept for me (Pinar, 2019). The learning process is inductive, that learning happens in a collaborative setting and that the teacher must learn with the students is not new. I have always worked this way in creating assignments with

students (Cancienne, 2013), conducting educational arts-based research (Bagley & Cancienne, 2001; Bagley & Cancienne, 2002), and in my approach to choreography (Cancienne & Snowber, 2003; Cancienne et al., 2008).

What changed for me was the power of the assignment in two ways: First, the purpose of the assignment was to uncover the excluded or null curriculum (Eisner, 1994) and that the audience was going to be global. Taken together, these two aspects of digital critical pedagogy and open transformed my perspective of the potential of teaching in learning for 21 century critical digital pedagogical literacies. In this format, the work became more meaningful; students worked longer hours, had more conversations, and asked for more feedback from their peers than before.

My theoretical lens is grounded in educational curriculum theory and specifically, the reconceptualist movement led by Freire (2018), Pinar (2019), Greene (1995), and hooks (1994). A re-conceptualist cares deeply about social justice and the inequities in society. Reconceptualist educators want to educate students on the systems of power and, in turn, empower students to name and understand their experience, develop their voice, and take ownership for their learning. To foster agency to those without a voice, the teacher must uncover the excluded curriculum with their students. In this process of unlearning and relearning, curriculum becomes a complicated conversation (Pinar, 2019).

The responses from our faculty colleagues also confirm Lambert's (2018) assertion that over time open educational research has fallen short in situating itself within or alongside established theoretical foundations within multiple fields. In the faculty responses, we can find insight into how to connect with theories from other disciplines. Using our framework, which values interdisciplinary knowledge-making, faculty have space to connect their theoretical background as they adopt and adapt the values of CDP and Open Pedagogy. We gain insight into the possible theoretical and methodological connections made as faculty engage in Open:

For me, praxis = teaching through the articulation of a concept that creates collaborative opportunities between student and professor. We workshop a concept through trial, revision, reflection, and action. Praxis is creation, collaboration, process, outcome, reflection, and ideally, action.

As an historian, there are a variety of ways in which we seek to understand the past. Due to the standardization of education, the ways in which public education has 'sold out' to a system that wants to measure learning as if it were a baking recipe, is highly problematic. It tells students that they and their communities are valid creators and makers of history.

I tell my students that we are embracing the emotions of lived experience in this class. We are deliberately textbook free. All of the readings for this class are available to my students on pdf so that it is economically accessible to everyone. I tell students that by collecting interviews of people we know, we are going to reshape what we know about history. Students not only collect interviews but they have to also ask an interesting question about at least three of the interviews and then try to answer it by bringing in valid outside materials that help them to do so.

It's important to note that faculty within the same broad discipline of Education have incredible nuance in the theories and frameworks they are grounding their work in. In a space of praxis that leverages the values of CDP and Open, we make room for interdisciplinary conversations, questions, and understanding of how these can support each other and develop shared understanding, which is invaluable as faculty evolve their teaching practices (Cronin, 2017).

For me, praxis = the intersection of theory and practice.

My experience guiding students to develop open educational materials was a slow, deliberate process. I entered the project quietly and as a listener. I wanted to know the "why" behind the project before I fully committed to it and more importantly, engaged my students in this process. After many months of listening and learning with the project team, I began to see not only the purpose and reasons behind the project, but also where I fit and where my students could fit.

It was really important that I set the context for the work through theories and curriculum design frameworks centered on equity and social justice in social studies education. We read and engaged with authors who write about equity and social justice. For example, we read Gloria Ladson-Billings on culturally relevant pedagogy, Bettina Love on abolitionist teaching, and Hasan Kwame Jeffries on teaching hard histories. Considering these theories and frameworks, we entered into the curriculum design process using the College, Career, & Civic Life (C3) framework and Inquiry Design Model (IDM) to construct social studies curriculum. These theories, pedagogies, and practices framed the development of the student's IDMs for the project. They developed an orientation toward critical pedagogy, which we then moved to considering this framing as it relates to Open and the digital world. I shared with my whole class that they had a chance to contribute to changing the narrative in social studies education in (state) by developing curricula that largely does not exist and is in support of the new 2022 history and social science standards in (state), which works to include African American histories, experiences, and voices in the curriculum. Students seemed motivated to transform social studies curricula and Open facilitated this process for us.

In his book *Radical Hope,* Kevin Gannon explores how teachers and scholars in higher education must better understand and operationalize *praxis* as posed by bell hooks and Paulo Freire. He states, "Too many times, pedagogical theory seems to focus on philosophical and attitudinal shifts while leaving the application portion unsaid" (2020, p. 49). Applying the values of CDP and Open Pedagogy guides us in making practical decisions that are "...courageous and flexible, as they scaffold the learning experience with the students..." (Pearce et al., 2022). This can address the challenges or questions students face when publishing openly:

I enjoyed the process of sharing responsibility to develop materials. To know that my work could be used to assist another student in their research was a very unique feeling and an opportunity I did not expect to have in a GenEd class. I understand this discipline to be about contributing your own story to a body of research and enabling your work to be seen.

I also felt a sense of personal responsibility for the quality of my research when I realized that other students would potentially be using my work to discover new insights as they developed their own projects.

However, it was very rewarding and humbling to be able to share someone else's story and perspective on history with my classmates, professor and anyone else who might visit the website. I felt responsible for telling and sharing my interviewee's story appropriately, accurately and with integrity.

Through this work, faculty (re)claim their spaces of praxis as they explore sharing power in their classrooms. They are connecting how the values of CDP and Open provide clear guidance on the decisions needed to develop a project that empowers students and themselves as indicated in these responses:

They and I took risks and created our best work. We were all changed by the process, the students, and the teacher. This project supports my teaching and learning perspective because I believe that the curriculum should be reconstructed. It is not a noun. It is a verb (Pinar, 2019), and curriculum and instruction must empower students (hooks, 1994).

I think the biggest take-away from Open Educational Practices has been how much is to be gained by breaking away from hierarchies of power, such as the "sage on the stage," approach to college-level education.

When we build spaces of praxis through the implementation and design of social justice projects that incorporate the values of CDP and

Open Pedagogy, we are bridging theory and practice in a way that can be replicated and used as a model for future projects. It's also critical to honor the ways in which faculty name the entire ecosystem of Open Education, Pedagogy, and Access as a broad term "Open" rather than referring to its discrete parts. Adopting the practice of using the big "Open" to talk about this work allows faculty and others to center the values and world view of open rather than create a barrier of technical definitions (Werth & Williams, 2022). The more ways in which barriers can be removed, the more ways the work of creating new knowledge also becomes a space of belonging for everyone in our communities. It's clear from faculty and student experiences that the values of CDP and Open resonate in their own contexts as learners, teachers, and knowledge producers. These values also support our understanding of how Open Pedagogy projects can build community, require trust, and create spaces to share power in order to dismantle systems of oppression.

Next Steps

As we consider the next steps for our work and the actions needed to push Open forward as a social justice movement, we can look to the values of CDP to develop our critical questions; CDP asks more questions than it answers, and "Without a doubt, Critical Digital Pedagogy energizes all of us to be an answer, if we choose to be" (Benjamin, 2020 p.xi). One next step is to continue to refine, research, and implement our framework in various contexts. Werth & Williams's (2022) work indicates the positive impacts of value-first frameworks for bringing faculty into the world of Open Education. Could the values of CDP and Open be leveraged to create spaces of praxis for teachers and students to garner and act on a collective sense of power? The framework we've created is a guide to doing so. We must also consider how institutions of higher education, which often state their purpose as contributing to the public good (Mushtare & Kane, 2021), can leverage their power and resources to build connections across the silos of the educational landscape. While there's risk in this work, having a collective and connected response is the only way forward. The next steps for the authors include gathering and sharing the stories of other cross-disciplinary projects in which we use this framework.

As research focuses on student experiences of renewable assignments and open pedagogy evolves (Clinton-Lisell & Gwozdz, 2023), we can explore other ways of assessing student feedback through formative assessment practices. By involving students in the process of sharing their experiences and amplifying their voices, there is space for future research and reflection in how we implement Open pedagogy. After gathering and sharing the experiences of faculty and students using our values-based framework, the authors propose exploring this further as a qualitative methodology in alignment with the critical research known as "bricolage" that focuses on empowerment and advancing social justice through qualitative research (Kincheloe et al., 2017).

We suggest critical conversations and reflection on the following questions to advance the open movement:

- How can we support students in and outside of the classroom as they are taking on the risks and responsibilities of publishing openly?
- How do we integrate this critical literacy into our work in academia and beyond?
- How might we change the ways we educate faculty about what it means to be Open that centers the common goals of Open initiatives rather than the discrete definitions that aren't even affirmed fully by our fields (Hyde & Hey, 2021)?
- Would this remove barriers, reduce cognitive load, and make Open more inclusive?
- How can we use the language of faculty and students to empower them as champions and co-conspirators of Open?

We have already begun to use the lessons learned through faculty and student reflections from this chapter in multiple spaces, including an [Open Pedagogy Fellowship](https://pressbooks.lib.jmu.edu/openpedagogy/), course design consultations, and broader conversations. Being an advocate for faculty and student perspectives creates an opportunity to break down barriers and foster equitable and inclusive learning environments. As we continue pushing forward the important work of Open, we ask you to deeply reflect on your own practices, projects, and spaces while considering how the values of CDP and Open Pedagogy might transform your praxis.

References

Bagley, C., & Cancienne, M. B. (Eds.). (2002). *Dancing the data*. New York: Peter Lang.

Bagley, C., & Cancienne, M. B. (2001). Educational research and inter-textual forms of (re)presentation: The case for dancing the data. *Qualitative Inquiry, 7*(2), 221-237. https://doi.org/10.1177/107780040100700205

Bali, M., Cronin, C., & Jhangiani, R. S. (2020). Framing open educational practices from a social justice perspective. *Journal of Interactive Media in Education, 2020*(1), 10. http://doi.org/10.5334/jime.565

Benjamin, R. (2020). Foreword. In J. Stommel, C. Friend, & S. M. Morris (Eds.), *Critical digital pedagogy: A collection* (pp. ix-xi). Hybrid Pedagogy Inc. https://pressbooks.pub/cdpcollection/front-matter/foreword/

Brown, B. (2010, June 1). *The power of vulnerability* [Video]. TED Talk. https://brenebrown.com/videos/ted-talk-the-power-of-vulnerability/

Brown, B. (2021a). *Atlas of the heart: Mapping meaningful connection and the language of human experience*. Random House.

Brown, B. (Host). (2021b, October 4). Brené with Charles Feltman on trust: Building, maintaining, and restoring it [Audio podcast episode]. In *Dare to Lead with Brené Brown*. Parcast Network. https://brenebrown.com/podcast/brene-with-charles-feltman-on-trust-building-maintaining-and-restoring-it/

Brown, B. (2023). *Dare to lead | the BRAVING inventory*. Brené Brown. https://brenebrown.com/resources/the-braving-inventory/

Cancienne, M. B. (Spring/Summer, 2013). Teaching spirituals in the American literature classroom. *The Virginia English Journal, 63*(1), 41-45.

Cancienne, M. B., & Bagley, C. (2008). Dance as method: The process and product of dance in arts-based educational research. In P. Liamputtong & J. Rumbold (Eds.). *Knowing differently: Experimental research methods in the health and social science* (pp.169-186). Nova Science: New York.

Cancienne, M. B., & Snowber, C. (2003). Writing rhythm: Movement as method. *Qualitative Inquiry, 9*(2), 237-253. https://doi.org/10.1177/1077800402250956

Clinton-Lisell, V., & Gwozdz, L. (2023). Understanding student experiences of renewable and traditional assignments. *College Teaching, 71*(2), 125-134. https://doi.org/10.1080/87567555.2023.2179591

Cronin, C. (2017). Openness and praxis: Exploring the use of open educational practices in higher education. *International Review of Research in Open & Distance Learning, 18*(5), 15–34. https://doi.org/10.19173/irrodl.v18i5.3096

De Fazio, G., Cancienne, M.B., Jaffee, A.T., Hegg, K., Kaye, E., & Wilson, N. (2021). Critical digital pedagogy and civic education: the experience of the racial terror: Lynching in Virginia Project. *Scholé*, 65-78. http://digital.casalini.it/5192608

Eisner, E. W. (1994). *The educational imagination: On the design and evaluation of school programs.* MacMillan.

Freire, P., Ramos, M. B., Macedo, D. P. 1., & Shor, I. (2018). *Pedagogy of the oppressed.* 50th anniversary edition. New York, Bloomsbury Academic.

Gannon, K.M. (2020). *Radical hope: A teaching manifesto.* Morgantown: West Virginia University Press.

Greene, M. (1995). *Releasing the imagination: Essays on education, the arts, and social change.* Jossey-Bass.

Hodgkinson-Williams, C.A., & Trotter, H. (2018). A social justice framework for understanding open educational resources and practices in the Global South. *Journal of Learning for Development, 5*(3), 204-224. https://doi.org/10.56059/jl4d.v5i3.312

hooks, b. (1994). *Teaching to transgress: Education as the practice of freedom.* Routledge.

Hyde, Z.W., & Hey, M. (2021, October). *The distance between us: How do open education & open research move forward together?* [Conference Session]. 2021 OpenEd global online conference. https://sched.co/moRX

Jhangiani, R. (2019, April 11). 5Rs for open pedagogy. *Rajiv Jhangiani, Ph.D.* https://rajivjhangiani.com/5rs-for-open-pedagogy/

JMU COE Curriculum Development Team. (2021). *Teaching hard histories for racial healing curriculum.* CC-BY-NC-SA 4.0. https://oercommons.org/courseware/lesson/86888

Kaye, E., Cancienne, M.B., Thompson, L., Wilson, N., Mlodynia, K., De Fazio, G., Jaffee, A.T., & Stone, A. (2021, October). *Teaching hard* histories for racial healing: The lynching in Virginia curriculum project [Presentation]. Open Education Conference 2021, Online. https://opened21.sched.com/event/moT8/teaching-hard-histories-for-racial-healing-the-lynching-in-virginia-curriculum-project

Kaye, E., & Wilson, N. (2022). Operationalizing values to create communities of care. *Journal of New Librarianship, 7*(2), 100–105. https://doi.org/10.33011/newlibs/12/19

Kaye, E., Wilson, N., McCleary K., & Mlodynia, K. (2021, October). *Emotional histories: Exploring social change in a Gen Ed history course through oral histories* [Presentation]. Open Education Conference 2021, Online. https://sched.co/moKc

Kincheloe, J. L., McLaren, P., Steinberg, S. R., & Monzó, L. (2017). Critical pedagogy and qualitative research: Advancing the bricolage. In N. K. Denzin & Y. S. Lincoln (Eds.), *The SAGE handbook of qualitative research* (5th ed.) (pp. 235-260). Thousand Oaks, CA: Sage.

Lambert, S. (2018). Changing our (dis)course: A distinctive social justice aligned definition of open education. *Journal of Learning for Development, 5*(3). https://doi.org/10.56059/jl4d.v5i3.290

Morris, S. M., & Stommel, J. (2018). *An urgency of teachers: The work of critical digital pedagogy.* Hybrid Pedagogy Inc. https://criticaldigitalpedagogy.pressbooks.com/chapter/chapter-1/

Mushtare, R. & Kane, J. (Hosts). (2021, August 11). Teaching for the public good (No. 200) [Audio podcast episode]. In *Tea for teaching.* https://teaforteaching.com/200-teaching-for-the-public-good/

Okun, T. (2022). White supremacy culture characteristics . *White Supremacy Culture.* https://www.whitesupremacyculture.info/characteristics.html

Pinar, W. (2019). *What is curriculum theory?* (3rd ed.). Routledge.

Pearce, L., Lin Hanick, S., Hofer, A., Townsend, L., and Willi Hooper, M. (2022). Your discomfort is valid: Big feelings and open pedagogy. *Knowledge Cultures 10*(2): 24–51. https://doi.org/10.22381/kc10220222

Roberts-Crews, J. for Open Education Network. (2022, September 7). *Jasmine Roberts-Crews: Creating a socially just open education* [Video]. YouTube. https://www.youtube.com/watch?v=vBUeagrtnps

Rorabaugh, P. (2020). Occupy the digital: Critical pedagogy and new media.

In J. Stommel, C. Friend, & S. M. Morris, *Critical digital pedagogy: A collection* (pp. 11-15). Hybrid Pedagogy Inc. https://pressbooks.pub/cdpcollection/chapter/occupy-the-digital-critical-pedagogy-and-new-media/

Social Change Interviews. (2023). Featured interviews. *Social Change Interviews.* https://sites.lib.jmu.edu/sc-interviews/category/featured-interviews/

Stommel, J., Friend, C., & Morris, S.M., (Eds). (2020a). *Critical digital pedagogy: A collection.* Hybrid Pedagogy Inc. https://pressbooks.pub/cdpcollection/?ref=hybridpedagogy.org

Stommel, J., Friend, C., & Morris, S.M. (2020b). Introduction: The urgency of critical digital pedagogy. In J. Stommel, C. Friend, & S.M. Morris (Eds.), *Critical digital pedagogy: A collection*, (pp. 1-8). Hybrid Pedagogy Inc. https://pressbooks.pub/cdpcollection/front-matter/introduction/

Watters, A. (2020). Maggie's digital content farm. In J. Stommel, C. Friend, & S.M. Morris (Eds.), *Critical digital pedagogy: A collection*, (pp. 24-28). Hybrid Pedagogy Inc. https://pressbooks.pub/cdpcollection/chapter/maggies-digital-content-farm/

Werth, E. & Williams, K. (2022). The why of open pedagogy: A value-first conceptualization for enhancing instructor praxis. *Smart Learning Environments, 9*(10). https://doi.org/10.1186/s40561-022-00191-0

Author Bios
Elaine Kaye, James Madison University

As an instructional designer, I'm strongly influenced by critical instructional design, critical digital pedagogy, open pedagogy, equity-based teaching, and social justice pedagogy. I have experience teaching undergraduate and continuing education courses. I'm interested, open, and committed to valuing experiences and understanding other ways of knowing.

Nicole Wilson, James Madison University

As an instructional designer, I am passionate about centering social justice in all projects that I work on. I approach my work from a critical instructional design perspective incorporating learning science, critical digital pedagogy, open pedagogy, and care. I have experience teaching multiple undergraduate courses.

Appendix: Interview Questions & Responses

For the interview process, we made a Google Doc for each faculty member and then one for each group of students with designated spaces to respond. We emailed everyone with their links and fielded questions as people worked through their responses.

Faculty questions:

1. Through this work how has your understanding of Open Educational Practices evolved? What have you learned about what it means for educational materials to be Open? What does a "world view of open" mean for you personally, as an educator, and/or as a scholar?
2. For me praxis = _____ (finish that statement). Describe your experience guiding students to develop open educational materials. How has this process being rooted in the values of CDP and Open supported and/or challenged your own perspective of teaching and learning? Can you share the theoretical or methodological pieces from your own discipline that inform and shape your processes, practices, pedagogy or approaches in relation to your specific project?
3. "Openness can be conceived of as an attitude or worldview which includes making oneself vulnerable, narrating one's own practice and sharing one's incomplete scholarship openly" (Bali and Koseouglu, 2016 as cited in Bali, Cronin, Jhangiani, 2020). We've asked about "a world view of openness" and it's impacts on your teaching but could you share about your experience of working in different ways with these projects that center open and how that has impacted your perceptions, thoughts, and processes in terms of telling our story and producing scholarship.

Student questions:

1. Through working on the ____ project, how has your understanding of Open Educational Practices evolved? After going through a process of choosing to publish content openly or not, how

would you describe what a "world view of open" means for you as a student? Describe how engaging with a project that centers Open Educational Projects compares to your other experiences in education (formal or informal).
2. Application of open education showcasing students as co-constructors of knowledge and problematizing open for certain contexts
   a. Throughout the semester you worked on a project that involved complex learning alongside your professor and peers. How did the process of sharing responsibility to develop materials feel for you? What do you understand or have a sense of about the discipline? Would you describe yourself as a co-creator of knowledge? Why or why not?
   b. As you were considering how you would engage in this open work, what kinds of considerations and challenges came up for you? Are there ways in which publishing or creating work in the open was problematic for you or others?

Question for all collaborators

1. As a learning community, we all have made commitments and been intentional about how we engage with each other and this work. We have used the values of Open and CDP to ground our work in trust, equity, the politicizing of education, vulnerability, and valuing all voices. Describe what it means to participate or have participated in this community through your work on the _____ project. What lessons do you take with you into other spaces?

Faculty responses describing and defining open educational practices

Question: Through this work how has your understanding of Open Educational Practices evolved? What have you learned about what it means for educational materials to be Open? What does a "world view of open" mean for you personally, as an educator, and/or as a scholar?

Kristen McCleary | Associate Professor, History; co-director of the JMU in Argentina Program

I think the biggest take-away from Open Educational Practices has been how much is to be gained by breaking away from hierarchies of power, such as the "sage on the stage," approach to college-level education. I also realize how embedded that ideology is in our students and part of the challenge of teaching in a collaborative way that contributes to Open Educational Practices is to convince the students that they can be co-creators in the classroom, that this is worthy of their time. The students have to be introduced to a different way of learning that is not the 'banking system' of education where the 'sage on the stage' deposits knowledge into them, as discussed by Paolo Freire and Bell Hooks.

My class, "*Emotional Histories*: Reshaping World History Through First Person Narratives," has evolved greatly over the years. At its heart was an oral interview assignment. Students prepared for, conducted, transcribed, contextualized and reflected upon an interview about social change.

By collecting the interviews on a public website, students create an alternative textbook to contemporary 'history.' This exercise helps them to deconstruct the textbooks of their past by seeing all of the small changes and events that were left out of their past history texts. It, thus, asks them to reimagine or re-envision the ways in which the educational system has prioritized the memorization of facts over other more nuanced historical analysis."

A particularly compelling interview theme has to do with changing gender roles in the twentieth century. Students see how women had limited choice of ways to shape their lives. Many women married and raised children. Working outside of the house was often limited at best to jobs like secretaries, teachers, and nurses, with very few of them attending college. Students comment that hearing women's voices tell their own stories made a great impact upon their understanding of social change. Contemporarily, students have conducted interviews that result in their analysis that women tend to change jobs much more to accommodate family life than do men. These are all topics that are seldom included in history classes. Open Educational Practice often results in student empowerment: their stories are now part of the historical record.

Mary Beth Cancienne | Professor of English Education; Director of Curriculum & Instruction for the Virginia New Teacher Support Program

When I began to work with curriculum collaborators (i.e., digital library projects colleagues, social justice and education colleagues, and graduate students), I had not heard of open educational practices. However, now that I have worked with this team on The Teaching Hard Histories for Racial Healing: The Lynching in Virginia Curriculum Project, and special thanks to the digital library projects colleagues who led the OER Commons curricular efforts, I now have an in-depth understanding of what it means for educational materials to be Open.

As an educator, "world view of open" means this grassroots endeavor gives students and the world writ large access to curriculum materials and resources without having to pay for them. As a result, all learners worldwide have access to educational curriculum and resources, which lessens the monetary value of receiving a high-quality education, and thus supports equality and educational opportunity globally.

Ashley Jaffee | Assistant Director, Social Studies; Teacher Prep Program:

Prior to engaging in this project, I had very little understanding of Open Educational Practices. My familiarity with Open was largely as a consumer. For example, I had accessed some resources on Open to support a book talk I was facilitating. My evolution of understanding regarding Open Educational Practices, therefore, was quite substantial during this project. I have learned why Open is important, discussed this importance with my students, learned about copyright, and engaged in the process of creating, editing, and uploading items to Open.

For me, I have learned that when educational materials are Open, they are accessible. Accessible in that they provide a space and place for educators to go to and engage with a community of Open authors, resources, materials, and institutions that may not have been easily available, if not due to Open. This accessibility provides a "window" into artifacts in museums, journals or videos created by authors and filmmakers, primarily source material, or lesson plans. These materials, now provided on Open, are no longer behind a paywall, but are now accessible to all who search, engage, reflect, and use the materials. This idea of a "window" into various places and spaces that might not have been accessible without Open, is how I would define a "world view of open" - one that offers consumers a place to access educational resources and materials that may not have been previously accessible as well as a place where consumers are now able to view (as well as engage with) new ideas, texts, strategies, etc. Also, once your "world view" is opened, due to Open, then you become not only a consumer, but also a producer or creator of educational materials. This producer or consumer of Open materials can happen in a variety of ways - e.g., using items in your own classroom or professional learning experience, reflecting on what you learned from the materials, and/or creating materials to also publish on Open. Open, therefore, becomes a community - where people go to learn, engage, reflect, and create.

Student responses describing their experiences with open educational practices

Question: Through working on the ____ project, how has your understanding of Open Educational Practices evolved? After going through a process of choosing to publish content openly or not, how would you describe what a "world view of open" means for you as a student? Describe how engaging with a project that centers Open Educational Projects compares to your other experiences in education (formal or informal).

Joaquin Dela Cruz

After Dr. McCleary's class, I think that my understanding of Open Educational Practices has evolved in that I did not know about them before. I am now exposed to various sources and materials that I would otherwise have not interacted within other classes. These types of open sources have allowed me to hear from authors with different backgrounds, and I find their voices invaluable to my work regarding social justice.

Mya Wilcox

Since working on the oral history project in Dr. McCleary's class, I have found Open Educational Practices to be a valuable and unique addition to my educational experience. I found that my prior research about a historical moment was enhanced by studying individual experiences that my classmates collected and shared, and I could see this process playing out successfully in other academic disciplines as well. I think "a world view of open" has meaningful applications for myself and my fellow students because it means we have the potential to engage with created content that represents a variety of worldviews and life experiences. Whereas some of my previous high school and college courses utilized a single textbook containing one perspective on historical events, the projects and resources I used for my oral history interview and essay contained many different understandings and remembrances of social change.

Carter Payne

I did not know a lot about Open Educational Practices before taking Dr. McCleary's class. This is a topic that I otherwise would not have had any exposure to in other classes. I think that a "world view of open" means experiencing and learning from various types of sources that allow students to broaden their perspectives. This project allowed me to learn and hear from others' perspectives about events that were occurring, or had occurred, in the world. This allowed me to develop a better understanding of what was going on in the world and how it was impacting people.

Mya Gonzales

After working on the Oral History project, I understood the value of Open Educational Practices. Prior to this class, I was never given the opportunity to use my peer's work for research purposes. I realized how important it is for every perspective to be seen and shared openly with others. When reflecting on what a "world view of open" means to me, I feel that it means to give everyone access to resources in the public domain and encourage people to share their stories. Having a project centered around Open Educational Projects was very engaging because I actively learned about someone else's history through their interview rather than simply reading a summary about them. The process was extremely thought-provoking and did require more effort but was extremely rewarding.

Michael Russo

I have taken plenty of project-based classes that are collaborative and allow for creativity, but usually within a tighter framework with more structured criteria and expectations. Before Dr. McCleary's class, I understood Open Educational Practices as a flipped classroom structure where students do most of the instruction for themselves and their peers. Now, I see Open Ed as a way for a professor and students to each contribute work and ideas and for students to find inspiration from other students' work.

I consider a "world view of open" to be a way to understand and value others' work, ideas and efforts. By choosing to make my oral history project public for anyone to see, it gives people an opportunity to learn about eras of history or topics from different and more personal, emotional perspectives unlike what one might find in a textbook.

The Open Educational Projects we completed in Dr. McCleary's HIST 150H class were incredibly valuable to my overall learning experience. They provided academic benefits through an inherently collaborative and flexible structure while also fostering deeper communication and interactions with my peers and their ideas

Ryland Jones

I had never heard of Open Educational Practices or Open Educational Resources before this project. This project has opened my eyes to a new way to accept, teach, and share resources and information. When we were reviewing the OER Commons website as a class, I didn't know how my ideas and subject matter would fit into something that seemed so history based. After working through the process to create these IDM based English lesson plans, I realized that there was a way to include myself in this bigger part of sharing resources.

I don't think there was ever a moment where I didn't want to openly publish this work. This work is something that I'm incredibly proud of and have spent a lot of time working on—why wouldn't I want to stick my name on it? I think that if I chose to not put my name on this work, it would be like hiding myself from the educational world. My lesson plan dealt with providing a voice to those that cannot tell their stories, and I think that if I left my name off, it would feel like I was deliberately choosing not to share my voice and ideas with others. This information isn't something to hide from or run from. It's something that we need to discuss and use to educate the masses.

This project was different from anything I have ever done in my brief educational career. I've never worked with a history format, and it was definitely daunting at first. I think the longer the English side worked with it, though, the more comfortable we found ourselves. Ideas became more free flowing and fleshed out. Rebekah and I would sit on the phone for hours talking through different ways to include newspapers or obituaries into novels and poems. This project helped to show me how we should be communicating throughout different curriculums in order to really showcase information.

Faculty responses reclaiming our praxis through reflection

Question: For me praxis = _____ (finish that statement). Describe your experience guiding students to develop open educational materials. How has this process being rooted in the values of CDP and Open supported and/or challenged your own perspective of teaching and learning? Can you share the theoretical or methodological pieces from your own discipline that inform and shape your processes, practices, pedagogy or approaches in relation to your specific project?

Kristen McCleary

For me, praxis = teaching through the articulation of a concept that creates collaborative opportunities between student and professor. We workshop a concept through trial, revision, reflection, and action. Praxis is creation, collaboration, process, outcome, reflection, and ideally, action.

As an historian, there are a variety of ways in which we seek to understand the past. Due to the standardization of education, the ways in which public education has 'sold out' to a system that wants to measure learning as if it were a baking recipe, is highly problematic. If I tell someone that I am a history professor, I always assure them that I will not be testing their knowledge of names, dates, and places. This class is the opposite of a textbook. It tells students that they and their communities are valid creators and makers of history.

I tell my students that we are embracing the emotions of lived experience in this class. We are deliberately textbook free. In fact, all of the readings I have chosen for this class are available to my students on pdf so that it is economically accessible to everyone. I tell students that by our work collecting interviews of people we know, we are going to reshape what we know about history. Students not only collect interviews but they have to also ask an interesting question about at least three of the interviews and then try to answer it by bringing in valid outside materials that help them to do so. The practice of an historian is then to identify questions (for both the interview preparation and the ways in which the interviews compare to other accounts of the past), to verify the strengths and weaknesses of source materials, and to write an analysis of this work, documented with proper citations.

Mary Beth Cancienne

For me, praxis is the relationship between theory and practice. One theoretical scholar, Freire (2018), defined praxis as the process of action and reflection to transform the curriculum. Like Freire, reconceptualist curriculum theorist, Pinar (2019), applied the notion of praxis to teachers by asking them to read theoretical curricular perspectives and then, based on the principles of the theory, asked teachers to construct curricular lesson plans, materials, and resources. This example is one way of engaging in praxis to reconceptualize and transform the curriculum for students.

The idea that curriculum must be reconceptualized for schools to succeed and for students to learn is not a new concept for me (Pinar, 2019). The idea that the learning process is inductive, that learning happens in a collaborative setting and that the teacher must learn with the students is not new. I have always worked this way in creating assignments with students (Cancienne, 2013), conducting educational arts-based research (Cancienne & Bagley, 2001; Cancienne & Bagley, 2002), and in my approach to choreography (Cancienne & Snowber, 2003; Cancienne, 2008).

What changed for me was the power of the assignment in two ways: First, the purpose of the assignment was to uncover the excluded or null curriculum (Eisner, 1994) and that the audience was going to be global. Taken together, these two aspects of digital critical pedagogy and open transformed my perspective of the potential of teaching in learning for 21 century critical digital pedagogical literacies. In this format, the work became more meaningful; students worked longer hours, had more conversations, and asked for more feedback from their peers than before. They and I took risks and created our best work. We were all changed by the process, the students, and the teacher. This project supports my teaching and learning perspective because I believe that the curriculum should be reconstructed. It is not a noun. It is a verb (Pinar, 2019), and curriculum and instruction must empower students (hooks, 1994).

My theoretical lens is grounded in educational curriculum theory and specifically, the reconceptualist movement led by Freire (2018), Pinar (2019), Greene (1995), and hooks (1994). A re-conceptualist cares deeply about social justice and the inequities in society. Reconceptualist educators want to educate students on the systems of power and, in turn, empower students to name and understand their experience, develop their voice, and take ownership for their learning. To foster agency to those without a voice, the teacher must uncover the excluded curriculum with their students. In this process of unlearning and relearning, curriculum becomes a complicated conversation (Pinar, 2019).

In the Teaching Hard Histories for Racial Healing project, one way to approach this work is an arts-based approach, as the arts are an expression of self, history, language, and culture. For example, spoken word poetry, songs, music videos, and visual art were artistic expressions used to convey racial terror in America in the English methods students' lesson plans.

Ashley Jaffee

For me, praxis = the intersection of theory and practice.

My experience guiding students to develop open educational materials was a slow, deliberate process. I entered the project quietly and as a listener. I wanted to know the "why" behind the project before I fully committed to it and more importantly, engaged my students in this process. After many months of listening and learning with the project team, I began to see not only the purpose and reasons behind the project, but also where I fit and where my students could fit.

For me, it was really important that I set the context for the work through theories and curriculum design frameworks centered on equity and social justice in social studies education. At the beginning of the semester, we read and engaged with authors who write about equity and social justice. For example, we read Gloria Ladson-Billings on culturally relevant pedagogy, Bettina Love on abolitionist teaching, and Hasan Kwame Jeffries on teaching hard histories. Considering these theories and frameworks, we entered into the curriculum design process using the College, Career, & Civic Life (C3) framework and Inquiry Design Model (IDM) to construct social studies curriculum. These theories, pedagogies, and practices framed the development of the student's IDMs for the project. They developed an orientation toward critical pedagogy, which we then moved to considering this framing as it relates to Open and the digital world. I shared with my whole class that they had a chance to contribute to changing the narrative in social studies education in Virginia by developing curricula that largely does not exist and is in support of the new 2022 history and social science standards in Virginia, which works to include African American histories, experiences, and voices in the curriculum. Students seemed motivated to transform social studies curricula in Virginia, and Open facilitated this process for us.

Faculty and Libraries colleagues' responses of what we carry into other spaces

Question: As a learning community we all have made commitments and been intentional about how we engage with each other and this work. We have used the values of Open and CDP to ground our work in trust, equity, the politicizing of education, vulnerability, and valuing all voices. Describe what it means to participate or have participated in this community through your work on the _____ project. What lessons do you take with you into other spaces?

Kristen McCleary

I just carried out an interview with my mom for this project and I learned how vulnerable the interviewees are to tell their stories in a way that requires them to reflect upon the past, often after a large part of their own life has been lived. I felt a bit intrusive and as if the questions were or might be thought of as judgemental. In one question, about why my mother stopped her formal education at the age of 16, when she graduated from high school, she took responsibility for this as if it were a bad thing. I explained to her later that my opportunities and hers were not the same, largely due to the massive support for public education that helped me to go to college. I think then that the lessons that I take away from this project have to do with the importance of listening, building empathy, being vulnerable, and allowing oneself to circle back to a conversation once that interview is over. This assignment allows me to always wonder about the grey areas of knowledge and that sometimes I wish things were not presented to us so definitively. I am also aware of the racial and gender dynamics of whose stories are told and whose are not told. I see the ways in which education presents its own bias towards the Western world and how so many small countries are overlooked and understudied. I have learned that some people want to tell their stories and are happy to have this opportunity to do so. Others might want to tell their stories only under a pseudonym. I think this assignment helps us explore questions about audience and open by exploring how people seek to differently expand and/or limit the audience for their stories.

Mary Beth Cancienne

Working with **a transdisciplinary team** on the Teaching Hard History for Racial Healing: The Lynching in Virginia Curriculum Project has deepened my commitment to social justice, enhanced my understanding of African American history, and connected me to open-authored publishing platforms. My experience with the digital library team to teach Open and the skills to be successful in 21-century digital literacies has transformed my assignments, my instruction, my students, and me. Collaborating with teams across campus to create innovative assignments for future high school English teachers is how I plan to work.

Lesson 1: Reconstructing the curriculum by including the excluded curriculum into the narrative is essential. Students want to know the truth to make sense of themselves and situate themselves as learners in an educational space that is honest with them and depicts a complicated history to them. The outcome is a complicated curriculum that tells the story of many voices. This approach teaches students to learn empathy, accept pain and joy as part of the learning process, and produce projects that include healing as part of the outcome.

Lesson 2: The students are fearless and ready for the challenge. English candidates want to work on meaningful projects that will make a difference for middle and high school students. Dominant narratives stifle them, and they do not want to teach them to students. They know that there are more perspectives to the stories and history, and they want to have access to the excluded curriculum to teach it.

For example, the graduate students were very interested in discovering the hidden history in their towns for the Teaching Hard History for Racial Healing project. For example, some of the English methods students chose to write a lesson plan on the racial terror case that took place in their community in Virginia. As a culminating project, the graduate students designed community-based projects to foster healing in their local communities. They were invested.

Lesson 3: I learn from my students, and they learn from me. We explored the excluded curriculum together, used our imaginations, and created something new based on what has been left out of the standard curriculum. Because the reconceptualist curriculum exists on the edge, the students become the experts, take risks, and create. The lessons are not about teaching an established curriculum, but are about reconstructing a curriculum. They are asked to reconceptualize the curriculum, which is a shift from what most professors asked them to do in education. Most education professors will only teach and assess on the standard curriculum. Most of my English methods students search for more and find meaning and joy in uncovering, discovering, and reconstructing.

Future: The lesson is that I will continue to have an open assignment for my students in my high school English methods course. English methods graduate students will explore open, learn to use it, discuss the strengths and weaknesses, and produce English education and interdisciplinary lesson plans with an open world view.

Ashley Jaffee

Participating in this community has been a learning experience. I have learned so much from the team about Open, CDP, and the history of lynching in Virginia (and in the U.S.). I have learned from my students about what it means to engage in this work and consider ways of approaching difficult and hard histories in the middle and high school classroom. For example, we discussed and reflected at length about the importance of not re-traumatizing students in what we teach and how we teach it, but humanizing our content and pedagogy with a lens toward "racial healing" (as is in the title of the project). This is not easy and takes patience, pause, and deep reflection (this is internal and external work). We did this, and in a remote teaching/learning environment no less. I am proud of the work we did and produced together, and I will continue to reflect on the curriculum we created. In my opinion, our work is not "finished," but fluid and will shift and change, depending on who engages with the work (on Open and within our project team) and as we continue to reflect on how to approach the narratives we aim to tell, why we tell them, and for whom?

Kevin Hegg | Director of Digital Projects

My participation in the "Teaching Hard Histories" project has unfolded along two different paths. First, I have provided deep technology support for the "Racial Terror: Lynching in Virginia" website, which is a repository for primary sources documenting lynching in Virginia and a focal point for researchers studying lynching in Virginia. Of course, technology is only a tool; content and its distribution matters. Secondly, I have engaged the materials and essays on the "Racial Terror" website as both a scholar and a member of the local community. On September 16, 2019, I attended an event sponsored by a local non-profit committed to promoting culture and history within the community. At the event, members of Virginia's Dr. Martin Luther King, Jr. Memorial Commission facilitated a discussion centered on Virginia's long and painful history of lynching. A member of the audience asked how she could teach lynching in her high school classroom. This was the impetus for my involvement in the "Teaching Hard Histories" collaboration at JMU. My work on the "Teaching Hard Histories" project has reaffirmed my commitment to understanding and using technology as an instrument for social justice work in the local community.

Liz Thompson | Open Education Librarian

When the team facilitators asked me to co-lead a session with the "Teaching Hard Histories" group about open licenses and publishing platforms, I felt excited! While I work with higher ed instructors frequently about adopting OER for use in their courses, I don't often get to work with pre-service teachers and current students about open education and OER. Students have a very different perspective about open education than instructors, and pre-service teachers in particular have a nuanced perspective that merges the student and instructor roles. During the session, the "Teaching Hard Histories" team, and especially the students, asked clarifying questions to distinguish between open licenses and what platform would be best for publishing their lesson plans.

While I only spent less than an hour with the "Teaching Hard Histories" team (April 22, 2021), I enjoyed the thoughtful discussion about open ed and open licenses. As a project, the "Teaching Hard Histories" team members gave thoughtful consideration to the open license options, potential for a shared lesson plan template, and the platform for publishing. I observed how they worked toward consensus and agreement, which can be complex and contentious. I also observed the "Teaching Hard Histories" facilitators leading with a focus on the values of trust, equity, and growth, which was evident in the session conversation as the students discussed the pros and cons of their licensing options.

Kirsten Mlodynia | Innovation Commons Specialist

In my work to support the Teaching Hard Histories work I've been blessed to work with a group of people with a wide variety of skill sets and expertise. It has been a gift to be able to see the rewards of working collaboratively and how effectively complex and nuanced projects can be successfully completed. The team held trust in each other to be vulnerable, honest, and candid as we engaged in the difficult topics associated with the Hard Histories curriculum. It was empowering to be able to lean on each other and also be afforded the space to learn and grow together.

Faculty responses to doing work in new ways

Kristen McCleary

It has been a long process for me to let go of the 'banking system' of education model. I have had to let go of the control that a textbook promises for shaping a class. I have found connections in unexpected places by looking at history from the margins. Part of the process of editing the interviews is 'tagging' them or creating subcategories. I remember that in 2020 a few interviews mentioned the British system of education (from India, Egypt, and Canada) and this made me see the impact of colonialism and language in a new way. It also made regional connections in a way that I would rarely find in a textbook. Ultimately, open education allows for the unexpected connections to occur in ways that are unlikely to happen in other contexts. Students also often interview family members about how their lives have been shaped by history. These engaging stories connect all of us to my discipline in unexpected, exciting, and emotional ways.

Mary Beth Cancienne

My English methods students are not just writing lesson plans for the instructor. They are writing lesson plans for teachers across America and around the world. As beginning teachers, they now have OER Commons that allows them to change, update, and add to their lessons as they decide what works best for their high school students. The open world view that curriculum can be used, revised, and remixed may produce globally differentiated lessons, materials, and resources.

Ashley Jaffee

The Open process wasn't easy or natural for me. Part of it is me constantly questioning, "is this ready to be shared with the world?" I worry. I worry it isn't ready, for the precise reasons I mentioned above. I want to create curriculum that is centered on equity, social justice, and challenges the status quo. I want to center historically marginalized and oppressed voices and do so in humanizing and beautiful ways. Does our work do this? I don't know. I think we are trying, and I think that is where we are headed, but we have to be okay with it being "open" while still involved in the process.

It isn't/won't be perfect and perhaps that is the point. We are engaging in a community of consumers and producers in the Open space, and things will likely shift and change, that is the purpose of Open afterall, right? This is my understanding, today, which has evolved over the course of this project and will likely continue to change once we move our curriculum into the Open space.

Student responses to being co-creators of knowledge

Question: Throughout the semester you worked on a project that involved complex learning alongside your professor and peers. How did the process of sharing responsibility to develop materials feel for you? What do you understand or have a sense of about the discipline? Would you describe yourself as a co-creator of knowledge? Why or why not?

Joaquin Dela Cruz

The process of creating these open materials was largely comfortable for me because I created them alongside my peers. If it were by myself, I would not have had the foundation that Dr. McCleary already had, and my classmates' ideas on how to make them better would not have been considered.

I am not exactly comfortable saying that I am a "co-creator" because the resources I used for my projects already existed, and I gathered them to share with the world.

Mya Wilcox

Within the process of developing my oral history interview and corresponding analytical essay, I really enjoyed using materials that my peers (and students in past versions of the course) developed in order to create new academic work. I also felt a sense of personal responsibility for the quality of my research when I realized that other students would potentially be using my work to discover new insights as they developed their own projects.

For this assignment in particular, sharing content openly allowed for other students and myself to recognize insights that may not have been easily discoverable from other forms of research—much of the knowledge shared came from anecdotes and/or personal experience with a historical moment. In a sense, I would describe myself and my peers as co-creators of knowledge—by sharing our content with one another, we were able to draw conclusions and develop new insights based on how we each synthesized our previous contributions.

Carter Payne

I liked that we were able to share our research with each other, as well as incorporate information that previous students had found in their projects. This made it easier to share information with each other and help create better and more informed projects. I would not necessarily use the word co-creator because the information I used in my projects was already available and had been compiled by other people. I worked more as an organizer and put the research together in my project.

Mya Gonzales

I enjoyed the process of sharing responsibility to develop materials. To know that my work could be used to assist another student in their research was a very unique feeling and an opportunity I did not expect to have in a GenEd class. I understand this discipline to be about contributing your own story to a body of research and enabling your work to be seen. In this instance, I would describe myself as a co-creator of knowledge because I did the work to create a cohesive interview with supplemented secondary research and helped a story be shared.

Michael Russo

The oral history project first seemed daunting and a lot to tackle with many pieces to compile. However, it was very rewarding and humbling to be able to share someone else's story and perspective on history with my classmates, professor and anyone else who might visit the website.

I felt responsible for telling and sharing my interviewee's story appropriately, accurately and with integrity. A critical factor during the process was simply being a good listener and allowing my interviewee to take as much time as they needed to tell their story.

Even though I completed the oral history interview and the other requirements of the assignment, I wouldn't consider myself a co-creator of knowledge for this Open Educational Project. I view my role as someone who elevated and shared my interviewee's knowledge with others more than a contributor to their knowledge.

Ryland Jones

I think we all felt comfortable sharing these materials with one another. Alia Stone was incredibly helpful in helping the English students figure out how our ideas worked with the IDM or what kind of materials we could bring in to pair with our texts. Rebekah Bloxom and I worked closely together on this material. This project had a learning curve, but by knowing that I had people like Alia or Rebekah to talk things out with, it made it easier to manage. I think I would consider myself a co-creator of knowledge. I didn't create any information from either discipline that people couldn't have already found on their own—I just put some of it together.

Student responses to challenges with open pedagogical practices

Question: As you were considering how you would engage in this open work, what kinds of considerations and challenges came up for you? Are there ways in which publishing or creating work in the open was problematic for you or others?

Joaquin Dela Cruz

Nothing about the process itself was challenging. However, I did think about the implications of my projects when viewed in the future. One of my projects was about racism, COVID-19, and their intersections within the theatre industry. I feared that I missed key facts or figures that showed my ignorance when I looked back in hindsight. Ultimately, I ignored these feelings because I deemed the subject matter more important than hypothetical scenarios.

Mya Wilcox

I did not have any problem publishing my interview openly, given the agreeableness of my interviewee, the topic of our interview, and the fact that we published the interview using pseudonyms. However, for interviews that revolved around particularly polarizing or emotionally charged historical moments, I could see how publishing content openly could be a challenge, especially as it relates to public perception of the interviewer or interviewee (regardless of anonymity.) Because of this, it was slightly more difficult for me to find quality sources for my analytical essay, which touched on a different historical moment than my interview.

Carter Payne

I did not have any challenges when I was creating my project, but I did consider how this information would affect people. My project focused on teaching during the COVID-19 pandemic, and how virtual learning was different from in-person learning. While I was researching my topic and conducting my interview, I could tell that the pandemic was going to have a big impact on learning and that it would continue to impact teachers and students for years.

Mya Gonzales

For my project in particular, I definitely was considerate about the timeframe. Everyone's story is contextualized by the time period they grow up in and social events that unfold around them, so being cognizant of that helped me better understand the interviewee. I interviewed someone whose first language was not English, so my biggest struggle was finding the balance of capturing who they were authentically while also editing their interview for clarity. When creating work in the open, my only concern was privacy. However, using anonymous names fully eliminated that fear for me because my interviewee was not a public figure, but I can see the difficulty in interviewing someone who is a well-known person but wants their story to not be traced back to them

Michael Russo

To my recollection, publishing the work was not problematic at any point over the course of the project. The subject matter (i.e. music therapy, working with people with disabilities, allergies) was not anything extremely sensitive that the interviewee wanted to keep private, and she was still able to retain some anonymity throughout the process by withholding key personal, identifiable information.

Ryland Jones

I was definitely nervous that I wasn't going to be able to produce anything worthwhile. Having my work published was a really strange feeling–I felt like it wasn't detailed enough and that no one would understand what I was trying to say. I know that that isn't the case, but it was still nerve racking. The format itself was a struggle in the beginning as it seemed more rigid than the normal lesson plans I make. As we went on, the process became a lot easier, and manipulating English techniques to fit the format became a breeze.

I can't speak for my peers, but I never really had any problems with publishing or creating this work. I think it's work that needs to be shared. This information has been buried for too long to have my internal problems stop it from being shared with as many people as possible.

2

Open Pedagogy Assignments in Theatre and History Courses to Promote Constructionist Learning and Digital Skills

Lisa Bernd, Cleveland State University
Shelley E. Rose, Cleveland State University
Heather Caprette, Cleveland State University

Abstract

Open pedagogy assignments benefit students in many ways and provide a means of expression for students that can be different from the mainstream. Open pedagogy assignments enhance transferable skills with digital tools for authoring and sharing content. Assignments in which students create presentational knowledge or knowledge checks involve active learning. They engage learners with course topics in a way that goes beyond listening to lectures, note-taking and traditional tests. Students explore their interests and synthesize new knowledge. By offering students choice and voice within a limited set of parameters, the instructor creates an environment conducive to constructionist learning.

In this article we demonstrate the use of digital authoring tools for open pedagogy assignments in the 100 and 200-level gateway courses Introduction to Theatre, Introduction to Geography, and Introduction to Historical Studies courses. These assignments include student creation of knowledge checks, interactive learning objects, in-depth explorations of geographic locations and their meanings, student narratives using historical images as primary sources, and press releases written on significant history publications. Digital authoring tools used by the students include

Pressbooks, H5P, Google Sites, Creative Commons images, and digital cameras to produce one's own images and video.

Keywords: open pedagogy assignments, H5P, Pressbooks, Constructionism, project-based learning, digital humanities

Suggested citation: Bernd, L., Rose, S. E., Caprette, H. (2024). Open pedagogy assignments in theatre and history courses to promote constructionist learning and digital skills. In T. Tijerina (Ed.), *Pedagogy opened: Innovative theory and practice* (pp. 49-78). University of North Georgia Press. https://alg.manifoldapp.org/read/pedagogy-opened-v1-a2/.

Background Information About the Institution and Courses

Cleveland State University (CSU), a public land-grant institution, is an urban campus in downtown Cleveland. The city has a poverty rate of 31.4%, which is 2.7 times the official national average (U.S. Census Bureau, 2021). We have a diverse student body. Approximately 25% are underrepresented minorities (CSU Institutional Research & Analysis Administrative Dashboard, 2022). 78% of full-time, degree-seeking undergraduate students were determined to have financial need in 2021 (CSU Institutional Research & Analysis, CSU Common Data Sets, 2022). In 2014, library director Glenda Thornton started an affordable learning initiative by partnering with the provost and other offices to support the development and use of open educational resources. Professional development talks, a Textbook Affordability Grant, and technology were implemented to encourage participation. One of the technologies was the installation of Pressbooks for CSU. Pressbooks provided an avenue for not only faculty to author open educational resources (OER) but also students to publish their own works.

Faculty within the Department of Theatre and Dance and the Department of History assign open pedagogy projects for introductory and mid-level undergraduate courses with good engagement and academic results. Introduction to Theatre is a general education humanities course and a gateway course at the university, meaning that it is a 100-level course that has more than 100 students enrolling over a calendar year. Its sections are almost always filled. It is an important course for Theatre majors because it contributes to the knowledge and skills necessary for further study in the department. It also draws diverse students from all over the university. Students in the course frequently did not buy the traditional publisher's textbook because of cost or because it was not their major area of study. Some students would have to wait until their financial aid was secured before they could purchase the textbook. This meant that students began the course already at a disadvantage because they would not be prepared for classes or assessments. Frustrated students would drop the course or stop coming, consequently failing the course. For these reasons, the instructor switched to using the open textbook, *Theatrical Worlds* (https://open.umn.edu/opentextbooks/textbooks/242) (Mitchell, 2014). The use of an open textbook improved student success rates and retention.

The Department of Theatre and Dance is housed at Playhouse Square, the country's largest performing venue outside of the Lincoln Center. While CSU promotes a liberal arts education, students in the department also receive a practical education working with Equity actors and union stagehands and participating as production leaders in all areas of theatrical work. Students in this program go on to work professionally in Cleveland as well as around the country or go on to graduate school. While pursuing their degree, 86% of majors hold jobs. Approximately 70% of white students with Pell Grants graduate from the department while less than 60% of Black or African American students with Pell Grants graduate. This is to say that theatre students' limited time and economic resources present challenges to creating a learning environment that is equitable and inclusive. In addition, theatre students' goals, passions, and drive are fundamentally different from other disciplines in that they need to express themselves creatively, often at a high cost to their confidence. Our society and educational system present enormous challenges to emerging artists because the systems undervalue their talent and their contributions to the community. In the classroom, this influences them in several ways. Some are unable to purchase books, and lack of access to course materials and outside commitments affect performance on traditional assessments such as quizzes and tests. Many students lack enthusiasm for traditional academic exercises and modes of delivery. Yet, theatre students must master an enormous amount of academic material in addition to their hands-on training. Theatre history, script analysis, and dramatic theory are all intense areas of study. The goals of this curriculum are to foster the development of intellectually engaged artists and citizens, competent critical thinkers, students with the "soft skill" set necessary in theatre and other professions and the ability to communicate clearly.

Introduction to Geography is a 200-level course for history and social studies education students. It is a comprehensive survey of the field of geography as it relates to the study and teaching of social studies and history and is required for all Early Education and Social Studies majors. The course investigates the core concepts of space, place, and environment and everyday uses of geographical knowledge and skills. Students practice using web-based GIS tools such as Google Maps, StoryMaps, and Google Earth. Introduction to Historical Studies is a gateway 200-level course tailored to history and social studies students. Considered the beginning bookend of the history and social studies majors, Introduction to Historical Studies prepares students with a foundation in historical thinking and research that is a prerequisite for the capstone research seminar. Students develop an understanding of the history discipline and how the transferable skills they will learn as history and social majors will apply to a variety of careers. It is particularly relevant for social studies students to master skills in the digital humanities because they will be teaching them to our youth. Assignments apply skills in communication, application of technologies, critical analysis of information, archival research, and historical thinking.

The Learning Theory behind Open Pedagogy Assignments

Seymour Papert was a mathematician, computer scientist and educator who developed constructionist learning theory in the late 1970s and early 1980s. Two tenets of constructionist learning theory are that we learn best when we are "actively engaged in constructing something that has personal meaning to [us] – be it a poem, a robot, a sandcastle, or a computer program," and learning "happens especially felicitously in a context where the learner is consciously engaged in constructing a public entity (Harel and Papert, 1991)." Theatre students were given a choice of what course topic interested them the most and could use any presented in class to create their interactive learning content with the H5P plugin in Pressbooks. History students, also, were given a choice of book/author, primary source image, and location they wished to create content for within the criteria of their assignments.

Open pedagogy assignments can build digital skills and require synthesis of knowledge about an academic topic. Moreover, they can be an outlet for a *student's voice*, expressing interests and concerns on topics not condoned by law makers in charge of higher education. I believe this could be one interpretation of what Harel and Papert were talking about. In *Situating Constructionism (*Harel and Papert, 1991*)*, Idit Harel and Seymour Papert said, "The presence of computers begins to go beyond first impact when it alters the nature of the learning process; for example, if it shifts the balance between transfer of knowledge to students (whether via book, teacher, or tutorial program is essentially irrelevant) and the production of knowledge by students. It will have really gone beyond it if computers play a part in mediating change in the criteria that govern what *kinds of knowledge are valued* in education." Publication of our students' voices supersedes restrictions on expressing and sharing valuable information about our nation's history. It also provides a means of representation through participation for minority groups, including LGBTQ+ students.

Support and Technology Used for Student Authoring

The digital authoring tools used for the open pedagogy assignments provide a public outlet for the students' values, ideas, and creativity. It is a path to sharing knowledge that is free of the traditional barriers to access. The increasing threat of discriminatory and inequitable laws and educational policies, such as Florida's recent ban on *The 1619 Project* in K-20 education (C.A. Bridges, 2023), along with anti-LGBTQ curriculum laws, means that instructors are looking for methodologies that do not rely on state-approved primary sources while creating a student-centered pedagogy. Developing outlets where students can create their own content to share with the class or publicly express opinions can serve as an alternative to repressive pedagogies. Moreover, the ambiguity of some anti-critical race theory laws leaves room for students to express their opinions about content related to course topics that do not include state government approved primary sources (Russel-Brown, 2022, p. 24). Pressbooks provides opportunities to accommodate students' comfort levels in sharing content and opinions. Students have the option of completing an assignment but excluding it from the public facing view of the book. In this way, students can participate without fear of retribution. In addition to this option, students can use pseudonyms in place of their legal name, if the student desires. Prior arrangements with the instructor will facilitate grading. In this way, a student can share and publish their ideas through an open pedagogy assignment with anonymity to the public. "Anti-woke" laws discourage the literacy and educational autonomy that the options available in Pressbooks may help preserve.

Pressbooks (https://github.com/pressbooks) is a free, open-source authoring platform that can be downloaded from GitHub and installed on an institution's server. It creates multiple sites on the server that are individual books. See the Pressbooks User Guide (https://guide.pressbooks.com/). It is used by many institutions for publishing open educational resources and specifically open textbooks. It allows for different user roles with varying privileges within a Pressbook. In our open pedagogy assignments, students are given the author role. This allows them to create a chapter (page) within the Pressbook for their assignment submission. A Pressbooks author can access and edit chapter pages of their own creation, but they cannot do so with other people's chapter pages. With group projects, one member can be designated to enter the combined assignment work into the Pressbook. The author role also allows them to create H5P content and upload images to the media library of the book. The H5P interactive learning objects and media can then be inserted into the chapter pages they create within the book. An editor role would allow editing of any chapter of the Pressbook. It was not assigned to students because of the risk of accidental deletion of other students' assignment content.

Within each Pressbook is the option to activate and use the H5P plugin. Once activated, an H5P content area is created on the main menu for interfacing with the book. H5P technology allows students to produce knowledge checks and interactive learning content for publication. In 2017, when we started using H5P, there were 43 content types. The developers have since added more and there are now 53. Examples include creation of quizzes and questions over course topics, interactive video with links to more information and questions interspersed on the timeline, course presentations that incorporate many of the other content types, branching scenarios, virtual tours with 360-degree photos, timelines, images with hotspots, juxtaposition of before and after imagery, and Agamotto sequences of images that change over time. For more information visit [H5P Content Types](https://h5p.org/content-types-and-applications).

Though instructors often turn to Pressbooks as a technology for student creation and publication, Google Sites is also a favorite tool for authoring. Google Sites can create a more aesthetically pleasing venue for the student content, given its ability to easily use images for backgrounds within a web page. There can be more than one editor of a Google Site for group work. Separate sites for separate student projects eliminates the risk of accidental deletion with the editor role. On one occasion, a history student admitted that he found it easier to work with Google Sites than to interact with the H5P forms that create content, though H5P.org provides plenty of documentation, examples, and tutorials. For the Introduction to Theatre open pedagogy assignment, an instructional designer visited with the Theatre classes and demonstrated how to access the Pressbook and create H5P content within it. She demonstrated how to search for images in the Public Domain or with a Creative Commons license. For the history classes, she produced video tutorials demonstrating how to create various H5P content of interest. The instructional designer also made herself available to support students with questions by sharing her contact information and by being part of class Teams sites. She also provided administrative support in setting up the Pressbooks and user accounts. Students were also required to generate an embeddable Google Map with their location biographies.

The library at the institution has a multimedia computer lab which students use to borrow digital cameras and utilize Adobe Creative Cloud applications. History students in geography utilized the multimedia lab to photograph their artifacts for their "Concentrates of Place" assignment. Some student film and media majors also have access to digital video cameras through their department. Students with cell phones were encouraged to use them for image and video creation for the assignments. Students could also use screen capture applications to produce location biographies as video presentations. The institution has Panopto Video integrated with Blackboard Learn for this purpose. Panopto allows a student to control the sharing permissions on a video. In this way, the student could make the video available for public viewing, if he or she wished. Some students used Screencastify to create video presentations. Students could also upload videos to YouTube for use in H5P or embedding in Pressbooks.

Overview of the Assignments

Note: For assignment instructions, please see Appendix B.

Theatre Student Development of Interactive Learning Content with H5P

Students were given a class Pressbook and asked to produce H5P knowledge checks and/or interactive learning objects over topics and content in the course. They could utilize their open-source textbook, *Theatrical Worlds*, information about Playhouse Square, presentations, articles, and plays assigned within the course. They were given a link to Playhouse Square's Digital Press Kit as a source for shared images and media. Students could also pull in YouTube videos covering course related topics, such as costume design. They were shown how to locate and use images with Creative Commons and Public Domain licensing.

The instructor facilitated engagement with the open resources. Students were encouraged to collaborate on larger endeavors, such as the creation of interactive video. If students chose simpler forms of H5P, such as multiple-choice questions, they were asked to do three. Students who struggled with Pressbooks were also given the opportunity to submit their assignment to Blackboard Learn. Students were told their assignments would live publicly in a Pressbook and were given the option to opt out of this.

The following learning objectives were supported by the assignment:
1. Explain and represent significant periods in theatre history.
2. Explain elements of theatre production and terminology, such as those found in costume design, lighting design, set design, theatre design, acting theory, and roles in theatre production.
3. Explain and create artifacts about theatre genres.
4. Explain the elements of a play.

Students were graded on both their engagement with the assignment and the appropriateness of the work to the course.

Use of H5P in Gateway Courses for History & Social Studies Majors

Both Introduction to Geography and Introduction to Historical Studies were designed with Robin DeRosa and Rajiv Jhangiani's frames of Open Pedagogy in mind. Conceptualizing these courses and the student-created OER models Open Pedagogy as a "site of praxis." Most importantly for students in these two courses, the instructor draws on their framework of Open Pedagogy as "an access-oriented commitment to learner-driven education AND as a process of designing architectures and using tools for learning that enable students to shape the public knowledge commons of which they are a part" (DeRosa & Jhangiani, 2023). As noted above, this combination is critical to teaching historical thinking in the 21st century United States.

Geography Students' Concentrates of Place Assignment

The "Concentrates of Place" (https://pressbooks.ulib.csuohio.edu/csugelab/chapter/concentrates-of-place/) assignment was given as a precursor to a "Location Biography" project. The concept of "place" is one of the most challenging for students to work with in the "Location Biography" project as reflected in their work and student evaluations from previous semesters. The "Concentrates of Place" project enables students to start thinking critically about the geographical concepts of location, space, and place at the start of the semester. In this assignment, the students

1. were asked to watch a video presentation on the concepts of space and place produced by Heath Robinson, Ph.D. The "Location, Space, and Place" video (https://youtu.be/Kg5uznUMSA0) resides on YouTube;
2. were given a Pressbook with the H5P plugin activated;
3. watched video tutorials on how to use Pressbooks, H5P content creation, and using Photoshop to edit images for use in Pressbooks;
4. received instruction from their instructor during face-to-face class lab time.

Students were asked to choose a location with meaning for them to illustrate place, lending to their ownership of the final product. The students also had a Microsoft Teams site to receive instructions and guidance and post their questions and creations to share with other students. Both the instructor and instructional designer created example assignments within the class Pressbook to show students what was expected. These and student submissions can be seen in "[Concentrates of Place—2022](https://pressbooks.ulib.csuohio.edu/geographyssed/part/place/)" in the Pressbook titled *Geography for Social Studies Educators: Learning Resources and Reflections—Fall 2022*.

Geography Student Location Biography Project

For this assignment, students created websites that are biographies about an absolute location. Google Sites was recommended because most of the education majors in the class will encounter Google Classroom in their teaching careers, but other website content management systems were accepted. This project is given in place of a traditional midterm and final exams in the course, and components are due at various points throughout the semester. Each student must demonstrate mastery of the geographic concepts of place, space, and environment. This assignment has been part of the Introduction to Geography course in some form for 10 years. With the addition of the H5P component and the "Concentrates of Place" assignment, student success in this course increased to 94%. See Appendix A for links to examples of student submissions.

H5P in the Archive: Historical Thinking and Primary Source Analysis

For this assignment, students were introduced to the special collections area at the institution's library. In this class meeting, students were given a box from special collections. They were asked to select one item from the box and, working as a group, answered historical thinking questions about sourcing, contextualization, corroboration, and close reading about the primary source (Stanford History Education Group). Some of the images in the special collections area are digitized and students were welcome to choose one for their "H5P in the Archive" assignment. They were asked to find an image as a primary source and provide an analysis of it. This took the form of writing within a chapter page of their class Pressbook, and inserting an H5P content type of their creation that narrated the image. Student assignment submissions can be seen in "H5P in the Archive" in the Pressbook titled *Intro to Historical Studies: Student Research and Resources—Fall 2022*.

Press Release: Historiography Edition

In the "Press Release" assignment, students created press releases for important contributions to the historical discipline within a class Pressbook. They utilized the Stanford History Education Group's "Historical Thinking Chart" (https://sheg.stanford.edu/sites/default/files/download-pdf/Historical%20Thinking%20Chart.pdf) as a guide to completing their assignment. Students selected a book/author to review from a spreadsheet of recommended books determined to be pioneering works of historical research by instructors in the CSU history department. As part of her open pedagogy method, the instructor completed the assignment herself as an example to demonstrate expectations and each step to the students. They also had a class Teams site for communicating questions about the assignment, receiving instruction, and sharing resources. Student assignment submissions can be seen in "Historiography Timeline" (https://pressbooks.ulib.csuohio.edu/historicalstudiesstudentresearch/front-matter/historiography-timeline/) in the Pressbook titled *Intro to Historical Studies: Student Research and Resources—Fall 2022*. A strength of these Pressbooks publications is that students and instructor alike now have shareable resources that demonstrate their historical thinking skills beyond the classroom. Students can also add links to these products in their resumes and teaching portfolios, increasing their engagement with the assignment, and helping them build a professional identity right from the start of their major.

Conclusion and Reflections on the Assignments

Before the open textbook and Pressbooks assignments, success rates (grade of C or above) in Introduction to Theatre topped out at 72% with 10% failures and 17% withdrawals. After the adoption of an open textbook and the Pressbooks assignments, success rates reached a high of 88% before the COVID-19 pandemic caused an institutional shutdown. As is evident from the results, students were interested in and enjoyed the Pressbooks assignments. Many students took the opportunity to work in teams to pursue projects that were more than the minimum assignment. Videos of department productions and enhanced videos with learning checks were popular choices by teams. Individual students pursued their interests by creating documents and learning checks in a variety of formats—crossword puzzles, fill-in checks, graphic identifications. Students were also appreciative that the previously created assignments offered them a way to check their own knowledge as well as provide insight into what other students found interesting.

The Introduction to Theatre "Interactive Learning Content Creation with H5P" assignment was first assigned in Fall 2017. With encouragement to record video with a cell phone for H5P content types, such as interactive videos, one student partnered with a master electrician to record and create a behind the scenes look at the student production of Steven Sondheim's *Company*. The video was posted to YouTube and used for the creation of an [interactive video](https://pressbooks.ulib.csuohio.edu/theater/chapter/chapter-1-2-interactive-learning-content-theatrical-roles/). Within the video, the student interviewed people in many distinct roles of the theatre production. He linked to the [American Association of Community Theatre's website](https://aact.org/other-key-positions) for further exploration of the roles he mentions along his timeline. He also shows the catwalks where the theatre lights are maintained. Other students utilized existing YouTube videos on costume design to create [interactive videos on costume design for various productions](https://pressbooks.ulib.csuohio.edu/theater/chapter/chapter-1-3-interactive-learning-content-costume-design/). Because of the flexibility of the assignment, students with varying skill levels could complete a content type that worked for them. Some unique uses of content types were implemented, such as the use of H5P's Timeline to illustrate the steps involved in the costume design process. Occasionally, there would be a problem with implementation. The setup of the Flash Cards content type is one. One student presented the acting term on the front of the card and required a short sentence answer, which was difficult for another to complete. This problem was noted and mentioned to subsequent classes of students when they were introduced to the assignment.

Another example from a pair of students who went above and beyond, was an H5P Course Presentation (https://pressbooks.ulib.csuohio.edu/theater-fall-2019/chapter/63/) which incorporated their video of the student production of *Into the Woods*. The viewer is asked to watch the video and then answer questions about it. This presentation interviews students in different acting roles, explains acting terminology, and shows a behind-the-scenes look at rehearsals and preparation for the musical portion of the play. The Course Presentation content type was used for other topics, including "The History of Ancient Greek Theater" (https://pressbooks.ulib.csuohio.edu/theater-fall-2019/chapter/chapter-1/) and "Tools of Lighting Design" (https://pressbooks.ulib.csuohio.edu/theater-fall-2019/chapter/chapter-1-6-interactive-learning-content-lighting-design/). As the development of H5P content types evolved, students in subsequent sections became more creative with the tools, including simple multiple choice question sets (https://pressbooks.ulib.csuohio.edu/theater-fall-2019/chapter/chapter-1-4-interactive-learning-content-costume-design/). Students started to embed YouTube videos on various theatre topics, such as costume design interspersed with their knowledge check questions. Find the Words content type was used for finding terms related to theatre production (https://pressbooks.ulib.csuohio.edu/theater-fall-2019/chapter/63/).

The Introduction to Historical Studies "H5P in the Archive" and "Press Release" assignments were added in Fall 2022. In the Fall 2022 course, student success peaked at an 88% pass rate out of 25 students, increasing from 69% pass rate in Fall 2020, 78% in Spring 2021, and 72% pass rate in Fall 2021. The H5P assignment introduced students to the H5P plugin, and the Image Hotspots content type allowed for an historical analysis of the chosen image and its content. Hotspots allowed for more context to be given, along with other writing within a Pressbook page. The ability to add embeds of YouTube videos with the hotspots, created the opportunity for further exploration of a subject, such as the links to a biography about Martin Luther King, Jr. and Malcolm X seen in the historical analysis of Martin Luther King, Jr's and Malcolm X's Press Conference (https://pressbooks.ulib.csuohio.edu/historicalstudiesstudentresearch/chapter/stadalskyh5p/). The history student authors explained the historical context of the image, demonstrating how this analysis fits the steps of historical thinking. This introduction to using Pressbooks served as a foundation for the "Press Release" assignment where students turned their attention to secondary source analysis. They were able to write press releases for pioneering works of historical research such as Kathy Peiss' *Hope in a Jar*, further reinforcing the digital publishing lessons learned in the H5P assignment. Students in this course noted the value of learning transferable skills through these assignments and that they could be applied to their own historical work as well as other disciplines.

The "Concentrates of Place" and "Location Biography" assignments gave students the opportunity to explore, research, and demonstrate their proficiency in geographic concepts using a specific geographic location. Students used the Image Hotspots H5P content type to explain objects they selected for their tin. Students explained the concepts of location, space, and place within a Pressbook page for assessment. Students learned how to create embeddable Google maps to illustrate their locations. The websites created for the "Location Biography" allowed students to research change over time in a specific location and explore place meaning. The impact of using open pedagogy and Pressbooks in Introduction to Geography is clear. Fall 2020 and Fall 2021 both had a pass rate of 78.8%. With the addition of the "Concentrates of Place" assignment and semester-long focus on open pedagogy student success in Fall 2022 increased to 94.3%. This result is promising for future cohorts in this required course for early education majors and social studies majors and reveals that the addition of the H5P assignment did the work of scaffolding the "Location Biography" project and providing all students with the skills and confidence to complete these digital projects.

The assignment designs facilitated active engagement with course content and collaboration with each other, especially with the creation of the videos on student productions. Completion and success with the assignments was high when they were engaged with projects that had personal meaning to them, demonstrating that voice and choice are critical components of open pedagogy design. Introduction to new technologies and media resources are built on digital skills, which are valued in many careers and by future employers.

References

Bridges, C.A. (2023, January 27). What is 'The 1619 Project' and why has Gov. DeSantis banned it from Florida schools? *The Daytona Beach News-Journal.* https://www.tallahassee.com/story/news/education/2023/01/27/1619-project-hulu-why-are-republican-states-banning-it-in-schools/69847374007/

DeRosa, R., & Jhangiani, R. (2017). Open pedagogy. In E. Mays (Ed.), *A guide to making open textbooks with students*. The Rebus Community for Open Textbook Creation. https://press.rebus.community/makingopentextbookswithstudents/chapter/open-pedagogy/

Harel, I., & Papert, S. (1991). *Constructionism: research reports and essays, 1985-1990.* Ablex Pub. Corp.

Mitchell, C. (2014). *Theatrical worlds*. University Press of Florida. https://open.umn.edu/opentextbooks/textbooks/242

Office of Institutional Research & Analysis, Cleveland State University. (2022). *CSU common data sets: 2021-2022.* https://www.csuohio.edu/iraa/csu-common-data-sets-cds

Office of Institutional Research & Analysis, Cleveland State University. (2022). *Administrative dashboard: Overall enrollment – headcount.* https://www.csuohio.edu/irtableau/administrative-dashboard-0

Russell-Brown, K. (2022). 'The Stop WOKE Act': HB 7, race, and Florida's 21st century anti-literacy campaign. *UF Law Faculty Publications, 1203.* 26. https://scholarship.law.ufl.edu/facultypub/1203

Stanford History Education Group. (2023, July 31). Reading like a historian. *Stanford History Education Group.* https://sheg.stanford.edu/history-lessons?f%5B0%5D=topic%3A7#main-content#main-content

U.S. Census Bureau. (2021, July 1). *QuickFacts for Cleveland, Ohio.* https://www.census.gov/quickfacts/clevelandcityohio

U.S. Census Bureau. (2021). *Poverty in the United States: 2021* (Report Number P60-277). https://www.census.gov/library/publications/2022/demo/p60-277.html

Author Bios
Lisa Bernd, Cleveland State University

Dr. Bernd received her Ph.D. from the University of Wisconsin-Madison in Theater History and is an Associate College Lecturer in the Department of Theatre and Dance at Cleveland State University. She teaches Introduction to Theatre, Theatre History, Script Analysis and Dramaturgy. A staunch advocate of open and hybrid pedagogy, she has worked with co-author Heather Caprette to create resources that eliminate textbooks in THE111, saving students over $25,000 annually.

Shelley E. Rose, Cleveland State University

Dr. Rose received her Ph.D. from Binghamton University and is Associate Professor and Director of Social Studies in the Department of History at Cleveland State University. Her research interests include digital humanities, pedagogy, protest movements, and gender history. She is a cofounder of the Cleveland Teaching Collaborative.

Heather Caprette, Cleveland State University

Heather Caprette, M.F.A. works as a Sr. Media Developer/Instructional Designer in CSU Online at Cleveland State University. She works with faculty on the design and development of open educational resources, and open pedagogy assignments. She also helps faculty design online courses that meet Quality Matters standards.

Appendix A: Links to Examples of Student Work
Pressbooks with Student Content
1. Fall 17 – Introduction to Theatre – Learning Resources (https://pressbooks.ulib.csuohio.edu/theater/)
2. Spring 18 – Introduction to Theater – Learning Resources (https://pressbooks.ulib.csuohio.edu/theater-spring-2018/)
3. Fall 2019 – Introduction to Theater – Learning Resources (https://pressbooks.ulib.csuohio.edu/theater-fall-2019/)
4. Geography for Social Studies Educators: Learning Resources and Reflections – Fall 2022 (https://pressbooks.ulib.csuohio.edu/geographyssed/)
5. Intro to Historical Studies: Student Research and Resources – Fall 2022 (https://pressbooks.ulib.csuohio.edu/historicalstudiesstudentresearch/)

Location Biographies Created by Students
1. EngagedScholarship @ CSU (https://engagedscholarship.csuohio.edu/locbio/)
2. Ken Kesey's Farm (https://sites.google.com/view/keseyfarmspace/home)
3. Saint Peter's Basilica (https://sites.google.com/view/jester-saintpetersbasilica/home?authuser=0)
4. Lakeview Estates (https://sites.google.com/view/tinker-phelps-lakeview-terrace/home?authuser=0)
5. Phillips Fones Cliff, Richmond County VA and the Return to the River Program (https://sites.google.com/view/phillipsfonescliff/timeline)
6. Pickett's Charge, Gettysburg, PA, site of a key battle during the American Civil War (https://sites.google.com/view/pickettscharge biography)
7. The Marble Room, Cleveland, OH, a building with beautiful architecture (https://sites.google.com/view/francescaklein/place)
8. The New Orleans Superdome site (https://sites.google.com/view/theneworleanssuperdome/home) & Video Presentation (https://watch.screencastify.com/v/JkKF080xvatSTnLEeLdI)

Appendix B: Assignment Instructions
The Interactive Learning Content assignment instructions given to the Introduction to Theatre students are below:

Instructor: Lisa Bernd, Ph.D.

Interactive Learning Content Creation with H5P

In this assignment, you will design interactive learning content for your fellow students to study from. These knowledge checks will be built with the H5P tool and presentations will have a public life in a Pressbook called *Introduction to Theater – Learning Resources*. You have the opportunity to build upon the open resources for Theater and teach the world what you know! Remember that if you cannot build the content in the Pressbook for any reason, you can still submit to this Blackboard assignment area to receive credit.

You can pick your topic of choice, but please write knowledge checks and interactive learning content relating to knowledge you have gained from your textbook, *Theatrical Worlds,* and that is presented in class. You can use open resources that permit reuse, such as images and video found on Playhouse Square's Digital Press Kit site, or theater images provided to you through a shared Google Drive folder established for this course. There are also images available through Wikimedia Commons (https://commons.wikimedia.org/wiki/Main_Page). Other places and ways you can search for re-usable media are suggested on the Creative Commons Search page (https://search.creativecommons.org/). These sites include YouTube, Flickr, Pixabay, and Google Images. Google Image search (https://support.google.com/websearch/answer/29508?hl=en) allows you to filter results by Usage Rights. To do this, run your search under Google Images (https://images.google.com/), select the Tools button, and then click on Usage Rights to get a drop-down menu. Select Creative Commons licenses from the drop-down menu. See Figure 1.

Open Pedagogy Assignments in Theatre and History Courses | 67

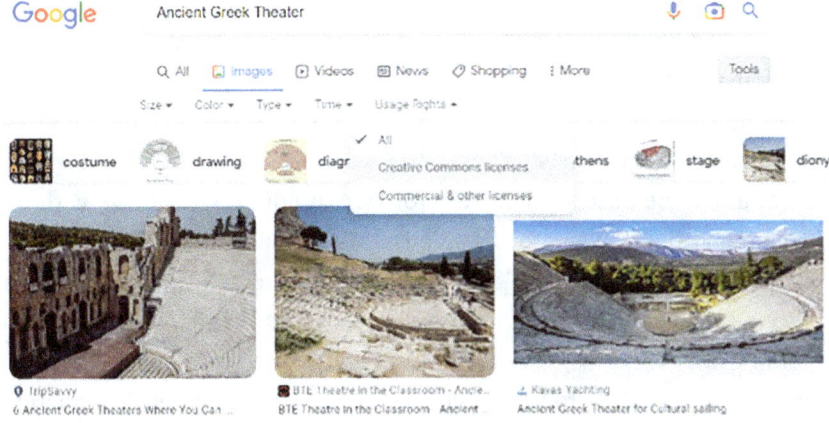

Figure 1: Google Image search

You might also try the Getty Search Gateway (http://search.getty.edu/gateway/search?q=&cat=highlight&f=%22Open+Content+Images%22&rows=10&srt=a&dir=s&pg=1) for public domain photographs of theaters.

Be sure to check for actual usage rights when you locate media you want to use and cite your sources for the media and other content. Purdue Online Writing Lab has an MLA Formatting Style Guide (https://owl.english.purdue.edu/owl/resource/747/01/) that will demonstrate how to properly cite your sources. Also, please credit yourself as well as others when you create the interactive content.

Your interactive learning content can be any of the types found on the H5P website (https://h5p.org/). Examples of content types you might create are:
1. Interactive Video with Questions to test viewers' attention with embedded links to other sites with further information (note: you can use YouTube and Vimeo URLs or import your own .mp4 video file)
2. Multiple Choice Questions
3. Fill in the Blank Questions
4. Drag and Drop Exercises that may test knowledge of Theater terminology associated with images that are open source and labeled for reuse

5. Timelines
6. Presentations of a topic

You will build these in a Pressbook called *Introduction to Theater—Learning Resources*, hosted by Michael Schwartz Library and then make a submission within your Blackboard course.

You will be sent soon (instructor will announce) an email with an invitation to join "Name of Pressbook." The email will contain a link to activate your user account. Please click the link to activate your account as soon as possible, because the invitation expires within three days. You should get an email with your username and password to login. If you do not get this and have trouble logging in, please contact [insert information for your Pressbooks administrator].

Once you are in the *Introduction to Theater – Learning Resources* book, look for **H5P Content** at the bottom of the left navigation column. Click on **H5P Content**, then click **Add new** at the top of the screen. In the first text entry box, give your content a descriptive title and pick the type of content you would like to create. Once you select a content type, you will have links to a tutorial on how to create it and examples on the H5P website (https://h5p.org/).

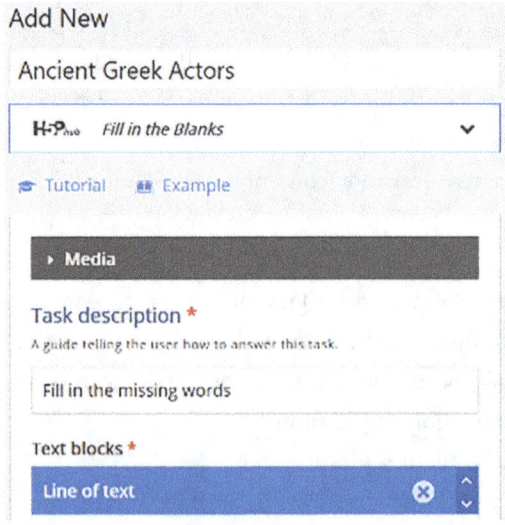

Figure 2: Screen for adding new H5P content

Follow the instructions on the H5P website (https://h5p.org/) for your content type. When you are done, note the ID given to your H5P content. The ID number will show in the ID column under the page for All H5P Content. See the examples below.

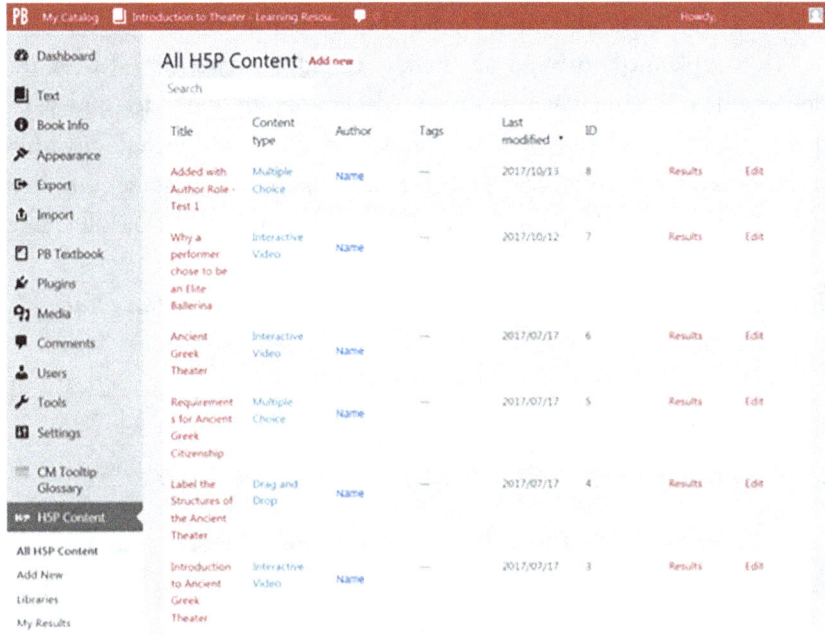

Figure 3: Screen showing all H5P content created within a Pressbook, with unique ID numbers

Next, to receive credit for the assignment and notify your instructor that you have completed it, log into your Blackboard Learn course and submit the assignment there also. Within the Blackboard Assignment, give the H5P **Content Title, Type, Date Created, and ID** for each interactive learning content you created in the Pressbook *Introduction to Theater – Learning Resources*. An example of this type of description you will submit to Blackboard, is:

Ancient Greek Theater, Interactive Video, 2017/07/17, ID=6.

If you have any questions or issues, please let your instructor know. You can also contact [insert your instructional designer contact information]. If you are unable to build the H5P content in the class's Pressbooks site, please let your instructor know and submit your ideas via the Blackboard Assignment. So, if you plan to build a multiple-choice question, write the question with its possible answers and note the correct answer.

If you planned to build an interactive video, write the URL of the online video, tell me when you planned on stopping the video and what question (with correct answer) you planned on asking, and include any links to outside resources that lead to more information about something that was talked about in the video. Describe your idea thoroughly for full credit!

Remember to pick content you enjoyed learning and have fun creating!

See an [example of the Word document you submit to the learning management system](https://docs.google.com/document/d/14WfB2722Dczw7vIOP2_V7pTmkJ6Tjt9rHZ2HIKDG_i4/edit?usp=sharing) (https://docs.google.com/document/d/14WfB2722Dczw7vIOP2_V7pTmkJ6Tjt9rHZ2HIKDG_i4/edit?usp=sharing).

The "Concentrates of Place" assignment instructions given to Introduction to Geography students are below:

Instructor: Shelley Rose, Ph.D.

This "Concentrates of Place" assignment is adapted from Marianne Braca's 2021 essay "[How My Geography Class Used Tins to Tell the Story of Place](https://blog.education.nationalgeographic.org/2021/11/17/how-my-geography-class-used-tins-to-tell-the-story-of-place/)" (https://blog.education.nationalgeographic.org/2021/11/17/how-my-geography-class-used-tins-to-tell-the-story-of-place/). Braca (a National Geographic Certified Educator) was inspired by artist Tanya Shadrick's project "[Concentrates of Place](https://tanyashadrick.com/concentrates-of-place/)" (https://tanyashadrick.com/concentrates-of-place/). In her creations, Shadrick curates "place" in small tins as a representation of the places she has visited. In her words, they are "memories made tangible." In geography, a space is an absolute location, such as GPS coordinates. Place is more ephemeral and different for each individual experiencing the space. Place is the character of a space, the feelings it inspires, the memories the space invokes.

This assignment is an excellent start on your journey of thinking critically about location, space, and place for the "Location Biography Project" (https://pressbooks.ulib.csuohio.edu/csugelab/part/location-biography/).

Learning Outcomes

- Students will understand and apply the geographic concept of "place"
- Students will practice digital publishing techniques, including H5P
- Students will write for a general audience

First, we need an overview of the concepts of space and place. For a detailed overview, watch this 12-minute video. "Location, Space, and Place" (https://www.youtube.com/watch?v=Kg5uznUMSA0) by Heath Robinson, Ph.D.

Figure 4: "Curating a Place," Shelley E. Rose, 2022

What Goes in Your Tin? Project Guidelines

Follow these steps to complete your "Concentrates of Place" Assignment:
1. Pick up a tin from your instructor in class or during student hours.
2. Choose a location with meaning for you and curate objects into the tin. NOTE: if you place perishable or natural objects, have a plan for their sustainability or removal from the tin.
3. Take a photo of the tin and contents (visit the Digital Design Studio or contact your instructor for assistance if needed).
4. Go to the GSSE Learning Resources and Reflections eBook and log in.
5. Create a page for your "Concentrates of Place" reflection following this tutorial (How to Create a Chapter Page within a Class Pressbook https://csuohio.hosted.panopto.com/Panopto/Pages/Viewer.aspx?id=ed79f490-40cf-4ae0-a98d-af10013e2dcb). Include the following elements in your Reflection:
    - What "place" did you curate?
    - What is the absolute or relative location (Share absolute location only if you are comfortable. For example, do not list the coordinates of your home but give a relative location description of the place you curate)
    - What did you include in your tin? (Use H5P to take us on a tour of your objects)
    - How do these items represent the "place" meaning of the location or space?
    - What does this place mean to you? What might it mean from someone else's perspective? Be sure to cite sources if you draw on secondary sources outside of your own experience with the location.

Potential H5P Content Types

Visit the H5P website (https://h5p.org/) for general information about curating content using H5P.
- Use Image Hotspots (https://h5p.org/image-hotspots) to post images of your tin and its items. You can use the hotspot for curating the sense of place

- Use [Agamotto](https://h5p.org/content-types/agamotto) to create layers or sequences as you analyze and curate place in your tin
- See [Appendix 1](https://pressbooks.ulib.csuohio.edu/geographyssed/back-matter/appendix/) in the Geography for Social Studies Educators student research eBook for a full collection of H5P and Pressbooks tutorials by the instructional designer working with the class

Additional Resource for Teaching Place

- Vicky Ellaway-Barnard, "[The Identity Game](https://www.jstor.org/stable/26455212)," Teaching Geography 43:1 (Spring 2018): 19-21. https://www.jstor.org/stable/26455212

The "Location Biography" assignment instructions given to Introduction to Geography students are below:

Instructor: Shelley Rose, Ph.D.

This project centers on **three core concepts** in geography: **space** (a location on the Earth's surface), **place** (form of bounded space- gives space meaning), and **environment** (what is the context of the location? how have humans changed or adapted the physical space of the location?)

- Choose a location in consultation with the instructor.
- Evaluate the geography of that location over time based on the concepts of place and space—in effect creating a "biography" of that location.
- Consider the following: Does this space have specific place meaning? Is that meaning the same for all people who use or interact with the space? Has the space been repurposed? Is it structurally the same?
- Evaluate the relationship between humans and this location. In what ways has the space changed over your timeframe and why?

Expectations and Due Dates

You will choose a location and specific timespan to evaluate. Turn in a thesis statement, an outline of your project, and a Chicago Style bibliography in class during Week 5. Between Week 5 and your assigned presentation date, you will determine the best digital format for your location; you may create a website for your location or consult the instructor about an alternative format. See the instructions for creating a "Location Biography" website (https://pressbooks.ulib.csuohio.edu/csugelab/chapter/locbiosite/) in this chapter.

Presentation

Each student will present their work to the class in a 5-10 minute presentation that is a recorded tour of your website. You may use Panopto on Blackboard to submit your assignment. For non-CSU students, there are also free apps for recording such as Screencastify (https://www.screencastify.com/) for Chrome Browsers, Open Broadcaster Software (https://obsproject.com/), or for some Macs visit How to record your screen (https://support.apple.com/en-us/HT208721). If you are unable to record audio, consider using a tool like Windows Steps Recorder (https://www.wikihow.com/Use-the-Steps-Recorder-in-Windows) and adding text narration.

Research Tips

- View this video on Location, Space, and Place (https://www.youtube.com/watch?v=Kg5uznUMSA0).
- Check the historical imagery on Google Earth.
- For Greater Cleveland locations check The Cleveland Memory Project (http://www.clevelandmemory.org/) and contact CSU's Special Collections department (https://library.csuohio.edu/speccoll/).
- For global locations check Old Maps Online (https://www.oldmapsonline.org/) or the Rumsey Historical Map Collection (https://www.davidrumsey.com/).
- Also check out the Cleveland Public Library Digital Collections (https://cdm16014.contentdm.oclc.org/digital/).
- Visit our CSU Research Guide (https://researchguides.csuohio.edu/HIS299/primary) for information on primary, secondary, and tertiary sources.
- See this list of digital GIS projects (http://anterotesis.com/wordpress/mapping-resources/dh-gis-projects/) for potential sources.

Grading

Projects will be graded on your ability to follow the directions above as well as formatting, organization, creativity, and understanding of the geographic concepts of place, space, and location.

The "H5P in the Archive" assignment instructions given to Historical Studies students are below:

Instructor: Shelley Rose, Ph.D.

In this historical thinking project, we will use H5P to explore a historical image as a primary source. In short, you will create a visual narrative of people, places, and things in the image and contextualize its journey in world history. This narrative method is characteristic of historian Timothy Brook's analysis in his 2008 book Vermeer's Hat (https://www.google.com/books/edition/Vermeer_s_Hat/2avtJqYc1eMC?hl=en&gbpv=0). See An Interview with Timothy Brook (http://www.essentialvermeer.com/interviews_newsletter/brook_interview.html).

This activity is an exercise in historical thinking about a specific material primary source.

Intro to Archives and Archival Sources

Archival Research Guiding Questions
1. What do you expect to find in the archive? (pre-primary source session)
2. What did you find? (post-primary source session) Students complete historical thinking worksheet (https://docs.google.com/forms/d/e/1FAIpQLScFXahKrDWeb7_kzFpgOyWtjBptw3w_wWUjj62xE5VGGuZoyA/viewform). (Or use the one provided in the library session)
3. How do you think historians can use this source for research? (pre-secondary source session)
4. How have historians used sources like this in secondary research? (post-secondary source session)
5. What subdisciplines, or "houses," of history are represented in the secondary sources you located? (post-secondary source session)

Historical Thinking and Primary Source Analysis

Your primary source analysis will include two main components:
1. A complete overview of your historical thinking as you analyze the primary source. This will include listing the steps of historical thinking (sourcing, contextualization, corroboration, and close reading) as part of your chapter, filling in your analysis as you go.
2. You will use H5P to elaborate on the contextualization step and visually analyze your source. See an [example of a completed assignment](https://pressbooks.ulib.csuohio.edu/historicalstudiesstudentresearch/chapter/roseh5p/).

H5P Project Lab

You will use H5P content types and your own written analysis to demonstrate the steps of historical thinking with this primary source.

H5P Instructions:
1. Choose an image to serve as your "lens" or a "door." See the Essential Vermeer for examples of how this works using the ["Officer and Laughing Girl"](http://www.essentialvermeer.com/catalogue/officer_and_laughing_girl.html) (1658). Be sure to scroll over the image of the painting to see the embedded narratives.
2. Go to your class [Pressbook](https://pressbooks.ulib.csuohio.edu/historicalstudiesstudentresearch/) and log in.
3. In the dashboard, create a "chapter" under the heading "H5P in the Archive." Label it with the title of your historical thinking project and your last name. You can edit the URL to be just your last name and H5P after the forward slash.
4. Browse the H5P site. Decide on how you would like to format your image to show sourcing, contextualization, corroboration, and close reading.
5. Click on "H5P Content" in the left menu of the Pressbooks Dashboard.
6. Click on "Add New."
7. Select your desired H5P Content Type from the menu and start filling in the fields.

8. When you are finished, click "Create" in the upper right corner of the dashboard.
9. Return to your chapter page. Navigate to where you want to insert the H5P content and click "Add H5P." Select your content from the list. Click "Insert."

The "Press Release" assignment instructions given to Historical Studies students are below:

Instructor: Shelley Rose, Ph.D.

This "Press Release" assignment can be used alone or as a planning assignment (formative assessment) for the Historiography UnEssay. It is intended as a brief, intense writing exercise for a general audience to have students practice career readiness (https://www.clestatecareers.com/post/are-you-career-ready) skills such as communication and application of information technology.

Instructions:
1. Choose a historian or historical publication/project that had a significant impact on the discipline of history. For example, Joan Wallach Scott's pioneering 1986 article, "Gender as a Useful Category of Analysis" in the American Historical Review.
2. Write a press release of around 500-800 words (notes not included). You may use any formats supported by Pressbooks and H5P.
3. Include your analysis of why this historian and/or publication is important to the field of history & which subdiscipline(s) it belongs to. Pitch it to a general audience.
4. Be sure to include the elements in the blue box in your press release and remember the sourcing and historical thinking skills outlined by the Stanford History Education Group at SHEG Chart (https://sheg.stanford.edu/sites/default/files/download-pdf/Historical%20Thinking%20Chart.pdf).

Inspiration for this assignment came from concluding comments by historian David Perry in *Drafting the Past* Episode 10, "David M. Perry Writes Out Loud."

Elements of a Press Release

Include the following sections in your press release:
- Historiography Connections
- Geographic Coverage
- Citation for First Edition/Printing (Chicago Style)
- Press Release (the analytical text of the press release, or the video and transcript, 500-800 words)

Sample formats for your press release:
- Written/Journalistic Style (https://pressbooks.ulib.csuohio.edu/historicalstudiesstudentresearch/chapter/rosepr/)
- VideoClip (https://www.youtube.com/watch?v=MQG6AR5diPw): See this clip with Kenn Michael on *Reading Rainbow* giving an overview of *Jumanji* for inspiration.
  Note: If you create a video you will need to be sure to have closed captioning and a transcript to post on your page with the video. Include any footnotes and a bibliography.

See examples of video tutorials created for students working on H5P and Pressbooks assignments (https://docs.google.com/document/d/1yP-qdGvxdcwpCZhyD1WLjlQnG6fOljM9newm2p3e8wY/edit?usp=sharing) by the instructional designer.

3

Culturally Sustaining Pedagogy & Open Educational Practices in K–8 Amidst High-Stakes Testing

Daniela R. Amaya, University of California, Los Angeles
Caroline E. Parker, SRI International
Krystal Thomas, SRI International

Abstract

Scholarship on open educational practices (OEP) and culturally sustaining pedagogy (CSP) challenges long-held dominant beliefs about what a classroom should look like. While OEP views knowledge as a public good that students ought to be a part of shaping, CSP situates its critique within a socio-political awareness of racial inequality. As the use of open educational resources (OER)—defined as materials with an open license that allows free use and adaptation—increases in K–8 education, there is an opportunity to implement OEP and CSP to enact a more equitable education for students. Through case studies of four full-course K–8 OER programs dedicated to inclusivity, this brief explores how the principles of OEP and CSP are mobilized in tandem to transform education.

Specifically, this brief discusses the complexities of leveraging the affordances of OER amidst the backdrop of nationwide standards and high-stakes testing that—in being used to inform students' grade advancement, graduation requirements, teacher evaluation, and school funding—narrowly dictate the content taught in schools.

Keywords: culturally sustaining pedagogy, open educational practices, open educational resources, high-stakes testing, open pedagogy, culturally responsive practices

Suggested citation: Amaya, D. R., Parker, C. E., & Thomas, K. (2024). Culturally sustaining pedagogy & open educational practices in K–8 amidst high-stakes testing. In T. Tijerina (Ed.), *Pedagogy opened: Innovative theory and practice* (pp. 79-96). University of North Georgia Press. https://alg.manifoldapp.org/read/pedagogy-opened-v1-a3/.

Theoretical background: Culturally sustaining pedagogy (CSP) and open educational practices (OEP)

Even as students of color now comprise a majority of U.S. public school enrollments (NCES, 2023), their communities' ontologies, or ways of being and knowing, are too often excluded from the classroom. Culturally sustaining pedagogy (CSP) is a theory in education that demands the de-centering of white middle-class norms[1]; that is, norms that permeate curricular content, definitions, and measures of success and behavioral expectations. In building on Ladson-Billing's (1995) original conception of culturally responsive practices, CSP views marginalized students' cultures as not only a *means* for delivering educational content but also the very content that should be taught and sustained through schooling (Paris & Alim, 2017). In this definition, culture is both the longstanding practices and belief systems of communities of color and youths' contemporary reworkings of that knowledge "to meet their current cultural and political realities" (Paris & Alim, 2017, p. 8). CSP further asserts that schools should develop students' ability to critique dominant discourse about real-world contemporary issues that affect them, a concept that Ladson-Billings (2014) refers to as sociopolitical consciousness.

CSP can be used to understand cultural norms even at the highest levels of the American education system; for example, the U.S. Department of Education's "mission is to promote student achievement and preparation

---

[1] Examples of white middle-class norms include favoring individualism over collectivism, indirect versus direct communication styles, and written traditions over oral traditions to reproduce knowledge.

for global competitiveness." Scholars of CSP document how this notion of competitiveness is a feature of individualistic culture common in white societies where individual achievement and independence are emphasized (Hammond, 2015). As a contrasting example, "traditional education from Indigenous centers strives toward the whole and ethical development of the person situated within the collective" (Holmes & González, 2017, p. 219). Collectivism is a common feature in cultures that value connections to communities, people, and histories. Collectivism supports community building through an understanding of the cultures within them; in the classroom, this entails strong relationships between teachers and students. Too often, the dominant culture values competition over collectivism (Hammond, 2015), which diminishes opportunities for teachers and student relationships in an increasingly-diverse student population. A classroom using CSP to center collectivism might have students collaborating to respond to test questions, whereas individualistic culture could label the same practice as cheating.

Scholarship on OEP has a natural affinity for the theoretical underpinnings of CSP. The OEP movement grew from OER, which are instructional materials with an open license that can be reused and adapted without permission from, or the need to pay royalties to, the copyright holder (Butcher, 2011). With the increased awareness and use of OER, OEP is now pushing to expand definitions of openness beyond materials and content and toward practices and processes (Bali et al., 2020; Ehlers, 2011). Conceptualizations of OEP are expansive; however, most hinge on centering students as knowledge generators who shape the knowledge commons (DeRosa & Jhangiani, 2017). OEP often include the usage, adaptation, and creation of OER, as well as collaborative pedagogies between students, between teachers, and between students and teachers (Ehlers, 2011).

While OEP is not inherently focused on centering diverse racial/ethnic and linguistic cultures, some scholars are pushing to explicitly reframe OEP through a social justice lens (Bali et al., 2020; Brown & Croft, 2020; Lambert, 2018). Lambert (2018) proposes a definition that states OEP should be "primarily by and for the benefit and empowerment of non-privileged learners who may be under-represented in education systems or marginalized in their global context" (p. 239). Bali et al. (2020) suggest a social justice framework whereby OEP address economic, cultural, and/or political injustice.

As this literature is emerging, CSP offers a critical lens to OEP outside of dominant white perspectives, which can in turn expand conceptions of the knowledge commons. CSP situates many concepts of equitable education present in OEP within a socio-political understanding of how and why academic settings aren't "open" to begin with. For example, OEP espouses a shift from teachers as the "dispensers of knowledge" to facilitators of student-centered learning (Geser, 2012, p. 40); CSP contextualizes that within a "legacy of genocide, land theft, enslavement, and various forms of colonialism," this top-down system of education serves to assimilate communities of color to dominant ways of thinking (Paris & Alim, 2017). Why do most Americans learn about Westward expansion as "manifest destiny" and not about the genocide of Indigenous peoples through this process? If Indigenous perspectives were honored as part of the knowledge commons, these lessons would include a more expansive account of U.S. history. OEP, in viewing knowledge as a public good, relies on collaboration and open sharing; CSP situates this collaboration as a natural component of communities of color's lifeways that are denied by hyper-individualism in the U.S. OEP encourages the constant updating of materials to ensure relevancy; CSP offers an understanding that culture is not static but instead being constantly re-defined by youth in real-time and should be circularized in academic settings. Why then is standardized Dominant American English (DAE) considered "academic language" while Latine and Black youth's linguistic practices are considered "inappropriate" (Rosa & Flores, 2017)? If students were centered as knowledge generators, their linguistic practices would contribute to how we define the English language.

The K–8 context: Standards and high-stakes testing

In the 1980s, state legislators across the country began promoting standards-based education in K–8 through policy changes. Over time, this policy evolved to hold teachers and schools accountable to standards using individual student performance on state standardized tests. In 2002, the Bush administration codified accountability through testing into federal law through the No Child Left Behind (NCLB) Act (Gonzalez & Vasudeva, 2021). NCLB was eventually replaced by the Obama administration's

Every Student Succeeds Act (ESSA) in 2015, which is still in effect today. While ESSA reduced test-based accountability requirements, it still requires states to set academic standards and test students annually in math and literacy during grades 3–8, as well as once in science during grades 3–5 and once during grades 6–9[2] (Lee, n.d.). These state standardized tests are often referred to as "high-stakes" because scores are used for students' grade advancement, graduation requirements, teacher evaluation, and school funding (Gonzalez & Vasudeva, 2021).

CSP scholars have identified the many ways in which the system of high-stakes testing, and its effects on teacher practices, disadvantage students of color. Dr. Gloria Ladson-Billings (2017) asserts, "educational research has shown that standardized tests are narrowly normed along white, middle-class, monolingual measures of achievement" (p. 143). Further, standardized exams are content-based and fail to measure "students' reasoning ability, problem-solving skills, and moral development" (Ladson-Billings, 2017, p. 143). Even more, high-stakes testing "undermine[s] teacher's autonomy, and de-professionalize[s] the teaching field" as educators are forced to tailor teaching to test preparation (Love, 2019, p. 101).

Research on OEP, being grounded in principles of student-centered learning, also discusses the limitations of this learning environment from the perspective of OER use. Ehlers (2011) describes that "the pure usage of OER in a traditional closed and top-down, instructive, exam-focused learning environment is not open educational practice" (p. 5). Indeed, a narrow focus on test preparation means that subjects that are not tested—such as social studies, art, and foreign languages—get devalued. This becomes especially troublesome considering that "evidence suggests, on average, schools that serve disadvantaged students engage in more test preparation" (Koretz, 2018, p. 23). Using OER in a high-stakes testing environment that forces teacher-centered instruction "will have little effect on equipping teachers, students, and workers with the competencies, knowledge, and skills to participate successfully in the knowledge economy and society" (Geser, 2012, p. 12).

---

2   At the high school level, states are required to test students once in math, literacy, and science.

Methods

In the context of the current ESSA policy, researchers worked in close collaboration with four participating non-profit organizations that develop OER to understand how they integrate CSP in their materials. The programs create full-course curricula that are standards-aligned and collectively span English language arts, mathematics, and science. The OER materials were originally developed through foundation grant funding; each organization now uses several methods to generate revenue. These methods include paid professional learning, digital tools for accessing content, and district partnerships that offer additional benefits and specialized support. Through in-depth case studies of the four programs described, researchers reviewed samples of their curriculum and professional learning materials and conducted a total of nine 1-1.5 hour focus groups with material developers, teachers, and students. The programs were identified in collaboration with the study's funder and opted into participating; their staff played active roles in choosing which materials they wished to have analyzed and in identifying study participants.

To review samples of each programs' curriculum and professional learning materials, researchers created a review protocol which was adapted from existing OEP and CSP protocols (Bali et al., 2020; Bryan-Gooden et al., 2019; Peoples et al., 2021). The team incorporated additional terms and definitions from the literature on CSP (Gay, 2018; Hammond, 2015; Ladson-Billings, 1995; Love, 2019; Paris & Alim, 2017) to ultimately identify seven constructs that illustrate these pedagogies: classroom culture of care, critical consciousness, free and open access, generating new knowledge, high and equitable standards, inclusive content, and student agency and ownership (see Table 1).

Table 1: Constructs associated with open educational practices and culturally sustaining practices

Construct	Definition
Classroom culture of care	Class materials and activities provide opportunities and guidance to develop strong relationships (e.g., safe space, ethics of care, respect between students and instructor, inclusive environment).
Critical consciousness	Class materials and activities (a) provide teachers and students with opportunities for self-reflection about their own biases and (b) encourage students to think critically about current or social justice issues (e.g., decolonized curriculum, explicit considerations of social justice).
Free and open access	Students and teachers can access materials for free and modify or adapt them to fit their specific needs.
Generating new knowledge	Class materials and activities allow opportunities for students and teachers to apply, evaluate, or create new knowledge, and this knowledge can become part of the open access materials (e.g., renewable or generative assignments).
High and equitable standards	Class materials and activities provide pedagogical and content tools to provide students opportunities to increase their intellective capacity.
Inclusive content	Class materials and activities contain inclusive content (e.g., bringing in diverse perspectives, providing teachers with tools to tailor content to students' backgrounds, needs, or interests).
Student agency and ownership	Class materials and activities allow for student agency or ownership (e.g., student has voice, choice, or leadership over what they learn, how they learn it, and how they share their learning).

Table 2 contains details on the materials reviewed for each K-8 OER program. Two researchers were assigned to each program and individually identified evidence of each construct from the material samples; they then collaboratively met to calibrate their analysis within each construct. The full team then met to compare examples and identify cross-program findings.

Table 2: Materials reviewed for each K-8 OER program

OER program	Student- and teacher-facing materials	Professional learning materials	Design principles
A	One grade 7 module, including student materials and teacher guides	One online professional learning module introducing the grade 6–8 curriculum	A blog post describing the program's approach to addressing race and culture
B	Two grade 8 modules, including student materials and teacher guides	Online freely available professional learning summaries on both academic content and teaching practices	Webpages describing program approach and design principles
C	One grade 5 unit, including student materials and teacher guides	One professional learning module introducing the program's collaborative learning approach	An implementation tool containing details on the program's instructional vision
D	One grade 5 unit, including student materials and teacher guides	*These materials were still in the development phase at the time of the study*	

To facilitate the focus groups, a liaison from each program provided a list of potential schools to participate in the study; these were schools that had experience implementing the program's OER curriculum for at least one year. Researchers then independently contacted these schools to submit research applications. Due to the study's short timeline and difficulties garnering school participation because of the COVID-19 pandemic, researchers ultimately used convenience sampling for the focus groups. Researchers conducted a total of four focus groups with material developers, three focus groups with teachers, and two focus groups with students. Altogether, 17 material developers, 13 teachers, and eight students participated in these focus groups. Table 3 contains further details on the participants from each OER program.

Table 3: K-8 OER program focus group participant details

OER program	Developer focus group	School characteristics	Teacher focus group	Student focus group
A	Two curriculum designers One professional learning designer	Midsized school in a city in the Northeast serving a majority English Language Learner students	Three grade 6-8 teachers One curriculum subject lead	Three grade 8 students with at least One year using the curriculum
B	Two curriculum developers Two professional learning developers Two state stakeholders involved in the material development	Small, predominantly white school in a town in the Midwest	Four grade 6 teachers One district curriculum director	Five grade 8 students with at least One year using the curriculum
C	Two curriculum developers Three professional learning designers	An invitation to participate was emailed to all of the program's newsletter subscribers. Teachers were chosen on a first-come, first-serve basis from four different schools across the country: • One small, predominantly Black, rural school in the South • One large, predominantly white, suburban school in the Midwest • One small, predominantly white, school in a town in the Midwest • One large, predominantly white, suburban school in the Northeast	Four grade 5 teachers	*No students participated due to the recruiting strategy across multiple schools*
D	One curriculum director Two curriculum developers	*This program's curriculum was still in the development phase at the time of the study. No students or teachers participated.*		

The study team conducted the focus groups using a semi-structured interview protocol with questions aligned to the seven constructs described in Table 1. Two-to-three researchers participated in each focus group, and the meetings were audio-recorded for reference during the analysis stage.

Observations from four case studies: Culturally sustaining OEP features of adaptability and collaborative learning face challenges amidst standards and testing

The OER program's adaptability of materials and student-led collaborative lesson design are two features with great potential to lead to culturally sustaining OEP. The following section describes findings observed through the case studies related to these features: both developers and users described challenges given the ongoing role of standards and high-stakes testing. They described being apprehensive of the OER feature of material adaptability at the classroom level because of a need to adhere to standards and identified challenges in changing teacher practice toward collaborative learning in an environment of high-stakes testing. By situating these learnings within the theory of CSP and OEP, this brief explores OER use in the larger systemic context of standards and high-stakes testing in grades K–8.

Attitudes toward material adaptations

The feature of adaptability in OER offers a promising vehicle for culturally sustaining OEP: what would K–8 curricular materials look like if they were adapted for students of color to drive learning and shape the public knowledge commons? Instead of a static textbook written by a publishing company, a teacher could use their own pedagogy to customize online materials to incorporate their students' cultures. In alignment with OEP, these adaptations could then be shared between classrooms to strengthen materials based on user experience. For example, if students were working on a unit about poetry using OER materials found online in a Word document format, it may be that all the poetry examples used to teach meter and rhyme came from Shakespeare's work. Teachers could then create an activity where students searched for spoken word poets that discussed themes that had an impact on their communities. Together, the class could adapt the materials with pieces from their favorite poets to re-share for other classrooms to use.

Researchers identified varying attitudes toward adaptations within and across OER program developers. Because the OER programs take great care in sequencing their materials to be standards-aligned, some material developers were apprehensive about teachers' ability to change materials while still maintaining standards. For example, one developer noted concern with "making sure that teachers understand where students are supposed to be coming from, understanding the progression of standards, the progression of learning, understanding prerequisite standards." In contrast, developers from a different program were concerned that teachers would abandon innovative elements of the material design that encourage student curiosity and learning through exploration in favor of the standards portion of the materials. Some programs release materials as editable text documents while others release them as HTML documents or PDFs—making adaptations significantly more cumbersome. Still, multiple developers said they "believe in teacher autonomy and their ability to make the best decisions for the children in their classroom."

The need to adhere to standards drives a top-down method of developing curricula that leaves little room for student-level input. The greatest resistance to material adaptations comes at the district level, where many decisions about curricula adoption are made. According to one curriculum developer, many districts "don't want to message to their teachers that they can change anything . . . they want the teachers to use the materials consistently" to ensure adherence to standards. In some instances, districts request customizations that incorporate their local communities' context directly from the OER programs; however, they avoid active messaging that encourages teachers to change materials. With the exception of the teachers from one school, all other teachers interviewed in the study adapted the way certain activities were implemented but did not make changes to the materials themselves. The school where teachers described making material adaptations builds all course curricula around interdisciplinary real-world projects that are intentionally grounded in addressing local inequities. A teacher from this school shared that "at our school, we've been given the freedom and the confidence to make our own decisions." Another teacher said, they "modify some of the tasks to make sure that every child's culture has some sort of entry point. . .we modify based on the year, based on who we have in front of us." However, teachers still center standards when making modifications. One teacher said they stick to the standards for the lesson then "add our own spice."

Collaborative learning

In alignment with culturally sustaining OEP, the four OER programs are dedicated to moving from traditional lecturing to student-led collaboration; however, changing teacher practice has proven to be a difficult task within a testing environment. In this model, teachers noted that they find themselves walking around the room to different student groups and asking them questions, as opposed to standing at the front of the room and lecturing for a full period. One of the programs has teachers maintain a space where students post questions that they are curious about related to the unit; students then work together to investigate these questions as part of the class. This practice is designed to allow students' natural curiosity to drive learning. In exploring these ideas by discussing them with their peers, students learn in a collaborative manner that resembles communication in many collectivist cultures.

Some teachers expressed concern with students' content knowledge in their ability to score highly on exams but universally agreed that this learning style leads to increased critical thinking and the development of practical skills for students. One teacher described that "It's taken a long time for me to realize that just because I'm up there standing doesn't mean the students are going to learn." Through collaborative methods, students spend more time on a given unit and can explore materials at a deeper level. Students explicitly identified that they are learning how to listen to others' ideas and enjoy problem-solving together through collaboration. For example, a student shared that "sometimes we have to work together to find an answer, one group has paper A, and another group has paper B, and we have to ask questions to get the answer from them." Students also express that they are learning more than in previous years of the same subject because they are more motivated and pay attention in class.

Standardized testing creates a culture of assessment where teachers constantly assess students on their learning progress against standards. Several material developers noted that this practice takes up limited class time and leads teachers away from collaborative learning. Because many teachers have become accustomed to a drill style of delivering content, and often see success in this method through higher test scores, changing this culture is difficult. Teachers implementing one of the programs expressed discomfort in abandoning traditional written assessment, even though it doesn't measure the critical thinking and practical skills that students are acquiring through collaboration. Developers from the program are working on expanding teachers' conception of formative assessment so that they can assess students' thinking by listening to them verbally problem-solve. Developers from another program have observed that the practice of constant assessment becomes especially problematic with students who are "below grade level" (often, these are students of color). When students are academically "behind," teachers more easily abandon the collaborative model and rely on a constant cycle of assessment and review of old material through drilling, which means students perpetually miss out on grade-level content.

Focus groups with teachers across six different districts revealed that the emphasis on standardized exams and "teaching to the test" is stratified by school resources and student demographics. The curriculum lead from a wealthier district with a relatively high concentration of white students explicitly noted being ok with lower standardized test scores because she believes in the curriculum. A teacher from a different white and wealthy district said, "Standardized tests don't affect my use of the materials; our students are high performing, so tests are something that we don't emphasize." The teacher further described that "there's really not a standardized test that aligns to the philosophy of student discovery . . . but unfortunately that's where money talks, is the tests." In contrast, a teacher from a rural district with lower resources and a relatively high percentage of Black students expressed that "all that's stressed is the state test, you're teaching to the test." This teacher then noted that their school is struggling to change teacher practice from traditional lecturing to student-led learning. A teacher from a school with a high percentage of students with disabilities said, "Yeah, we're basically instructed to teach to the test." Another teacher who also has a high percentage of students with disabilities said, "Our state testing and our standards are just jammed down our throats all the time . . . it is just data-driven test test test."

Discussion

As state politicians and local school boards are increasingly restricting the knowledge that is considered acceptable in schools,[3] CSP and OEP offer frameworks for envisioning a transformative education. Scholars from both fields have documented how top-down systems of education with restrictive testing requirements disadvantage students of color and restrict the generation of new knowledge. The programs studied present innovative approaches to address these challenges through OER by offering free materials with an open license and designing lessons to feature student-centered collaborative learning models, but their full implementation is hindered by high-stakes testing systems.

The need to be standards-aligned drives a top-down process for creating curriculum whereby districts and OER developers are resistant to teachers adapting materials, because of a worry both that standards won't be properly addressed and that teachers will abandon innovative design elements in favor of teaching standards. This creates a rigid structure within which student input and knowledge outside of what is tested on standardized exams gets devalued. High-stakes testing encourages traditional models of teachers as lecturers which limits student-centered collaborative learning. Teachers are concerned with students' abilities to score highly on exams despite evidence of their growth as curious learners. This study illustrates how standards and high-stakes testing in K–8 are major impediments to OER's ability to be implemented with culturally-sustaining OEP. Dr. Gloria Ladson-Billings (2017) reminds us that "The (r)evolution will not be standardized" (p. 141). How might we then imagine an *open* understanding of diverse students' brilliance?

---

3   See book bans (https://www.nytimes.com/2022/01/30/books/book-ban-us-schools.html) and anti-critical race theory laws (https://time.com/6192708/critical-race-theory-teachers-racism/).

References

Alim, H. S., & Paris, D. (2017). What is culturally sustaining pedagogy and why does it matter? In D. Paris. & H. S. Alim (Eds.), *Culturally sustaining pedagogies: Teaching and learning for justice in a changing world* (pp. 1–21). Teachers College Press.

Bali, M., Cronin, C., & Jhangiani, R. S. (2020). Framing open educational practices from a social justice perspective. *Journal of Interactive Media in Education, 2020*(1), 1–12. https://doi.org/10.5334/jime.565

Brown, M., & Croft, B. (2020). Social annotation and an inclusive praxis for open pedagogy in the college classroom. *Journal of Interactive Media in Education, 2020*(1), 1–8. https://doi.org/10.5334/jime.561

Bryan-Gooden, J., Hester, M., & Peoples, L. Q. (2019). *Culturally responsive curriculum scorecard*. Metropolitan Center for Research on Equity and the Transformation of Schools, New York University. https://steinhardt.nyu.edu/metrocenter/ejroc/services/culturally-responsive-curriculum-scorecards

Butcher, N. (2011). *A basic guide to open educational resources (OER)*. Commonwealth of Learning (COL) & United Nations Educational, Scientific, and Cultural Organization (UNESCO). https://unesdoc.unesco.org/ark:/48223/pf0000215804

DeRosa, R., & Jhangiani, R. (2017). Open pedagogy. In E. Mays (Ed.), *A guide to making open textbooks with students* (pp. 7–20). The Rebus Community for Open Textbook Creation. https://press.rebus.community/makingopentextbookswithstudents/chapter/open-pedagogy/

Ehlers, U.-D. (2011). Extending the territory: From open educational resources to open educational practices. *Journal of Open, Flexible, and Distance Learning, 15*(2), 11–10. https://doi.org/10.61468/jofdl.v15i2.64

Gay, G. (2018). *Culturally responsive teaching: Theory, research and practice* (third edition). Teachers College Press.

Geser, G. (Ed.). (2012). *Open educational practices and resources: OLCOS roadmap 2012*. Salzburg Research; EduMedia Group. https://www.olcos.org/english/roadmap/

Gonzales, D., & Vasudeva, A. (2021). *Looking back to accelerate forward: Toward a policy paradigm that advances equity and improvement.* Carnegie Foundation for the Advancement of Teaching; The Aspen Institute Education & Society Program. https://www.aspeninstitute.org/publications/looking-back-to-accelerate-forward/

Hammond, Z. (2015). Culturally responsive teaching & the brain: Promoting authentic engagement and rigor among culturally and linguistically diverse students. Corwin.

Holmes, A., & González, N. (2017). Finding sustenance: An indigenous relational pedagogy. In D. Paris, & H. S. Alim (Eds.), *Culturally sustaining pedagogies: Teaching and learning for justice in a changing world* (pp. 207–224). Teachers College Press.

Koretz, D. (2018). Moving beyond the failure of test-based accountability. *American Educator, 41*(4), 22–26. https://eric.ed.gov/?id=EJ1164385

Ladson-Billings, G. (2017). The (r)evolution will not be standardized: Teacher education, hip hop pedagogy, and culturally relevant pedagogy 2.0. In D. Paris, & H. S. Alim (Eds.), *Culturally sustaining pedagogies: Teaching and learning for justice in a changing world* (pp. 141–156). Teachers College Press.

Ladson-Billings, G. (2014). Culturally relevant pedagogy 2.0: a.k.a. the remix. *Harvard Educational Review, 84*(1), 74-84. https://www.proquest.com/scholarly-journals/culturally-relevant-pedagogy-2-0-k-remix/docview/1511014412/se-2

Ladson-Billings, G. (1995). Toward a theory of culturally relevant pedagogy. *American Educational Research Journal, 32*(3), 465–491. https://doi.org/10.2307/1163320

Lambert, S. R. (2018). Changing our (dis)course: A distinctive social justice aligned definition of open education. *Journal of Learning for Development, 5*(3), 225–244. https://doi.org/10.56059/jl4d.v5i3.290

Lee, A. M. I. (n.d.). *What is the Every Student Succeeds Act (ESSA)?* Understood for All Inc. https://www.understood.org/en/articles/every-student-succeeds-act-essa-what-you-need-to-know

Love, B. (2019). *We want to do more than survive: Abolitionist teaching and the pursuit of educational freedom.* Beacon Press.

National Center for Education Statistics. (2023, May). *Condition of education: Racial/ethnic enrollment in public schools.* U.S. Department of Education, Institute of Education Sciences. Retrieved July 21, 2023, from https://nces.ed.gov/programs/coe/indicator/cge

Peoples, L. Q., Islam, T., & Davis, T. (2021). *The culturally responsive-sustaining STEAM curriculum scorecard.* Metropolitan Center for Research on Equity and the Transformation of Schools, New York University.

Rosa, J., & Flores, N. (2017). Do you hear what I hear? Raciolinguistic ideologies and culturally sustaining pedagogies. In D. Paris, & H. S. Alim (Eds.), *Culturally sustaining pedagogies: Teaching and learning for justice in a changing world* (pp. 175–190). Teachers College Press.

Author Bios
Daniela R. Amaya, University of California, Los Angeles

Daniela Amaya uses mixed methods infused with critical theory to analyze systemic educational inequality and its effects on students of color and from low socioeconomic backgrounds. Amaya earned her B.S. in economics from Duke University and is a Ph.D. student at the UCLA Graduate School of Education & Information Science.

Caroline E. Parker, SRI International

Caroline (Carrie) E. Parker, EdD, leads research to improve learning for culturally and linguistically diverse students, with a particular interest in how language learning intersects with disabilities. Parker received an MEd from Framingham State College, and EdM and EdD degrees from the Harvard Graduate School of Education.

Krystal Thomas, SRI International

Krystal Thomas, PhD, brings a developmental psychology and equity lens to research and capacity building. Her projects span issues of teacher quality and practices, students' academic and social identities, and patterns of contextual inequality in the classroom. Thomas holds a PhD and master's in developmental psychology from Virginia Commonwealth University.

Positionality Statement

I, Daniela Amaya, am unapologetically dedicated to the intellectual liberation of students of color. I am a Latina woman who was raised by a single immigrant mother. I have had the great privilege of attending public, charter, and private schools where I learned the necessary tools to survive *economically* in the U.S. empire. However, it was radical educators—that challenged these institutions' narrow notions of "knowledge"—who taught me the critical consciousness necessary to survive *spiritually* in this country.

4

Creating a Gender and Sexuality Inclusive OER World Language Course

Federica Goldoni, Georgia Gwinnett College
Kristina Watkins Mormino, Georgia Gwinnett College

Abstract

Diversity and inclusivity are imperatives in world language classes because teaching and learning a foreign language entails intimacy and engagement of various identities and preparation for immersion in the target language and culture. World language instructors who use OER must keep abreast of real-world developments and issues and incorporate them into lessons, practice, and assessments. Gender inclusive language specifically is one cultural and linguistic issue that instructors face—especially when teaching gendered languages—and that has been rapidly changing hand-in-hand with socio-cultural developments.

This article shows how inclusive education instruction draws on open educational practices. World language instructors using OER can increase diversity and acceptance of all sexualities and gender identities and dismantle the concept of universal values. OER-based culture lessons can be added highlighting female and queer figures, vocabulary lists can be expanded to embrace gender inclusive terms, and inclusive notions can be integrated into activities, course goals, and assessments throughout the course using backward design. Creating an inclusive space while drawing on open educational practices helps students see the target culture with greater nuance, the language as living and evolving, and the people who speak it as more real and less stereotypical.

Keywords: world languages and cultures, diversity and inclusivity, gender inclusive language, sexuality, inclusive pedagogy, open educational resources

Suggested citation: Goldoni, F., & Mormino, K. W. (2024). Creating a gender and sexuality inclusive OER world language course. In T. Tijerina (Ed.), *Pedagogy opened: Innovative theory and practice* (pp. 97-127). University of North Georgia Press. https://alg.manifoldapp.org/read/pedagogy-opened-v1-a4/.

Introduction

Diversity and inclusivity are a challenge and an imperative in world language classes because teaching and learning a world language entails intimacy and engagement of various identities on the part of instructors and learners and preparation for immersion in the target language and culture. World language instructors who use open educational resources (OER), which are not always up-to-date, have an added duty to keep abreast of real-world developments in the target language and culture and to incorporate them into lessons, practice, and assessments. Gender inclusive language specifically is a complex cultural and linguistic issue, especially in gendered European languages. Gender inclusive language has been at the forefront of people's attention, and it has been rapidly changing together with socio-cultural developments, like gender equality and non-conformity of gender and sexual orientation, as language reflects culture, power, and societal biases.

This article shows how inclusive education instruction draws on open educational practices. World language instructors using OER can increase and normalize diversity and acceptance of all sexualities and gender identities, dismantle the concept of universal values and enable students to see culture with greater nuance. OER-based culture lessons and vocabulary lists can be added and/or expanded, and inclusive language and ideas can be integrated into activities, course goals, and assessments throughout the course using backward design, therefore leading each lesson toward assessment and a demonstration of proficiency in each learning outcome. The implications of this discussion are important: Creating an inclusive space while drawing on open educational practices has the potential to help students see the target language as living and evolving and the people who speak it as more real and less stereotypical; students may experience a deeper sense of belonging and a greater appreciation of the complexity and nuances of cultures and societies. Finally, sharing these OER among instructors can potentially transform world language teaching by bringing gender and sexuality inclusivity to a greater number of classrooms.

What Do Gender and Sexuality Inclusivity Look Like in a World Language Class?

Because culture and identity permeate the world language curriculum in both subtle and overt ways, there are innumerable points at which there may be inclusion or exclusion. In many fields, it would be sufficient to explore minority, women, and LGBTQ+ figures and works or achievements associated with them. In world language classes, however, students are directed to communicate about their own lives and opinions using the target language. For example, if students are learning vocabulary dealing with relationships, they must practice by speaking and writing about their own relationships, be they familial, friendly, professional, residential, or romantic. So too, if they are learning vocabulary and grammar used in describing people, they apply that knowledge by describing themselves and people they know. In brief, students develop proficiency with vocabulary and grammar by communicating about themselves. Moreover, while there are other disciplines—anthropology, geography, and religious studies, for example—that analyze varying types of societies and cultural norms from an external perspective, world language classes must prepare students to immerse themselves in the target language and culture. In short, it is personal. The intimacy entailed in learning a world language requires instructors and learners to engage with a range of identities. Thus, inclusivity presents a particular challenge and a special imperative in world language classes compared to other academic subjects.

Inclusivity Using Open Educational Resources for World Language Instruction

World language instructors who use OER have a particular duty to focus on diversity and inclusivity in their pedagogical practice. The profit motive in professional publishing incentivizes and enables updating textbooks on a regular basis, such that for-profit books are more likely to reflect recent developments in culture and language. By contrast, the tremendous amount of work required and the relative paucity of support available for the writing, editing, and revision of open educational texts increases the likelihood that they will lag behind contemporary shifts in the target language and culture, not to mention developments in U.S. culture. Students coming of age in the wake of the #MeToo and Black Lives Matter movements and the mainstreaming of Gay Pride have questions about social movements abroad that may not be addressed in OER textbooks, particularly those that have not been kept up-to-date. It then becomes incumbent on the classroom instructor or course supervisor to (1) keep abreast of real-world developments—including those that take place in virtual spaces, such as in social media—and (2) incorporate those developments into lessons, practice, and assessments.

To determine whether OER are lacking gender inclusivity, one may start by considering the following:

- Are all people portrayed in the text cisgender and heterosexual? Do materials assume that the learner is cisgender and heterosexual?
- Are sexist stereotypes propagated—even jokingly—in the text?
- Are gender and sexuality issues in the target culture ever directly addressed? Does the text explore how LGBTQ+ people or women may be received when visiting the target culture for work or pleasure?
- Does the OER textbook highlight the contributions of cis-women and LGBTQ+ people in the target culture? Are movements and developments impacting women and queer communities addressed?

For the moment, the number of OER textbooks world language faculty can choose from is more limited than what is available through for-profit publishing companies, at least in widely-spoken European languages.

Because best practices in world language pedagogy require integrating instruction in vocabulary, grammar, and culture, it is impractical to try to teach with a hodgepodge of OER materials taken from here and there, especially at the elementary levels during the first two to three semesters of instruction in a language. With the need to select a single text or program from a restricted number of options, professors considering factors such as scope and sequence, multimedia resources, and instruction style may feel compelled to select texts that come up short in terms of inclusivity.

However, users of OER are also creators of OER, because they can make a coherent and effective course by adopting a main text or program and incorporating supplementary materials that can be borrowed, adapted, or created new. These supplementary materials can then be shared with others, in particular those who have adopted the same textbook or program. This kind of sharing, be it through Creative Commons, conferences, communities on social media, or instructor-to-instructor exchanges, has the power to transform world language instruction on a larger scale, bringing gender and sexuality inclusivity to a vastly greater number of (virtual and literal) classrooms.

Gender Inclusivity as a Cultural and Linguistic Issue
The Importance of Gender Inclusive Language

The United Nations broadly define gender inclusive language as "speaking and writing in a way that does not discriminate against a particular sex, social gender, or gender identity, and does not perpetuate gender stereotypes" (United Nations, n.d.). The background of inclusive and genderless language in the context of specific languages and cultures is complex. Progress toward gender inclusivity has been made in the last fifty years, and inclusive language has become more widespread. Lately, gender identity and gender inclusive language have been at the forefront of people's attention, and gender-free language has been changing rapidly. Nevertheless, inclusive language remains contested and rejected, and much work remains to be done to build more inclusive and unbiased societies. In the sections that follow, instructors may glean both general and detailed information about recent changes to make certain European languages more inclusive and the arguments for and against those changes. This information can inform instructor-created vocabulary, grammar, and culture lessons for classes using OER.

While the development of inclusive language is sometimes contentious in English, it is understandably more fraught in languages with gendered nouns and adjectives, such as Spanish, French, German, Italian, and Portuguese. In these languages, gender agreement may be essential for clarity to the extent that syntax and style of expression are dependent on gendered features of language. How can one refer to persons in a gender-neutral fashion when even places, things, and ideas belong to gendered categories? How can there be gender inclusivity in a way that does not simply default to masculine forms, as has always been done? Yet, numerous Western societies that use these gendered European languages also embrace—or at least tolerate—concepts like gender equality and non-conformity of gender and sexual orientation. In these contexts, linguistic norms are being shaped by socio-cultural developments.

Gender Inclusive Linguistic Developments: Examples in Spanish, French, German, Italian, Portuguese, and English

One way to explore gender inclusivity is to look at language in the Spanish-speaking world, including Spanish in the U.S., through the experience of nonbinary people, the American civil rights agenda, and American cultural politics. Like other romance languages, Spanish has binary grammatical gender: Every noun and modifier, animate or not, is marked with either feminine or masculine gender. The gender of animate nouns generally corresponds to the apparent biological sex of the referent. Gender ambiguous individuals struggle to express themselves in Spanish due to the binary grammatical gender that is required. In addition, masculine generics dominate the Spanish language, and here mixed groups of individuals are referred to in the masculine form. This has been criticized for its erasure of women and gender diverse individuals by feminists and activists, like Irene Montero, Minister of Equality of Spain, who strongly advocated in 2021 for gender-inclusive language and stated, "Lo que no se nombra, no existe" ("what is not named, does not exist"), thereby questioning the use of masculine generics in Spanish (Pino, 2021).

Inclusive language in Spanish generally appears in four forms: Doublets, the inclusive marker -@, the gender inclusive -x, and the morpheme –e (Banegas & Lopez, 2021; Slemp, 2020; 2021; Stetie & Zunino, 2022):

- In the 1980s, the doubled forms started to become a popular option for inclusive language, even though this option is not in line with the economy of the language. One example of the doubled forms is *bienvenidos y bienvenidas a todos y todas* for "welcome everyone."
- With the use of computers, the inclusive marker -@ has become another popular option as it indicates both masculine and feminine gender simultaneously (with an *a* surrounded by an *o*). The @ facilitates writing, but it is generally pronounced orally as a masculine generic. Examples include *bievenid@s a tod@s* and *Latin@s*.
- In 2004, the -x was incorporated in inclusive language, mostly in writing, to express gender identity outside of the traditional male-female dichotomy. The word *Latinx* is a familiar example.
- In the mid-2010s, the gender-inclusive morpheme -e has been used in both speech and writing. The incorporation of -e has increased significantly. Phonologically, there is no criticism as to its pronunciation, and it mimics existing nouns and adjectives in Spanish like *estudiante* (student) and *inteligente* (intelligent) that are not marked for gender. Besides *Latine* and *bievenides a todes,* other examples are *elles* (they), *nosotres* (we), *les amigues* (the friends), *les hijes* (the sons and daughters), *les niñes* (the children), and *les alumnes* (the school children).

In the U.S., Latin@s, Latine, and Latinx are widespread labels that are not mutually exclusive; rather, they complement one another and are employed by Hispanic people in different settings and environments. The "x" in Latinx stands for the unknowable or undefinable (similarly to Malcolm X and Gen X), and it seems to represent gender binary politics and intersectional identities (Mora et el., 2022). For example, the term "Latinx" opens discussions about inclusivity and diversity and the impact of ethnoracial identities in reifying gender binaries, and it is not just used in elitist spaces and academic environments where these discussions are likely to take place. Rather, those without college degrees employ the label "Latinx," perhaps thinking about gender politics and fluidity in intersectional ways and therefore indexing ethnoracial identification and representation.

In other gender-marked languages like Italian, French, Portuguese, and German (which has three genders, but primarily uses the feminine and masculine genders when referring to people), gender inclusive language can appear in various forms such as:

- Doublets
- The use of *todes*, *amigues*, the morpheme x and the marker @ used in Portuguese similarly to Spanish (Auxland, 2020)
- The use of the asterisk *, the marker @, and the gender inclusive "schwa" (/ə/ taken from the international phonetic alphabet) used in Italian (Orrú & Vitiello, 2022)
- The use of the *point médian* in French, comparable to the "gender-star" in German for inclusive writing (*écriture inclusive*) and consisting of a dot, or an asterisk, that combine the masculine and the feminine endings of a word like *lycéen·lycéenne* (male highschooler·female highschooler) or *Zuhörer*innen* (the listener, he*the listener, she) (Nöstlinger, 2021; Pilon, 2020)
- The use of linguistic innovations in oral communication that the German language has recently experienced, namely 1) the pronoun *Sier* [a combination of *sie* (she) and *er* (he), 2) *Per* (abbreviation of *Person*), 3) *they* (English borrowing), 4) and *x* (U.S. Spanish borrowing from "Latinx" used similarly to "they" as a gender-neutral pronoun). The German youth language has also introduced final -i as inclusive language such as *Schüli* und *Lehri* (school-aged children and teachers) (Kofler, 2022).

The doubled forms can be problematic because they take up space, especially in an online interface, and because they perpetuate the binary masculine versus feminine dichotomy without offering a gender-neutral alternative. The asterisk, the marker @ and the *point médian* in French or the "gender-star" in German can be useful in writing, but they pose accessibility issues orally, namely for text screen readers, and reading-impaired and dyslexic people find them challenging to read. Other strategies for gender neutral language in gender-marked languages are the use of periphrases, the passive voice, or collective or neutral and invariable nouns, including gender neutral professional language. Some examples are offered below:

- For "people" (rather than men and women)
  - Italian: *popolazione, persone, individui, o membri*
  - French: *population, personnes, gens, individus, membres*
  - Portuguese: *pessoas*
  - German: *Leute, Person, Menschen, Mitglied, Genenüber, Alle*
  - Spanish: *personas*
- For "staff" (rather than specific job names with gendered associations)
  - Italian: *personal, equipe*
  - French: *personnel, équipe*
  - Portuguese: *equipe*
  - German: *Personal, Team*
  - Spanish: *personal, equipo*
- For "faculty and students"
  - Italian: *corpo studentesco e corpo insegnante/docente*
  - French: *corps enseignant/professorat et corps étudiant*
  - Portuguese: *corpo docente e corpo discente*
  - German: *Studierende und Lehrende*
  - Spanish: *cuerpo estudiantil y cuerpo de docentes*

Unlike Italian, French, Portuguese, Spanish, and German, English is a largely gender-neutral language, and advocates for gender-neutral language have pushed for the use of the gender-inclusive, usually plural, pronoun "they/them" to stand in for the singular "she/he". However, English does express gender through word endings and stereotypes associated with the words and a masculine generic. One example is the feminine morpheme "-ess" employed to modify masculine versions of nouns such as "waiter" versus "waitress". The endings -man and -woman perform a similar function: "chairman" versus "chairwoman" is in common use in the U.S. Congress. One way to overcome these issues is to replace gendered nouns, using words like "server," "chairperson," "legislator," "workforce," "folks," "child," "owner," "firefighter," "first-year student," and "partner," instead of "waiter/waitress," "chairman/chairwoman," "congressman/congresswoman," "manpower," "ladies or gentlemen," "boy or girl," "landlord," "fireman," "freshman," and "boyfriend/girlfriend." As indicated above, there are also nouns that, through stereotypes, are often associated with male and female attributes. For example, "nurse" is perceived as a more feminine profession (Teresa-Morales et al., 2022), but "doctor" is often associated with a male physician. Regardless, there has been a push for acceptance of nurses and doctors of any gender.

Linguistic Change and Resistance

The ability of a language to change and adapt is a sign of health; languages change all the time while remaining recognizable as the same linguistic system. Most of these changes and innovations come from the community. Recent research on the use of gender-inclusive language in Spanish (Sczesny et al., 2015; Slemp, 2020, 2021) indicated that (younger) age and (female) gender can have significant correlation with the use of inclusive language. The use of gender-inclusive language is typically linked to people who:

- Perceive ease in utilizing inclusive language;
- Understand the consequences of using exclusive versus inclusive terms; and
- Hold non-sexist attitudes and embrace the idea that gender-inclusive language is about human rights, social justice, compassion, representation, and visibility of gender minorities.

Overcoming Barriers to Genderless Language and Interventions

There are multiple barriers toward the use of gender-inclusive language. One barrier is the novelty of gender-fair forms, which conflicts with speakers' linguistic habits and practices. Language usage that deviates from the norms that were taught in the past may be perceived as "incorrect." Another is the challenge of using inclusive language consistently, mostly relying on the individual speaker's efforts and intentionality, since gender-neutral solutions can be hard in grammatically gendered languages like French, Spanish, and Italian. Sexist beliefs and attitudes constitute another barrier because they impact inclusive language use; speakers tend to avoid inclusive language because they are reluctant to change their linguistic habits so may deliberately use a form of language that treats males as the norm and makes women less visible. The opposition to gender inclusive language can also be correlated with social conservatism and a novel politization of gender. Specifically, in Western Europe parties of the political right have framed "gender" as a tool for conservative mobilization, especially focusing on issues of gender and sexual identity, trans and non-binary identities, and feminism. This turn against "gender ideology" or "woke/cancel culture" is seen as a fruitful strategy for conservative politicians and radical right parties to get traction and votes among large shares of the electorate that are generally opposed to a linear trend towards more culturally progressive societies (Abou-Chadi et al., 2021).

Resistance to linguistic change remains strong because variation is perceived to destabilize the language, create ambiguity, and hinder communication; therefore, understanding could be impaired and legal clarity could be compromised. One form of resistance comes from institutions, linguistic authorities, and even education. One example is the French language authority, the Académie Française (the French Academy), a group of intellectuals charged with overseeing and steering the evolution of the French language. The Académie Française has criticized gender-inclusive language, calling it an "aberration" (Dodman, 202) and stating that it threatens the French language. The inclusion in 2021 of the French genderless pronoun *iel* by the online version of *Le Robert* (Le Robert, n.d.), one of France's leading dictionaries, generated heated debate in the French press, on social media, and among politicians despite extensive research conducted among French native speakers evidencing increased usage of the pronoun. The French government and the Education Ministry have resisted the gender-fair pronoun and attempts at incorporating inclusive language in the school curriculum. French president Emmanuel Macron stated that there are two fine pronouns in French, *il* and *elle*, and that the French language is beautiful as it is (Atkinson, 2022). Lawmaker François Jolivet, a member of the socially left-of-center Renaissance Party founded by Macron, also opposed the inclusion of the pronoun *iel*, calling the actions of *Le Robert* an ideological intrusion undermining French and its linguistic and cultural influence. Jolivet went even further: He introduced a bill banning gender-neutral spelling among government employees (Nöstlinger, 2021). Another example of resistance to inclusive language in France comes from far right-wing National Rally politician Laurie Lavalette who called proponents "highly subsidized activists who seek to spread a grotesque and mendacious ideology" (Gallagher, 2022).

Gender-inclusive language in French took hold in Canada earlier than in France, and while France has not been very receptive, the Canadian government has approached the issue differently. In fact, the Canadian government website has made available a set of bilingual guidelines for using gender-neutral language, stating that "The Guidelines for Inclusive Writing are designed to help the federal public service and any other organization produce writing that is free of discrimination based on sex, gender, sexual orientation, race, ethnicity, disability or any other identity factor" (Government of Canada, 2022). Similarly, the Quebec Office of the French Language (Office québécois de la langue française, OQLF), in contrast with the French Academy for European French, has a long history of supporting feminist language reform efforts and the feminization of Canadian French (Pilon, 2020), and it has inspired academic milieus like McGill University and the University of Montreal that have shifted toward more inclusive language. Overall, the Canadian civil rights agenda aligning with similar agendas in the U.S. may explain why Canada has a more positive view on inclusive language than France. Additionally, since Canada is a bilingual country (French and English), one could claim that Canadian English speakers shape expectations for gender inclusivity in government texts, all of which must be available in both English and French.

Another form of resistance to inclusive language is represented by the Royal Spanish Academy (RAE), the body that presides over prescriptive Spanish grammar, syntax, morphology, and mostly lexicon. The RAE has not welcomed favorably the inclusion of genderless options in Spanish, be they in writing or oral discourse (Burgen, 2020; Piser, 2021). For example, in the 2018 style guide, the RAE stated it is not considered valid to use the -@, the –e, or the –x to refer to the two sexes: *l@s Latin@s, les Latines, lxs Latinx*. In fact, the RAE uses the term "sex" rather than "gender" and affirms that there are only two biological sexes. The style guide also stated that the unmarked character of the masculine makes duplication unnecessary (Real Academia Española, 2018).

The official authority of the German language is the *Düden* dictionary, which has been open to gender-neutral and gender-inclusive language in its publications, but not without pushback. The German Language Society (The Verein Deutsche Sprache*)*, a German language association with the aim of preserving and promoting German as an independent cultural language, has shown a fundamental resistance to language inclusivity, which has been seen as destructive interventions into the German language. The *Verein Deutsche Sprache* stated that grammar and sex/gender are separate entities, and inclusive language is untenable on both linguistic and social grounds, leading to no social change. Walter Krämer, leader of the *Verein Deutsche Sprache,* led a petition to "save German from the *Düden"* over including gender-neutral language, with Krämer calling the gender-star a "modern Hitler salute" for "left-wing idealogues" (Piser, 2021). In contrast, the Gesellschaft für Deutsche Sprache, the Society for the German Language supported by the German Conference of Ministers of Education and the Minister of State for Culture, is tasked with promoting and researching the German language. As reported in Luck (2020), for the Gesellschaft für Deutsche Sprache, gender-fair language plays a key role in ensuring equal treatment of all individuals in society. However, reservations were expressed about the visualization of the third sex/gender and the fact that gender-fair language must comply with current rules. To be beneficial to the speech community, gender-fair language must be understandable, legible, readable, and grammatically correct, and ensure accessibility, legal clarity, and unambiguousness. Finally, Christian Democratic Union (CDU) and Alternative for Germany (AfD), respectively a conservative and far-right party in Germany, strongly opposed any attempts to modify the German language or to use the feminine generic (Nöstlinger, 2021), specifically when the Social Democratic Party (SPD)-led Ministry of Justice introduced a draft bill that the CDU-led Interior Ministry promptly shut down over fears it would only apply to women.

Like the *Düden*, the Oxford English Dictionary has served as the official linguistic authority for the English language, and it has rectified exclusive or derogatory language around gendered terms like "man" and "woman". In 2015, the Oxford English Dictionary introduced the gender-neutral title "Mx.," pronounced as "mix," a title that matched more closely with some of the members of the transgender and gender non-conforming community (Martin, 2015). The Oxford English Dictionary has also defended the use of singular "they/them" as a fact of speech (Baron, 2018). In the U.K, the British House of Lords Hansard held important debates around linguistic norms and neutral drafting of U.K. Government bills, which led to gender-free language in legislation in the U.K. and Ireland. As a result, since 2007, the pronoun "he" cannot be employed anymore as an inclusive term for "he and she".

Finally, the Accademia della Crusca (Academy of the Bran), the official linguistic academy of Italian, approved the feminization of Italian, including job titles like *avvocato* and *avvocatessa* (lawyer). However, in Italy, the political acceptance and opposition of gender-inclusive language seem to fall on the same partisan lines as in Germany and France. Georgia Meloni, the Italian Prime Minister elected in 2022 and leader of the Italian far-right party, has used the masculine *il ministro* instead of the feminine *la ministra* in her official capacity (Stewart, 2022). The scarce literature available on gender-inclusive Italian and the lack of knowledge of and experience with non-binary gender identities in Italy has led to instances of deadnaming and misgendering suffered by genderfluid individuals (Rosati et al., 2022).

Language as a Reflection of Culture, Power, and Biases

Language is a reflection of culture and power in society, and one could claim that a binary system perpetuates gender stereotyping and enforces and solidifies social hierarchies, patriarchal practices, and heterosexual norms. Even a gender-unmarked language like English tends to embrace masculine generics and put masculine first, rather than feminine, in paired expressions like "boys and girls", "men and women", "husband and wife", "sons and daughters", "brother and sister", "Mr. and Mrs." except for "ladies and gentlemen." Gender inequality exists in the form of unconscious bias instilled in the language and, therefore, affects our thoughts. In the English-language context, Lakoff (1973) and Spender (198) discussed the connection between language and reality, linguistic disparity, social positioning, and how language reflects and perpetuates power structures assigning women a more subordinate position than men. The psychological damage of derogatory or exclusive language on speakers' perceptions is palpable, as corroborated by empirical data (Bem & Bem, 1973; Born & Taris, 2010; Everett, 2011; Martyna, 1980; McConnell & Fazio, 1996; Moulton et al., 1978; Reali et al., 2015; Schneider & Hacker, 1973; Stout & Dasgupta, 2011). A special edition of the academic journal *Linguistische Berichte* explained how the German language fundamentally obscures women's skills, intellect, and accomplishments; it belittles women, relegating them to inferior status or subordinate to men, as if women were unworthy or incapable of existing outside of stereotypical roles (Guentherodt et al., 1980). Empirical studies conducted in German confirmed that women were put at a conceptual advantage if the pair form/gender-balanced form was employed as opposed to the masculine generic (Gabriel and Mellenberger 2004, p. 276). Concurrently, "[w]hen stereotypically male occupations had been presented in pair forms, children of both genders perceived women's and men's success in a more balanced way than if titles had been presented in generic masculine forms" (Vervecken et al., 2013, p. 213). There are signs of progress elsewhere, too. In Germany and France, women no longer must declare their marital status via their title. Editorial style guides, legislation drafting guidelines, and government communications (letters, forms, and legal documents) employ unbiased and gender-fair language. Even national anthems have been revised. The Austrian anthem now includes *Töchter* (daughters) in the first verse: "Heimat großer Töchter und Söhne" [Home of great daughters and sons] while previously Austria was referred to as "Heimat bist du großer Söhne" [Home are you of great sons] (Bundeskanzleramt Österreich, n.d.). Progress has been made in educational materials, schoolbooks, and job advertisements in German that now contain more gender fair language and equal representation of women and men.

In the U.S., the House Resolution 8 of the 117th Congress changed the title of the Office of the Whistleblower Ombudsman to the Office of the Whistleblower Ombuds, established the Office of Diversity and Inclusion, and amended the Rules of the House to use gender-neutral language (House Resolution 8 Section 2(e), 117th Congress), and the rules package of the 118th Congress does not reverse it (House Resolution 5, 118th Congress).

In the Spanish-speaking world, progress toward inclusive language, and the inclusion of women and diverse gender identities has been made. In Ecuador, President Daniel Noboa's administration, constituted in November

2023, is an example of gender inclusivity: Women were designated at the head of the most important Departments, including e*l Ministerio de la mujer y de los derechos humanos* (the Department of women and human rights). In Spain, Chile, and Argentina there are now institutions such as *el Ministerio de la mujer y de la igualdad de género* (the Department of women and gender equality); *el matrimonio igualitario y la adopción* (legal gay marriage and adoption); and the use of social names for transgender people. Additionally, the Socialist Workers Party (PSOE), who were once in charge of the Spanish government, pushed for a rewriting of the Spanish constitution to use gender-neutral language. In Argentina, legal protections for gender-neutral language have been pursued by "mak[ing] explicit and visible the relationship between language and the right to gender identity and diversity" (Stetie & Zunino, 2022, p. 8).

Gender and Sexuality Inclusivity in the Classroom

What are the pedagogical implications of language evolution away from a gendered binary that privileges masculinity? How must teaching change in the face of increasing diversity and growing acceptance of a range of sexualities and gender identities? These are questions that world language professionals must answer. But why? If, as has been made clear in this article, inclusive language is a matter of some controversy, wouldn't it be better for the classroom instructor to stay out of the political fray? Perhaps not. Since identity is not merely a political positioning but also a reflection of personal experience, the recognition and validation of human diversity—politically charged, though it may be—is essential to creating an inclusive environment, one in which each individual "feels fully present and involved, believes that others recognize and appreciate his or her contributions, and feels both safe and open about his or her social identities" (Ferdman, 2010). On the other hand, one might argue that world language teachers should not concern themselves with the issue of inclusive language, because it is so much a product of North American ideas, movements, social media, and events. Would it not be more respectful to resist the impulse to impose U.S. and Canadian ideas in courses focused on cultures in which such concepts have little traction? Not exactly. Educators whose students reside in North America should absolutely give them the tools to position themselves as North Americans to dismantle the myth of universal values. That is, students must first examine culturally bound perspectives and practices of the place where they live before they can begin to analyze those of other cultures. Adopting an antiracist, inclusive, and equity-minded pedagogy enables language learners to see their own culture as well as others with greater nuance.

Two Pedagogical Paths to Gender and Sexuality Inclusivity

There are two ways to modify an OER-based language course to introduce or increase gender and sexuality inclusivity. First, non-inclusive OER can be expanded by adding culture lessons, supplementary vocabulary, and instruction about inclusive language in the target culture. Secondly, inclusive language and ideas can be baked into activities and assessments throughout the OER-based course. The first approach educates students about gender and LGBTQ+ issues in a direct fashion. The second has a day-to-day impact on the culture of the classroom, thus normalizing and embracing gender and sexuality inclusivity. Whether an instructor adopts the first approach, the second, or both, it is vital to employ backward design (Wiggins & McTighe, 2011). That is, the instructor should start with 1) a learning outcome of the course (what the student should be able to do at the end of the course) and work backward through 2) assessment (how the student demonstrates their achievement of the outcome), then on to 3) practice activities (how the student prepares for the assessment), and finally to 4) the introduction of the OER material (how the student is first exposed to the OER content they will practice and be assessed on).

Gender and sexuality inclusive instruction can be incorporated into any language course at any level, but whereas an intermediate or advanced world language course may have a learning outcome specifically related to gender or sexuality issues, in most elementary and intermediate classes, the instructor will be focused on linguistic and cultural course objectives. It is also true that intermediate-high learners can more readily develop cultural understandings regarding gender and sexuality through authentic resources (that is, resources intended for a native-speaking audience, such as websites, popular music, and podcasts) and compilations of native-speaker interviews, such as those available through The Center for Open Educational Resources & Language Learning (COERLL) at the University of Texas at Austin including the [Spanish in Texas Project](https://www.coerll.utexas.edu/spintx/), the [Hindi in America Collection](http://goo.gl/yBWId), and the [Cultural Interviews with International Business Executives](http://sites.utexas.edu/culturalinterviews/) video archives. Beginning students generally lack the linguistic ability and the cultural learning framework to gain a nuanced understanding of LGBTQ+ and women's issues through resources in the target language. Nevertheless, OER-based activities in elementary-level classes can still be designed to be gender and sexuality inclusive.

Perhaps the simplest way of making an OER-based world language class more inclusive is by adding content related to culture, especially lessons that are not integrated with specific linguistic objectives. For example, historical lessons could spotlight feminist or LGBTQ+ movements or gay and/or female historical figures. Literary selections might include works by cis women or queer authors. Even works that do not primarily tackle gender and sexuality issues can be analyzed through a gender studies lens. Similarly, the instructor can take gender inclusivity into account when selecting films, art, and music for classes. The instructor must be particularly careful to employ backward design when it comes to this kind of cultural instruction, so that the lesson leads toward assessment and a demonstration of proficiency in each learning outcome. Culture lessons that are not well embedded in the course can come off as mere trivia to students or worse, a distraction from what "really counts" towards passing the class. By contrast, assignments that direct students to write or speak about cis women and LGBTQ+ people, their achievements, and their concerns integrate gender inclusivity well with linguistic and cultural course goals.

Presuming instructors or curriculum leads keep abreast of developments in the target culture(s), they can create culture and linguistic OER that focus on the contentious evolution of gender inclusive language. For example, a professor covering subject pronouns, adjective agreement, or words for professions can glean information from this article (at least for a few years) to teach about the steps being made towards gender inclusive language in countries with Western European languages. Even as the instructor strives for an inclusive world language course, it is essential to convey to the students what is generally accepted versus what is considered controversial, radical, or even illegal in the target culture(s). For example, students in a French class must learn to use the gendered pronouns "*il*" and "*elle*" in accordance with the conventions of the Académie Française. If not, their French will be considered not gender inclusive but simply wrong. However, by discussing the existence of the novel pronoun "*iel*" and the controversy surrounding its inclusion in *Le Robert*, the instructor creates an inclusive space for those students who do not themselves see gender in binary terms. Moreover, attention to linguistic tension and innovation helps students to see French as a living and evolving international language, used and contested in different nations by real individuals who not only appear less stereotypical, more nuanced, and less fixed but also vary in perspective.

World language classes should prepare female, gay, and non-gender-conforming students for what to expect while traveling, studying, or living in countries where the target language is spoken. Certainly, the vocabulary lists of most OER textbooks require addenda to enable students to express that someone is gay or trans, although widely-used gender inclusive terms ought to have a place in their lexicons. To take another example from the French curriculum, lessons about dress should go beyond vocabulary lists and the verb *mettre* (to put on). Particularly for women, certain modes of dress may be tacitly encouraged or discouraged and officially required or banned, depending on where one is in the francophone world. Thus, from a purely practical standpoint, students should be made aware that mores and taboos around self-presentation exist. Moreover, a discussion of clothing items such as head scarves, burkinis, and abayas, and their use in public spaces, reveals a wide spectrum of francophone perspectives influenced by religion, politics, geography, feminism, history, generational attitudes, public health, and current events. Such a discussion would allow students to see a complexity in French-speaking societies that mirrors the intricacies of their own world and would permit students to be exposed to points of view that may be entirely new to them (e.g., the concept of *laïcité*, the exclusion of religion from civic life). If the instructor does not feel prepared for or comfortable with lecturing on topics such as these, guest speakers, cultural informants, Collaborative Online International Learning (COIL), and native-speaking language partners can be extremely helpful for addressing legal and quotidian conditions for LGBTQ+ people and women.

While the use of OER on historical topics is a reliable way to increase gender and sexuality inclusivity, teaching about cultural developments presents special challenges. As discussed above, attitudes, practices, language, and laws are constantly in flux. World language instructors who do not have the ability to frequently immerse themselves in the target cultures must settle for immersion at a distance through a regular diet of authentic sources like news reports, blogs, films, television shows, and music to keep abreast of cultural shifts. Just as information may have an expiration date so also can OER become inaccessible over time. For example, the Center for Global Business – Texas McCombs' Cultural Interviews with International Business Executives video repository assembled a trove of native-speaker interviews in Chinese, Japanese, Spanish, and Turkish on topics such as "Machismo," "Race, Color, and Gender," and "Women Executives." These videos are no longer accessible and organized through the Center's YouTube channel, which has been suspended, or the project website, which is deemed not secure. If time places limits on an instructor's cultural knowledge and resources, geography does also. After all, trends impacting women in Spain may be unknown or rejected in Honduras or Venezuela. The instructor who incorporates OER about contemporary culture must provide caveats to students about the temporal and geographic specificity of the information and resources shared in the course. Regardless, sexuality inclusivity requires teaching about contemporary culture. While it is possible to celebrate the achievements of historical women, old taboos make it difficult to identify gay and trans figures as such.

An alternative to the additive approach to making a world language course more inclusive is to alter the OER materials used throughout the course for instruction, practice, and assessment. This approach focuses on the incidentals of the course rather than the content itself and is appropriate since world language classes use social contexts as the framework for language learning. For inductive instruction, deductive instruction, or practice activities, model sentences and discussion prompts can incorporate LGBTQ+ identities and relationships. Likewise, tests may employ plausible scenarios in each section that provide a gender inclusive context. For example, if an examination of OER materials reveals a pattern of gendered stereotypes, it would not be very difficult to change the doctor in an exercise on health vocabulary from a man to a woman or, vice versa, change the nurse from a woman to a man. In a test section on food vocabulary, it could be the father rather than the mother who is seeking items in the grocery store and then preparing dinner for the family. In a section on household, it could be the dad rather than the mom who could be the stay-at-home parent in charge of the house chores while the mother is employed, or it could be the dad who is the one on paternity leave after a newborn child. If there is a pervasive assumption of heteronormativity, it is simple enough to place a fictional "Juan Carlos," "Manfred," or "André" in dialogue with his *boy*friend, rather than his *girl*friend in an activity.

While such changes may be simple to make, the consequences may be profound. On the positive side, representation across the spectrum of gender roles and sexual orientations can make students feel that the classroom is a more welcoming environment and that the instructor embraces equity-minded practices. While learners should always retain the prerogative to reveal as much or as little about their private lives as they wish, when inclusivity is modeled in the course materials, they may feel more at ease being open about themselves, their lives, and their loved ones. However, there can be negative reactions, particularly from students whose conservative worldviews oppose feminism and homosexuality. With smartphones and social media, this pushback can certainly spill beyond the classroom, and the current politically-motivated attacks on academic freedom in many parts of the U.S. might make even minor course modifications risky. For those who are willing and able to take on that risk, the worksheet in the Appendix can help generate more inclusive OER materials that integrate well with the overall curriculum of a course.

Erasing Discriminatory Hierarchies and Biases in the OER World Language Classroom

Using gender inclusive language really matters in the academic setting. Likewise, classroom inclusion of all sexual orientations creates a safe space for learners who desperately need it, since biased language, such as sexist and homophobic statements, perpetuate prejudice, discrimination, and even homelessness and violence, and is harmful to transgender and gender nonconforming individuals (National Center for Transgender Equality, 2021). The use of gender-inclusive language, instead, promotes gender equality and inclusivity. No student deserves to feel excluded or unsuited. Everyone deserves to be recognized, accepted, and respected, and to feel equal and proud of who they are, especially when facing the vulnerability it takes to stumble through learning an unfamiliar language. Ideally, those educators using OER who feel empowered to revise their courses with an eye to gender inclusivity will share their ideas and materials with the wider OER community so that everyone will find some new practice and inspiration—however small—that give their students a deeper sense of belonging and a greater appreciation of the complexity of cultures and peoples and their diverse perspectives and practices.

References

Abou-Chadi, T., Breyer, M., & Gessler, T. (2021). The (re)politicisation of gender in Western Europe. *European Journal of Politics and Gender, 4*(2), 311–314. https://doi.org/10.1332/251510821X16177312096679

Atkinson, E. (2022, December 13). Brigitte Macron hits out at gender-neutral French grammar system. *The Independent.* https://www.msn.com/en-gb/news/world/brigitte-macron-hits-out-at-gender-neutral-french-grammar-system/ar-AA15dZO4

Auxland, M. (2020). Para todes: A case study on Portuguese and gender-neutrality. *Journal of Languages, Texts, and Society, 4,* 60–83. https://www.nottingham.ac.uk/research/groups/languagestextssociety/documents/lts-journal/issue-4/lts-issue-4-article-auxland.-m.-para-todes-a-case-study-on-portuguese-and-gender-neutrality.pdf

Banegas, D. L., & López, M. F. (2021). Inclusive language in Spanish as interpellation to educational authorities. *Applied Linguistics, 42*(2), 342–346. https://doi.org/10.1093/applin/amz026

Baron, D. (2018, September 4). A brief history of singular 'they.' *Oxford English Dictionary.*

Bem, S. L., & Bem, D. J. (1973). Does sex-biased job advertising "aid and abet" sex discrimination? *Journal of Applied Social Psychology, 3*(1), 6–18. https://doi.org/10.1111/j.1559-1816.1973.tb01290.x

Born, M. P., & Taris, T. W. (2010). The impact of the wording of employment advertisements on students' inclination to apply for a job. *The Journal of Social Psychology*, *150*(5), 485–502. https://doi.org/10.1080/00224540903365422

Bundeskanzleramt Österreich - Bundeskanzlerin und Bundeskanzler seit 1945 (n.d.). Retrieved March 6, 2023, from https://www.bundeskanzleramt.gv.at/bundeskanzleramt/geschichte/kanzler-seit-1945.html

Burgen, S. (2020, January 19). Masculine, feminist or neutral? The language battle that has split Spain. *The Observer*. https://www.theguardian.com/world/2020/jan/19/gender-neutral-language-battle-spain

Dodman, B. (2021, February 25). 'Françaises, Français': Could the French language be less sexist? *France 24*. https://www.france24.com/en/culture/20210225-fran%C3%A7aises-fran%C3%A7ais-why-the-french-language-need-not-be-so-sexist

Everett, C. (2011). Gender, pronouns and thought: The ligature between epicene pronouns and a more neutral gender perception. *Gender and Language*, *5*(1), 133–152. https://doi.org/10.1558/genl.v5i1.133

Ferdman, B. (2010). Teaching inclusion by example and experience: Creating an inclusive learning environment. In *Leading across differences: Cases and perspectives—Facilitator's guide,* edited by Kelly M. Hannum, Belinda McFeeters, and Lize Booysen, 37–49. San Francisco: Pfeiffer.

Gabriel, U., & Mellenberger, F. (2004). Exchanging the generic masculine for gender-balanced forms—The impact of context valence. *Swiss Journal of Psychology*, *63*(4), 273–278. https://doi.org/10.1024/1421-0185.63.4.273

Gallagher, T. (2022, December 14). What's the boeuf? Gender neutral pronouns spark fury of French establishment. *Euronews*. https://www.euronews.com/culture/2022/12/14/whats-the-boeuf-gender-neutral-pronouns-spark-fury-of-french-establishment

Government of Canada (2022, September 14). *Inclusive writing—Guidelines and resources.* https://www.noslangues-ourlanguages.gc.ca/en/writing-tips-plus/inclusive-writing-guidelines-resources

House of Lords Hansard—UK Parliament. (2013, October 10). Retrieved March 4, 2023, https://hansard.parliament.uk//Lords/2013-10-10

House Resolution 8, 117th Congress (2021-2022). *Adopting the rules of the*

House of Representatives for the One Hundred Seventeenth Congress, and for other purposes. Retrieved March 4, 2023 from https://rules.house.gov/bill/117/h-res-5

House Resolution 5, 118th Congress (2023-2024). *Adopting the rules of the House of Representatives for the One Hundred Eighteenth Congress, and for other purposes.* Retrieved March 4, 2023 from https://rules.house.gov/bill/118/h-res-5

Kofler, B. (2022, March 30). *Gender-Inclusive Language Project: German.* UX Writers Collective. Directed by Carlos Vives. https://www.youtube.com/watch?v=Qdvf4XoitC0

Lakoff, R. (1973). Language and woman's place. *Language in Society, 2*(1), 45–79. https://doi.org/10.1017/S0047404500000051

Le Robert. (n.d.). *Dico en ligne.* Retrieved July 12, 2023, from https://dictionnaire.lerobert.com/

Luck, C. (2020). Linguistics and literature. In *Rewriting Language: How Literary Texts Can Promote Inclusive Language Use* (pp. 14–52). UCL Press. https://doi.org/10.2307/j.ctv13xpsg6.5

Martin, R. (2015, May 10). Oxford dictionary proposes gender-neutral title. *NPR.* https://www.npr.org/2015/05/10/405624481/oxford-dictionary-proposes-gender-neutral-title

Martyna, W. (1980). The psychology of the generic masculine. In S. McConnell-Ginet, R. Borker, & N. Furman (Eds.), *Women and language in literature and society,* (pp. 69–78). Praeger.

McConnell, A. R., & Fazio, R. H. (1996). Women as men and people: Effects of gender-marked language. *Personality and Social Psychology Bulletin, 22*(10), 1004–1013. https://doi.org/10.1177/01461672962210003

Mora, G. C., Perez, R., & Vargas, N. (2022). Who identifies as "Latinx"? The generational politics of ethnoracial labels. *Social Forces, 100*(3), 1170–1194. https://doi.org/10.1093/sf/soab011

Moulton, J., Robinson, G. M., & Elias, C. (1978). Sex bias in language use: "Neutral" pronouns that aren't. *American Psychologist, 33*(11), 1032–1036. https://doi.org/10.1037/0003-066X.33.11.1032

National Center for Transgender Equality. (2021, April 22). *Housing & Homelessness.* https://transequality.org/issues/housing-homelessness

Nöstlinger, N. (2021, March 8). Debate over gender-neutral language divides Germany. *Politico*. https://www.politico.eu/article/debate-over-gender-inclusive-neutral-language-divides-germany/

Orrú, A. & Vitiello, R. (2022, June 23). *The gender-inclusive language project. Italiano*. UX Content Collective. Directed by Carlos Vives. https://www.youtube.com/watch?v=sohPNXgao8w

Pilon, S. (2020). Toward a more gender-inclusive and gender-neutral French language. *The French Review*, *94*(2), 193–205. https://doi.org/10.1353/tfr.2020.0281

Pino, M. C. (2021). Más glotopolítica del sexismo lingüístico: Ideologemas de la argumentación de los defensores del lenguaje inclusivo de género. *Erebea: Revista de Humanidades y Ciencias Sociales*, *11*, 127–149. https://doi.org/10.33776/erebea.v11i0.6904

Piser, K. (2021, July 4). Aux armes, citoyen·nes! *Foreign Policy*. https://foreignpolicy.com/2021/07/04/france-gender-language-ecriture-inclusive-aux-armes-citoyennes/

Real Academia Española. (2018). *Libro de estilo de la lengua española: Según la norma panhispánica*. Espasa.

Reali, C., Esaulova, Y., Öttl, A., & von Stockhausen, L. (2015). Role descriptions induce gender mismatch effects in eye movements during reading. *Frontiers in Psychology*, *6*, 1–13. https://doi.org/10.3389/fpsyg.2015.01607

Rosati, F., Lorusso, M. M., Pistella, J., Giovanardi, G., Di Giannantonio, B., Mirabella, M., Williams, R., Lingiardi, V., & Baiocco, R. (2022). Non-binary clients' experiences of psychotherapy: Uncomfortable and affirmative approaches. *International Journal of Environmental Research and Public Health*, *19*(22), Article 22. https://doi.org/10.3390/ijerph192215339

Schneider, J. W., & Hacker, S. L. (1973). Sex role imagery and use of the generic "Man" in introductory texts: A case in the sociology of sociology. *The American Sociologist*, *8*(1), 12–18. https://www.jstor.org/stable/27702068

Sczesny, S., Moser, F., & Wood, W. (2015). Beyond sexist beliefs: How do people decide to use gender-inclusive language? *Personality and Social Psychology Bulletin*, *41*(7), 943–954. https://doi.org/10.1177/0146167215585727

Slemp, K. (2020). *Latino, Latina, Latin@, Latine, and Latinx: Gender inclusive oral expression in Spanish* (29247791) [Master's thesis, The University of Western Ontario (Canada)]. ProQuest Dissertations Publishing. https://www.proquest.com/openview/917facff59ec416f1d066839c766125b/1?pq-origsite=gscholar&cbl=18750&diss=y

Slemp, K. (2021). Attitudes towards varied inclusive language use in Spanish on Twitter. *Working Papers in Applied Linguistics and Linguistics at York*, *1*, 60–74. https://doi.org/10.25071/2564-2855.6

Spender, D. (1985). *Man Made Language*. Routledge.

Stetie, N., & Zunino, G. (2022). Non-binary language in Spanish? Comprehension of non-binary morphological forms: a psycholinguistic study. *Glossa: A Journal of General Linguistics*, *7*(1), Article 1. https://doi.org/10.16995/glossa.6144

Stewart, D. (2022, October 25). Giorgia Meloni stirs controversy in Italy by announcing she wants to be called «the prime minister». *MSN*.

Stout, J. G., & Dasgupta, N. (2011). When he doesn't mean you: Gender-exclusive language as ostracism. *Personality and Social Psychology Bulletin*, *37*(6), 757–769. https://doi.org/10.1177/0146167211406434

Teresa-Morales, C., Rodríguez-Pérez, M., Araujo-Hernández, M., & Feria-Ramírez, C. (2022). Current stereotypes associated with nursing and nursing professionals: An integrative review. *International Journal of Environmental Research and Public Health*, *19*(13). https://doi.org/10.3390/ijerph19137640

United Nations. (n.d.). *United Nations gender-inclusive language*. Retrieved August 14, 2023, from https://www.un.org/en/gender-inclusive-language/

Vervecken, D., Hannover, B., & Wolter, I. (2013). Changing (s)expectations: How gender fair job descriptions impact children's perceptions and interest regarding traditionally male occupations. *Journal of Vocational Behavior*, *82*(3), 208–220. https://doi.org/10.1016/j.jvb.2013.01.008

Wiggins, G., & McTighe, J. (2011). *The understanding by design guide to creating high-quality units*. ASCD.

Author Bios
Federica Goldoni, Georgia Gwinnett College
Federica Goldoni is a Professor of Spanish in the Department of Political Science, Criminal Justice and International Studies at Georgia Gwinnett College. Her Ph.D. is from the Department of Language and Literacy Education at the University of Georgia. Her interests are identity issues in second language, foreign language pedagogy, and study abroad.

Kristina Watkins Mormino
Kristina Watkins Mormino is a Professor of French in the Department of Political Science, Criminal Justice and International Studies and an associate dean in the School of Liberal Arts at Georgia Gwinnett College. She earned her Ph.D. from the Department of French and Italian at Emory University. Her interests are medieval studies, women's writing, and issues in foreign language pedagogy.

Appendix: A Worksheet for Creating a Culturally Relevant and Inclusive Activity Through Backward Design

Step One: Pick a Course – Any Course!

Culturally relevant activities can be incorporated into any course at any level. Which course would you like to start with, and why?

Step Two: Outcomes-Driven Planning

Course activities should be driven by learning outcomes. Here are the outcomes for FREN 1001 courses at Georgia Gwinnett College with the outcome related to culture highlighted:

Upon completion of this course, students will:
1. Demonstrate basic comprehension of information or instructions conveyed orally in French.
2. Communicate orally in the present tense using common French words and phrases and comprehensible pronunciation.
3. Use learned French vocabulary and cognates to derive information from readings and familiar topics.
4. Relate information in writing using simple French sentences in the present tense.
5. **Identify various parts of the world where French is spoken and relate information about francophone cultural products and practices.**

What cultural outcomes do you have in your chosen course? Do you feel your course currently moves students effectively toward meeting the outcome? If not, why not? If you do not have a cultural goal among the learning outcomes for your course, what is your personal objective regarding cultural knowledge, intercultural competence, or inclusivity?

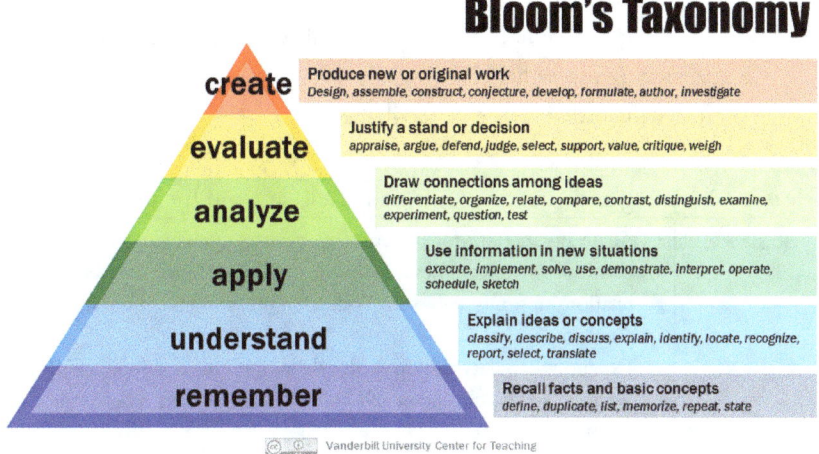

Armstrong, P. (2010). Bloom's Taxonomy. Vanderbilt University Center for Teaching. Retrieved June 3, 2022 from https://cft.vanderbilt.edu/guides-sub-pages/blooms-taxonomy/.

While you might plan your activity to advance students toward your desired cultural outcome(s), alternatively, you could create an activity designed around a different course objective that coincidentally exposes students to cultural difference or cultural issues. Examples would be a reading comprehension activity for which the selected passage features an LGBTQ character or a writing activity that incorporates a non-Western context.

Which course objective(s) do you intend to address with this activity instead of/in addition to your cultural goal(s)?

What should your students be able to do once they meet your chosen objective(s)? Circle the relevant verb(s) (e.g. define, compose, contrast, etc.) in the objectives you wrote above.

Step Three: Assessment (Formal or Informal?)

1. Will your activity be graded?
2. At the end of your course, will you have a product (student work or data) to reveal whether or not your chosen learning outcome/objective has been met? If so, what will your product be? If this

activity will not generate data to allow you to determine whether a learning outcome has been met, will it help prepare the students for such an assessment?
3. How will students receive feedback?

Ideas for Adapting and Creating Culturally Relevant and Inclusive Activities

Adapted Activities	• Adapt instructions for pre-existing activities to include culturally/ethnically diverse names and images and LGBTQ identities and relationships. Diversify your discussion prompts and example sentences. • Expand vocabulary dealing with celebrations, history, food, clothing, weather, and describing people to include terms appropriate to a variety of cultures. • Give tests an overarching and plausible scenario as a context that introduces diversity. • For assignments requiring research, have students use at least one non-U.S., non-Western, or non-normative (but trustworthy!) source. • Generate a list of topics for reports that requires or encourages students to branch out. For class presentations, set a limit of one student per topic so that all students are exposed to a range of topics.
Created Activities	• Incorporate an artistic work that introduces cultural difference or social issues into your course. This could be a poem, a song, a narrative, a film (short or feature-length), or a visual work. Introduce the work and its creator to the class. Create speaking, listening, culture, reading or writing activities using this work as a basis. • Identify a contemporary issue to explore in the course. Create mini-lectures, readings, or class discussions around this issue. Alternately, create assignments for which students write, converse, read, or present about this issue. • Create brief written or oral activities based around an assortment of short videos, such as commercials, music videos, sports interviews, and human-interest reports. • Make an assignment that requires interaction with a person from the target culture *who is not in the class*. In a heterogenous location, this could entail a site visit or an oral interview. Collaborative Online International Learning (COIL) or Talk Abroad could be used in a less diverse setting. • Invite a guest speaker, and make your students accountable for asking questions or doing something with the information from the guest's presentation.

Step Four: Adapt or Create Your Activity

Brainstorm possible activities. Use the chart above if you need ideas. Ask yourself . . .
- Will the activity be in English, in the target language, or in a combination of the two?
- Do I need to do some cultural research to inform this activity?
- What materials or resources will be needed?
- What classroom methods might be entailed?
- Do I need to scaffold the activity?
- Do I need to create a rubric? Do I need to create samples of appropriate work?

5

A Hybrid Model of Media Entrepreneurship Using Open Pedagogy Principles

Michelle Barrett Ferrier, Media Innovation Collaboratory
Geoffrey Graybeal, University of South Carolina

Abstract

This case study examines the use of open pedagogy practices to develop open educational resources and a community of practice around media entrepreneurship and innovation. The case study describes both online and physical space co-creation practices to build a knowledge base to test and revise the open educational resources. One emerging community of practice is developing in Ethiopia using a hybrid modality of face-to-face and digital delivery of the open educational resources. Internet shutdowns and rolling power outages across Ethiopia make development of an independent media sector a challenging one. The goal is to enhance the open education resources for a non-Western, professional context and co-create materials for media innovation in challenging digital environments. The authors adapted their pedagogy to ensure they stayed true to the core principles of open pedagogy: low-cost, low-risk, access to the materials, flattened design to ensure easy downloads of videos or content for offline reading and viewing, and adoption of digital tools that were free or open-source to build our distributed network. Finally, the case study also examines the use of various design practices that help to make visible open pedagogy and group sense-making practices.

Keywords: open pedagogy, journalism, media entrepreneurship, media innovation, community-led media

Suggested citation: Ferrier, M. B., Graybeal, G. (2024). A hybrid model of media entrepreneurship using open pedagogy principles. In T. Tijerina (Ed.), *Pedagogy opened: Innovative theory and practice* (pp. 128-155). University of North Georgia Press. https://alg.manifoldapp.org/read/pedagogy-opened-v1-a5/.

Introduction

Open pedagogy, according to the editors of this collection, is defined as teaching and learning practices and environments that promote equity, collaboration, and innovation and invite students to create and share knowledge with future publics, often in association with the use of Open Educational Resources (OER). Wiley (2013) defined open pedagogy as a set of teaching and learning practices made possible by free access and the OER 5R characteristics of reuse, redistribute, revise, remix, and retain permissions (Wiley, 2013).

Open educational resources allow students and instructors more control over the educational material, customizing it and sharing it in ways that make sense, as the material from the textbook can be retained, reused, revised, and redistributed. OER allows for customization and localization of resources and material that work for varying teaching styles and hopefully have students perform as well or better than they would have with an off-the-shelf publisher resource (Robinson et al., 2014). Open pedagogy and our OER resources also bring other affordances to our students, such as deeper learning and critical ability to evaluate and defend sources, write more concisely, collaborate with others around the world, provide and receive constructive feedback, enhance digital literacy, and communicate ideas to a general audience (Farazan & Kraut, 2013; Marentette, 2014; Karney, 2012; Ibrahim, 2012; Silton, 2012; and APS, 2013).

OER is also valuable in a dynamic environment such as media and technology to keep the materials current and relevant for our various practitioners. This case study examines the development and use of open educational resources around media innovation and entrepreneurship and communities of practice in a non-Western context. The case study also examines the use of various human-centered design practices that help to make visible open pedagogy and group sense-making practices. Finally, the case study describes both online and physical space practices to build communities of practice in media innovation and entrepreneurship using open-source technologies and co-creation strategies.

Previous research has largely been centered around use in a traditional academic setting, e.g. college courses, and focused on satisfaction of adoption from student and faculty perspectives as well as quality and performance measures. Some studies suggest that OER may indirectly improve student performance through increased satisfaction, engagement, and interest in the subjects (Colvard, Watson & Park, 2018; de los Arcos et al., 2014; Farrow et al., 2015; Pitt, 2015). Colvard, Watson & Park (2018) studied OER use and student ethnic origin and found a statistically significant difference in academic performance between white and non-white students in a university setting.

To help prepare students and professionals for the changing media environment, educators in journalism and communication courses developed and designed digital media and media entrepreneurship courses that were often experiential in nature, bringing venture creation experiences and product development skills to students (Pittaway, et. al. 2017, 2020, 2021). These courses also emphasized design thinking and hands-on development skills—key skills the new digital marketplace was looking for (Graybeal & Ferrier, 2023; Graybeal & Sindik, 2016; Hoag, 2008; Sindik & Graybeal, 2017). Media entrepreneurship education generally integrates traditional entrepreneurial format with media-specific information. Media entrepreneurship courses are designed to introduce students to what it means to be an entrepreneur and create their own company (Ferrier, 2013).

Educators previously cited the lack of teaching resources specific to the media and communication fields around technology, media innovation, and entrepreneurship (Ferrier, 2013), and researchers had been examining community-based physical and virtual practices for creating online communities. Educators created online groups to discuss new courses and skills for journalism and media students in computational journalism, technological innovation, and media entrepreneurship that helped educators with peer-to-peer exchanges on pedagogy and other challenges to teaching the new curricula (Examples: Facebook Disruptive Journalism Educators Network established 2011, the Media Entrepreneurship Facebook Group established 2014, the Journalism Entrepreneurship Facebook groups formed around the Scripps Howard Journalism Entrepreneurship Institute cohorts, and the Journalism That Matters Create or Die May 26, 2011 Facebook group) (Graybeal & Ferrier, 2023).

From these online communities of educators, media entrepreneurs, and intrapreneurs, a learning community of more than 25 authors, more than 12 peer reviewers, and 12 faculty beta testers created an open educational resource, *Media Innovation and Entrepreneurship*, edited by Ferrier and Mays (2017). The modular resource is designed as a workbook, moving students through design thinking to venture creation in a 15-week design sprint. This first "community of practice" developed from the open education and open pedagogy strategies as described in "Free + Freedom: The Role of Open Pedagogy in the Open Education Movement" by Rajiv Jhangiani and Robin DeRosa and included communities, learner-driven education, access, and public contexts (Jhangiani & DeRosa, 2016).

A community of practice (COP) is a group of people who share a concern or a passion for something they do and learn how to do it better as they interact regularly (Lave and Wenger 1991:98). Cognitive anthropologists Jean Lave and Etienne Wenger coined the term "community of practice" when studying apprenticeships as a learning model – the term referred to the community that acts as a living curriculum. Many communities of practice rely on face-to-face meetings as well as web-based collaborative environments to communicate, connect, and conduct community activities (Edmonton Regional Learning Consortium, 2016).

Our initial community of practice snowballed as we reached into our emerging media entrepreneurial landscape and connected with other higher education institutions, business incubators and accelerators, and the larger entrepreneurial ecosystem. Our processes mimicked our co-creation philosophy "Nothing about us without us," and we invited the voices of entrepreneurs, students, financiers, and others to contribute to the final open textbook. These ever-widening communities of practice ensured that our final product would not only be useful to our initial cohort but also find value beyond the media/journalism classroom in other venture creation programs.

1. The first community of practice was born from the needs of several journalism educators seeking an accessible and flexible educational resource. The community of practice developed shared syllabi and resources and created an open educational resource: the *Media Innovation and Entrepreneurship* textbook published by the Rebus Foundation in 2017.
2. The second community of practice became the beta testers of that open textbook, that is, the journalism educators and faculty members that took the first draft into the classroom. The community met weekly to discuss the upcoming draft chapter with the chapter author and discuss how to assess student learning.
3. The third community of practice evolved following adoption of the OER, largely through new faculty members adopting the materials on its first release in 2017. There were at least two dozen initial adopters.
4. The fourth community of practice developed from other specialized programs that appreciated the creation and development framework and open access of the OER and have adapted the resources for graduate, professional, and executive programs.

Within these communities of practice, journalists and educators have been practicing co-creating knowledge using a variety of open technologies for knowledge creation. Our goal was to help journalists, technologists, and educators navigate an ever-changing digital environment and co-create media products and innovations for community news and information needs.

The Development of Media Innovation and Entrepreneurship Curriculum

College campuses and institutions of higher education have been building entrepreneurial ecosystems to address venture creation by students from a variety of creative industries. Higher education began to use digital tools to reach students through online and other digital modalities and began to think of how to make these spaces experiential, collaborative, and student-centered. Upheavals in the communications, information, and technology spaces would create shifts in what was taught within journalism and media programs across the United States (Ferrier and Batts, 2016; Ferrier and Mays, 2017). As digital spaces exploded in the early 2000s, more communication and creative industries were finding a need to re-visit their curricular offerings and determine what new emerging industries needed in workforce skills (Ferrier, 2009; Graybeal & Sindik, 2016). Disciplines and degree programs in journalism, business, art, entrepreneurship, music, theater, media, communication, information technologies, and other creative industries began to revisit how to bring access to education to new populations and make higher education more equitable.

Journalism and communication educators were also wrestling with new technologies and their ongoing impact on the work of communicators. Florida educators began curriculum changes in 2006 to address the emerging fields in digital media, interactive content, immersive and augmented media, simulations and other technologies like cloud computing, mobile technologies, and other transformations to communication like social media, video, and digital content creation and sharing. The University of Central Florida (UCF) attracted transfer students from a wide range of community colleges across Florida because of its unique undergraduate and graduate programs in digital media. In order to ensure that transfer students from all of these sources entered the program with the core knowledge of digital media principles, the university's digital media department and UCF Regional Campuses embarked on a different approach—to work with several community college partners to develop consensus around a core set of competencies that would become the basis for a common set of courses offered across the state. The educators shaped the curriculum, first defining the student learning objectives, then second defining the skills and knowledge necessary to form the basis of a new discipline that brought a convergence of technology, media, journalism, and communication skills and knowledge (Ferrier, 2009).

In the intervening decades since courses on media entrepreneurship were introduced in journalism schools across the U.S. in the early 2000s, a community of practice developed around media innovation and entrepreneurship through educator training programs like Jan Schaffer's New Media Women's Voices grant program for women media entrepreneurs

(Schaffer writes the forward to the *Media Innovation & Entrepreneurship* open textbook); Journalism Interactive, a rotating conference for educators working with emerging technologies; the "Create or Die" media venture creation gatherings of a nonprofit organization called Journalism That Matters; the gatherings sponsored by the City University of New York that focused on journalism entrepreneurship; and weeklong training programs for educators like the Scripps Howard Journalism Entrepreneurial Institute, housed at Arizona State University and sponsored by the Scripps Howard Foundation. From 2012 to 2019, the program brought together journalism educators for a weeklong training on strategies for teaching media entrepreneurship. Educators were expected to create and introduce new courses on media entrepreneurship at their universities after participation in the program (Ferrier, 2013; Ferrier, 2014; Ferrier & Batts, 2016; Graybeal & Ferrier, 2023; Hang & van Weezel, 2007; Hang, 2020; Sindik & Graybeal, 2017). Ten years later, we see many of the syllabi centered around courses with "media entrepreneurship," "media innovation," "disruptive entrepreneurship," "digital media innovation," "social entrepreneurship" and other course titles that have moved away from "journalism entrepreneurship" to the broader framing of innovation within the media, technology, and communication industries (Graybeal & Ferrier, 2023).

Our initial OER, the *Media Innovation & Entrepreneurship* open textbook, was outlined in a spreadsheet with potential chapters and contributors vetted, with an intentional effort to find diverse contributors and expand the "public contexts" involved in our community of practice. Feedback and dialogue from the community was solicited throughout the development process. Hypothes.is, an experimental tool itself developed by an open education publisher, was used for annotations in beta testing of the initial material and some peer review. Quizzes and interactive material were later added in subsequent editions of the textbook using HP5. Students could access the OER in multiple formats in digital and print, so that the materials could be downloaded, viewed on a mobile phone, or purchased through low-cost print-on-demand options.

In the second community of practice, the faculty educators became beta testers before our release and used the open textbook in their Fall 2017 classes in media entrepreneurship. Biweekly calls using Zoom were held so educators teaching the subject could develop pedagogical ideas for delivering the curriculum as it unfolded over the semester. These sessions included a mentorship "how I teach this" portion, which attendees found valuable.

Peer review was used to gather and incorporate feedback. Faculty were invited to biweekly calls with authors to ask questions, discuss the content, and allow authors to revise their chapters. A Google Form was used for submission of suggested edits (most were incorporated), and single anonymous peer review was used. The textbook also underwent two independent reviews by OER repositories before they were adopted into their knowledge base for use. The book is distributed on Amazon, but it is also available on open resources like LibreTexts (https://socialsci.libretexts.org/Bookshelves/Communication/Journalism_and_Mass_Communication/Media_Innovation_and_Entrepreneurship_(Ferrier_and_Mays)) and Center for Open Education (https://open.umn.edu/opentextbooks/textbooks/507) (Ferrier & Mays, 2020). We also used the beta group to garner feedback from students themselves on the structure and language of the open textbook. Hypothes.is was used for both student and faculty feedback. Finally, the weekly calls allowed novice educators to get pedagogical suggestions and engagement strategies to use in the classroom and suggestions on how to implement the syllabi and textbook materials into a hands-on, experiential media innovation course. In addition to the textbook page, a project page with reviews was established along with a YouTube channel, blog post, and report page from the OER publisher, Rebus (https://press.rebus.community/media-innovation-and-entrepreneurship/).

Since its release in 2017, the open text has been widely adopted by more than 36 universities for use in the curriculum to date with more than 2,000 downloads of the open textbook. Educators have used the open textbook in courses like "Journalism Innovation", "Journalism Entrepreneurship", "Media Innovation", "Product Development" and other innovation and venture creation courses within the media/journalism/communication disciplines. Some courses, like existing "Media Management" courses, were amended to include "Media Management and Entrepreneurship" and included business venture creation as a final assessment for the course. The communities of practice members shared syllabi for how the OER textbook material could be incorporated into various journalism courses. While journalism educators made up the core of the implementation beta group, the book development was shepherded by a diverse group of educators from journalism, computer science, and business; entrepreneurs; students; college administrators; accelerator managers; venture capitalists; angel investors; and others. In short, the OER textbook includes the voices and stories of all parts of the media innovation and entrepreneurship ecosystem (Ferrier and Mays, 2020).

The OER textbook has served as the linchpin and catalyst for the creation of new courses, but also additional communities of practice tailored to specific geographies. In Fall 2021, a group of African media executives enrolled in an Executive Master's in Media Leadership and Innovation course at The Aga Khan University. The open textbook was used for the program and the chapter authors were solicited to present their materials each week. Textbook contributors led virtual course sessions with the executives enrolled in the program. Now, the book editors continue to update the book to deepen the international context on building news and information in other economies.

Case Study Using the Community of Practice/OER Approach

In Fall 2022, one of the editors of the OER material received a federal U.S. government grant for a national nonprofit, the Media Innovation Collaboratory, for which she serves as executive director. This grant led to the establishment of the Ethiopian Media Innovation Accelerator program in partnership with the United States Embassy-Addis Ababa. Brought together by the Media Innovation Collaboratory, the U.S. Embassy-Addis, Addis Insights and other local partners, the program by the Media Innovation Collaboratory created an apprenticeship model designed to build regional cooperative networks and strengthen the news and information ecosystem across Ethiopia. Our goal: Reimagine news, communication, and information in ways that sustain our communities to thrive.

The program also supports another of the objectives of the U.S. Embassy grant: To strengthen independent and state media through digital literacy—to learn about how to discern reliable sources of information, how to identify mis- and disinformation, and how to stay safe as a journalist building in digital spaces. Digital journalists in Ethiopia have been subjected to an ongoing crackdown in Ethiopia in 2022, some resigning their posts in state media and others enduring false arrests and long detentions of two to three weeks.

Our objectives with the Ethiopia program:
1. Build local networks for sustainability, mutual self-aid, and digital resilience.
2. Create localized solutions for communication needs of residents and the region.
3. Develop deeper reporting and localized stories of critical issues such as climate change, economic sustainability, and global health crises.
4. Build regional skills and capacity for news and information.

The Ethiopia Media Innovation Accelerator hybrid program which was conducted from February 2023 to May 2023, consisted of face-to-face engagement and virtual tools to connect for 11 weeks. To reach a diverse group, we produced our application materials in English and Amharic. More than 250 professionals, students, and media workers applied for the accelerator program. Participants were selected to reflect the geographic diversity and gender diversity of Ethiopia (Figure 1). Participants also came with skills and interest in deepening the news and information available in their communities and brought to our dialogues the key issues facing the residents in their region such as sanitation, corruption, gender-based violence, poverty, transportation, and other concerns. The word cloud captured the most often repeated words; however, it was not able to capture the Amharic words and characters that show as rectangle blocks in the diagram (Figure 2). The face-to-face Ethiopia Imagine Camp in Addis Ababa brought together more than 50 media workers, journalists, technologists, and educators to imagine new media innovations for community news and information. A diverse group came together from across Ethiopia to design and co-create communications that help residents to learn from each other in a hybrid face-to-face and online venture development program.

138 | Pedagogy Opened: Innovative Theory and Practice

Figure 1: A map of the regions of Ethiopia and the location of the media professionals participating in the Ethiopia Media Innovation Accelerator Program. Program participants were selected from an applicant pool of more than 250 applications and provide diversity in geography, gender and working environment.

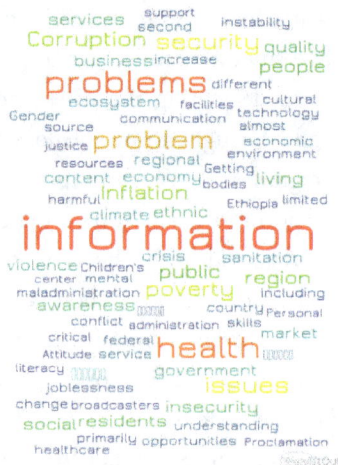

Figure 2: Word cloud of issues across Ethiopia generated from the 250 application responses received for the Ethiopia Media Accelerator Program. Some respondents used Amharic to write their responses, and these were not properly translated in the word cloud program. The responses appear as rectangles in the graphic.

The 2023 program began in Addis Ababa with a face-to-face, four-day design-build sprint with Ethiopian media innovators and professionals (dubbed Imagine Camp). Participants created concept posters where they crystallized their concepts and pitched their media venture to the public (Figure 3). Coaching and development continued virtually for 12 weeks after the face-to-face workshop using synchronous and asynchronous tools, coaching the media entrepreneurs to build and launch their media enterprises. Our program concluded with a Pop-Up Awards Ceremony, where we celebrated the completion of the program and awarded cash prizes to five emerging entrepreneurs and their projects.

Figure 3: Concept poster of educator Yordanos Gizachew of Jijiga University and the community radio laboratory she is creating for her students.

In our bi-weekly, 90-minute co-working sessions, the objectives were:
1. To demonstrate some community-oriented enterprises using applied technology that supports innovation and collaboration in community development and entrepreneurship, civic leadership, and public management.

2. To create an innovation laboratory—a design-build workshop for journalists, communicators, technologists, artists, community activists, and others to reimagine new products and services for diverse communities.
3. To engage participants in sharing ideas and concepts and developing ideas through intensive team building, idea development, design, and build sessions.
4. To provide a showcase for projects in development by Ethiopian innovators and entrepreneurs.
5. To provide instruction and coaching for media innovators/entrepreneurs to connect with each other and with alumni.
6. To serve as a resource and mentoring hub for just-in-time education for media startups.

Table 1: Curriculum for the 12-week program

Week & Modality	Days, Dates: Objectives	Readings
Week 1 Addis Ababa F2F Imagine Camp	Thursday, 2/9: Opening Friday, 2/10: Grounding Saturday, 2/11: Seeding Sunday, 2/12: Nurturing	Chapter 11: Entrepreneurship Abroad: Cultural and International Perspectives
Week 2 Online	Monday, 2/13: Grounding Thursday, 2/16: Grounding	• Forward; • Chapter 1: Developing the Entrepreneurial Mindset; • Taking Risks and Building Resilience; • From the Field: Q&A with a Young Innovator; • What's an Intrapreneur?; • Looking Ahead
Week 3 Online	Monday, 2/20 Thursday, 2/23	• Chapter 2: Ideation; • Chapter 3: Customer Discovery; • Science Museum: Futurecasting; • 50 Ways to Make Media Pay

Week & Modality	Days, Dates: Objectives	Readings
Week 4 Online	Monday, 2/27 Holiday, 3/2: Victory of Adwa Thursday, 3/2	• Chapter 4: Business Models for Content and Technology Ventures; • Ethiopian context, philanthropic entrepreneurial venture giving; • Telegram/WhatsApp Adoption; • Napkin Sketch/Business Model Canvas/social canvas
Week 5 Online	Monday, 3/6 Thursday, 3/9	• Chapter 5: Nonprofit Model Development; • Chapter 8: Pitching; • Community Radio: Frieda Warden, Pamela Morgan, Birgitte Jallov; • My Cell Phone Cinema: Engagement Work and Community Collaboration
Week 6 Online	Monday, 3/13 Thursday, 3/16	• Chapter 6: Freelancing as Entrepreneurship; • Chapter 7: Startup Funding; • Solopreneurship: What does that look like?; • Successful Telegram, TikTok Ethiopian media
Week 7 Online	Monday, 3/20 Thursday, 3/23	• Chapter 6: Freelancing as Entrepreneurship; • Chapter 7: Startup Funding
Week 8 Online	Monday, 3/27 Thursday, 3/30	• Chapter 9: Marketing Your Venture to Audiences; • Theatre of the Oppressed/ Sociodrama & Community Radio
Week 9 Online	Monday, 4/3 Thursday, 4/6	Chapter 10: Product Management

Week & Modality	Days, Dates: Objectives	Readings
Week 10 Online	Monday, 4/10 Thursday, 4/13: Good Thursday Sunday, 4/16: Easter Sunday	Holiday—Easter Week
Week 11 Online	Monday, 4/17 Thursday, 4/20	Licensing and Registrations: Operations
Week 12 Online/Pitch Day	Sunday Monday, 4/24 Thursday, 4/27: Online Program	Program End

Adapting Our Open Pedagogical Practices to Ethiopia

Our design strategy involved creating the cohort bond through the face-to-face activities in Addis Ababa. Then, we used online technologies such as videoconferencing, cloud computing and other communication tools like Google Drive to virtually deliver instruction and coaching through the design/build process. The face-to-face Imagine Camp in Addis Ababa led participants through different design and dialogue practices to engage and build communication tools with and for communities. From the use of design thinking and small-group sense-making practices, participants were able to learn community-led design and action strategies to take back to their communities. Participants learned new ways of thinking, listening, systems thinking and creating with their communities from some of the practices we used in the program:

1. **Hosting and Group Processes:** One of the goals of the program was to introduce participants to face-to-face and online engagement practices for hosting community listening and dialogue meetings and other design sessions. The program used processes like setting the room in a circle, engaging in small-group activities, and attentiveness to the whole person.
2. **Stakeholder Mapping:** The Imagine Camp utilized several human-centered design and group processes to create cohort cohesion, knowledge sharing, and intelligence gathering. Stakeholder Mapping is a visualization tool introduced to participants to

bring diverse voices and views together in small groups to tackle community issues. Using broad topics like corruption, poverty, violence and others, small groups worked together to make visible the system at work and how communication and power flows and where they may be able to effect change with their interventions.
3. **Concept Poster:** Participants used poster board, visuals, and text to create a concept poster or advertisement for their business or media venture. These posters were presented in a gallery for others to provide comment, resources, and other feedback.
4. **Entrepreneurial Mindset—"Mad Libs" Pitch:** In a quick round of pitches, participants have to fill in the blanks, describing their company and the value they intend to bring. In this "tweet-like" format, participants have to succinctly and quickly describe their concept.
5. **Field Trip: The Science Museum—Imagining the Future:** The Imagine Camp brought participants to the newly opened Science Museum in Addis Ababa. The museum demonstrates the use of technologies in communication, surveillance, governance, and other commercial uses of artificial intelligence and technologies in home and city design. The Imagine Camp also provided a glimpse into the future for participants to imagine new ways future residents might get news and information.
6. **Make it Visible:** The program also used graphic recording to create key takeaways from our work. The liberal use of low-tech tools such as markers, sticky notes, and paper allowed participants to contribute their unique experiences to the whole group sense-making activities (Figures 4,5).

144 | Pedagogy Opened: Innovative Theory and Practice

Figure 4: During the training, the program participants learned human-centered design and design thinking strategies to design localized solutions to community news and information needs.

Figure 5: Graphic recording of our daily sessions during the Imagine Camp helped participants make sense of the system and key takeaways from the day's activities.

The four-day Imagine Camp created many opportunities for participants to see their work inside the larger media ecosystem, learn, and apply new skills in listening, engagement, systems thinking, design, and hosting. Participants were asked to reflect on the face-to-face component, to determine what had been key takeaways and practices they would implement in their project or professional work. One participant wrote:

> I found our stay in Addis Ababa to be better than I expected. Because the recruitment and selection of participants were different and their experiences and capabilities were very interesting, this is one of the things that made me love the training even more. I found it to be a platform of experience, skill, and knowledge. This boosted my motivation.

Or this participant's reflection:

> The Imagine Camp enables me to clearly identify my project goal in line with the very needs of the community I am targeting. It enables me to make a stakeholder mapping, to clearly identify the persona, the value proposition etc. The Imagine Camp was therefore very valuable for both my personal and professional career path.

Another media worker said,

> As a journalist, I've come to understand that my reports should include original information in addition to the typical government requirements. I am aware that I must approach my work with a new perspective, especially in light of professional ethics.

Several participants expressed how their projects changed, but they changed too, during the time together imagining something better. One participant wrote,

> It was a pleasure meeting with you at the Ethiopian Media Acceleration Fellowship Program and discussing the importance of freedom of speech, freedom of write and freedom of expression in the digital world. You

have inspired me to use my resources to help create a better community through the use of digital media. Your appreciation and enthusiasm to learn have been eye-opening and motivating. I am thankful for your support in taking the first steps to start our journey together and am grateful for everyone's commitment and open-mindedness to the digital media space. Looking forward to continuing the progress of this fellowship program and all the amazing opportunities it can bring.

Internet Shutdowns and Dancing with Uncertainties

As the authors embarked on the virtual 12 weeks of the accelerator program, they had to adapt to ensure they stayed true to the core principles of open pedagogy – access to the materials, low-tech design of the course content, flattened design to ensure easy downloads of content for offline reading and viewing, and digital tools that were free or open-source for our creation suite of tools. Government Internet shutdowns across Ethiopia, shutdowns on specific social media channels such as Facebook, Twitter, and Google services, and rolling blackouts which broke streaming connections forced much of our communication with participants to WhatsApp, telephone, and cloud computing for OER materials and conversations.

The program funded telecom data for all of the participants for a year so that they could participate in the bi-weekly co-working sessions. Participants have access to the learnings and co-created materials after the official program has terminated in May 2023. However, the participants still experienced connectivity issues for the synchronous portions of the program. Our program took place in Ethiopia right after a peace agreement was negotiated in the conflict in the Tigray region in 2022. Protests continue to plague the streets and the government response was to limit communication channels to disrupt organizing efforts. The cellular networks were overloaded during our stay in Ethiopia with residents and visitors scrambling to download virtual private networks to dodge the new Internet bans across Addis Ababa. To solve for the instability of the network, our online video conference sessions were recorded and uploaded to our shared Google Drive folders within hours to participants so they can view offline when they are able. However, we were able to use WhatsApp as a channel for communications of links to our shared resources, ensuring the program has an open channel for discussion and ongoing connection between participants.

The Ethiopia Media Innovation Accelerator Program team continued to adapt the program structure to ensure the safety and creative space to model open pedagogy, shared knowledge, and venture creation with the new community of practice in Ethiopia. We limited exposure of our participants by not identifying them by name or location in our materials or online mentions, unless we received consent. We added monthly check-in sessions with the cohort for the remainder of the year, to continue to share our learnings and support each other as we build our ventures.

What We Learned—Together

In our closing program evaluation, participants wrote of their frustrations with the connectivity issues and their frustrations with participation in our online bi-weekly sessions:

> In our country, the internet connection is still locked because of political and ethnic conflict. It was a big challenge. To tell you the truth, I was very happy with the introductory training session held in Addis Ababa in person at the Ethiopia Media Innovation Program group, and I was happy with the package data gift that was given to all of our trainees so that we could attend the online training program. Especially on the first day, the questionnaire given to us to start the online training program was very interesting and made us look at our own inner vision. Therefore, when the online training came, it was a challenge for me because the electricity and network were frequently cut off in the area where I live. As a result, I was not able to participate due to network and electricity problems, which lowered my score by 1 level.

However, participants took advantage of the recorded co-working sessions and the open materials and notes from other participants. Even without a consistent connection, one participant diligently worked offline to complete the program: "I didn't receive the yearly internet package. Due to that I missed a few sessions. However, I decided to manage myself to listen to the recorded sessions and get back to the program. And submit all the assignments and produce a good pitch deck."

Despite the Internet shutdowns, participants persisted to the end of the program and used the offline resources and the OER to continue to engage and produce the final deliverables of their community media ventures. From our original cohort of 50 participants in Addis Ababa for our Imagine Camp,

- 47 started our virtual program in Week 2.
- 36 participants persisted to the final Week 13 Pitch Day.
- 19 participants completed the final deliverables of a pitch deck and video.
- 36 participants will receive certificates of completion.
- 5 program participants were awarded with $2,500 in support toward their projects.

Twenty participants completed the post-program evaluation which asked participants to reflect on the whole program and the implications for their projects and professional work. Overall, participants ranked the program a 9 on a scale of 1-10 in program delivery and impact. In particular, participant responses to the following impact indicators show how participants' confidence in their abilities to effect change have been altered as a result of their participation in the program.

- 18 out of 20 indicated they are more confident in their ability to make a difference in their workplace or business.
- 19 out of 20 indicated they are more confident in their ability to make a difference in their community.
- 17 out of 20 feel they are more confident in their ability to make a difference in their country.
- And 17 out of 20 are more confident in their ability to make a difference in the global community.

On professional skills, program participants noted the following enhanced skills from participation in the program: leadership skills, communication skills, listening skills, self-awareness skills, self-confidence, resourcefulness, decision-making skills, problem-solving skills, project management skills, business management skills, human-centered design skills, entrepreneurship skills, journalism skills, teaching skills, creative skills, science competence, technology competence, engineering competence, mathematics competence, digital safety and resilience, cloud computing skills, distributed work skills, artificial intelligence, humanity and respect.

Our second goal was to build a resilient independent media network in Ethiopia. We measured our impact by the level of engagement between our participants. All of the survey respondents had made contact with someone in the program, and they planned on keeping in touch after the program ended. In addition, participants noted the feedback they received from fellow participants and the program team as pivotal to their engagement with the program. Many of the participants have already launched their community projects in Amhara, Oromia, Somali, Sidama and Afar and Tigray regions of Ethiopia. Several participants are building professional organizations to continue to support the growth of the independent media sector in Ethiopia. The newly formed Ethiopia Business Journalists Association was created by one cohort member, and another created a new women's journalist network through the International Association of Women in Radio and Television, supporting our program goal of building networks for mutual aid and learning.

Conclusion

These key insights may help others building OER resources and communities of practice or engaging in co-creation practices in communities. Sustaining our communities of practice helps to continuously infuse and update our OER with new knowledge to remain relevant, current, reliable, and accurate:

1. **Group Sense-Making Activities**. Consider the knowledge and experience you bring and honor the situated knowledge of others. Create opportunities for group sense-making and solutions generation.
2. **Listen deeply**. Bring a whole systems view to co-creation practices, by making visible the stakeholders and the issues at stake. Use engagement and hosting skills to bring new people to the table.
3. **Make the invisible visible**. Discover the factors that affect the capacity of community members to connect to each other and the geographie(s) in which they interact. Assess the constraints and assets of local infrastructure, making visible the gaps.

4. **Build support for digital resilience and mutual aid.** Journalists are under attack in digital and physical spaces as a result of their work (Ferrier, 2018). We purposefully did not publish our participants' names or details of their locations, for their safety and protection. We encouraged an environment of mutual care, sharing resources, support, and assistance through our WhatsApp group channel.
5. **Anticipate disruptions and threats.** Building independent media innovations in a state-controlled media environment can be dangerous and disruptive. Participants used their new skills in deep listening to collaborate with local partners and their new digital literacy skills to create alternative platforms for communication and delivery of news and information.

This case study shares the difficulties of building shared communities of practice and OER materials in a challenging digital environment. We learned from prior work in media deserts that our work must confront and interrogate local geographies, infrastructure, politics, and local cultures (Ferrier, 2023). Both physical and digital geographies must play a role in our calculus of how and what communities need to thrive and how to build a safe space for civic communications.

One participant wrote:

Some concrete practices and ways of thinking and seeing that I learned at Imagine Camp that I can use in the future include viewing problems from different angles, being aware of the context of my work, and leveraging the power of collaboration. I also learned to think creatively and innovatively, to consider how every aspect of a project can be tightly optimized, and to use effective visuals to tell a story and create powerful user experiences. Additionally, I learnt the importance of taking time for self-reflection, to gain clarity on my motivations and purpose. By utilizing these techniques, I can develop best-in-class project solutions, foster meaningful partnerships, and actively shape the kind of world I want to live in.

References

Association for Psychological Science [PsychologicalScience]. (2013, May 23). *2013 APS convention video: The benefits of traditional vs. Wikipedia research assignments* [Video]. YouTube. https://www.youtube.com/watch?v=6YBdQH0eIEQ&t=66

Colvard, N. B., Watson, C. E., & Park, H. (2018). The impact of open educational resources on various student success metrics. *International Journal of Teaching and Learning in Higher Education, 30*(2), 262–276. https://eric.ed.gov/?id=EJ1184998

de los Arcos, B., Farrow, R., Perryman, L.-A., Pitt, R., & Weller, M. (2014). OER evidence report 2013–2014. *OER Research Hub*. http://oerresearchhub.files.wordpress.com/2014/11/oerrh-evidence-report-2014.pdf

DeRosa, R., & Jhangiani, R. (n.d.). Open pedagogy. *Open Pedagogy Notebook*. https://openpedagogy.org/open-pedagogy/

Edmonton Regional Learning Consortium (ERLC). (2016). What is a community of practice? *Creating Communities of Practice*. Retrieved August 21, 2023, from https://www.communityofpractice.ca/background/what-is-a-community-of-practice/

Farrow, R., Pitt, R., de los Arcos, B., Perryman, L. A., Weller, M., & McAndrew, P. (2015). Impact of OER use on teaching and learning: Data from OER Research Hub (2013–2014). *British Journal of Educational Technology, 46*(5), 972–976. https://doi.org/10.1111/bjet.12310

Farzan, R., & Kraut, R. E. (2013). Wikipedia classroom experiment: Bidirectional benefits of students' engagement in online production communities. *CHI'13: Proceedings of the ACM conference on human factors in computing systems* (pp. 783–792). New York: ACM Press. https://doi.org/10.1145/2470654.2470765

Ferrier, M. B. (2009). *Deliverable 5: Industry-Driven Digital Media Certification, Final: Version 1.0.*, Florida Digital Media Banner Center. Originally provided July 27, 2009.

Ferrier, M. B. (2013). Media entrepreneurship: Curriculum development and faculty perceptions of what students should know. *Journalism*

& *Mass Communication Educator, 68*(3), 222–241. https://doi.org/10.1177/1077695813494833

Ferrier, M. (2014). AEJMC showcases a leap toward entrepreneurial learning at J-Schools. *Mediashift*. http://mediashift.org/2014/08/aejmc-showcases-a-leap-toward-entrepreneurial-learning-at-j-schools/

Ferrier, M. (2018) *Attacks and harassment: The impact on female journalists and their reporting*. TrollBusters and the International Women's Media Foundation. https://www.iwmf.org/attacks-and-harassment/

Ferrier, M. (2023). Co-creating news oases in media deserts. *Media and Communication, 11*(3), 355–359. https://doi.org/10.17645/mac.v11i3.6869

Ferrier, M. B., & Batts, B. (2016). Educators and professionals agree on outcomes for entrepreneurship courses. *Newspaper Research Journal, 37*(4), 322–338. https://doi.org/10.1177/0739532916677054

Ferrier, M., & Mays, E. (Eds.). (2017). *Media Innovation & Entrepreneurship*. Rebus Publishing. Retrieved from https://press.rebus.community/media-innovation-and-entrepreneurship/

Ferrier, M., & Mays, E. (2020, November 12). *Building a community while building an OER* [Presentation]. Open Education Conference 2020.

Graybeal, G. M., & Ferrier, M. B. (2023). Examination of pedagogy and instructional innovation to create entrepreneurs in the media and technology fields. *Entrepreneurship Education and Pedagogy, 6*(1), 110–134. https://doi.org/10.1177/25151274211033155

Graybeal, G., & Sindik, A. (2016). University partnerships with area entrepreneurial efforts produce shared benefits. *Newspaper Research Journal*, 37(4), 344–355. https://doi.org/10.1177/0739532916677053

Hang, M., & van Weezel, A. (2007). Media and entrepreneurship: What do we know and where should we go? *Journal of Media Business Studies, 4*(1), 51–70. https://doi.org/10.1080/16522354.2007.11073446

Hang, M. (2020). Media and entrepreneurship, a revisit with a decade of progress: A bibliometric analysis of media entrepreneurship research between 2005 and 2017. *Nordic Journal of Media Management, 1*(2), 187–207. https://doi.org/10.5278/njmm.2597-0445.4295

Hoag, A. (2008). Measuring media entrepreneurship. *International Journal on Media Management, 10*(2), 74–80. https://doi.

org/10.1080/14241270802000496

Huang, R., Liu, D., Tlili, A., Knyazeva, S., Chang, T. W., Zhang, X., Burgos, D., Jemni, M., Zhang, M., Zhuang, R., & Holotescu, C. (2020). *Guidance on open educational practices during school closures: Utilizing OER under COVID-19 pandemic in line with UNESCO OER recommendation.* Beijing: Smart Learning Institute of Beijing Normal University. https://iite.unesco.org/wp-content/uploads/2020/05/Guidance-on-Open-Educational-Practices-during-School-Closures-English-Version-V1_0.pdf

Ibrahim, M. (2012). Reflections on Wikipedia in the classroom. *Observer,* 25(1), 29–30. https://www.psychologicalscience.org/observer/reflections-on-wikipedia-in-the-classroom

Jhangiani, R., & DeRosa, R. (2016, November 3). *Free + freedom: The role of open pedagogy in the open education movement.* [PowerPoint slides]. Slideshare. https://www.slideshare.net/thatpsychprof/free-freedom-the-role-of-open-pedagogy-in-the-open-education-movement

Karney, B. (2012). Feedback from the whole world. *Observer,* 25(3), 45–46. https://www.psychologicalscience.org/observer/feedback-from-the-whole-world

Lave, J., & Wenger, E. (1991). Situated learning. *Legitimate peripheral participation.*
Cambridge, England: Cambridge University Press.

Marentette, P. (2014). Achieving "good article" status in Wikipedia. *Observer,* 27(3), 25–37. https://www.psychologicalscience.org/observer/achieving-good-article-status-in-wikipedia

Pitt, R. (2015). Mainstreaming open textbooks: Educator perspectives on the impact of OpenStax college open textbooks. *International Review of Research in Open and Distributed Learning, 16*(4). http://www.irrodl.org/index.php/irrodl/article/view/2381/3497

Pittaway, Luke & Ferrier, Michelle & Aïssaoui, Rachida & Mass, Paul. (2017). Trends in Entrepreneurship Education: Innovation Infrastructure. https://www.researchgate.net/publication/321193843_Trends_in_Entrepreneurship_Education_Innovation_Infrastructure

Pittaway, L., Aissaoui, R., Ferrier, M., & Mass, P. (2020). University spaces for entrepreneurship: a process model. *International Journal of*

Entrepreneurial Behavior & Research, 26(5), 911–936. https://dx.doi.org/10.2139/ssrn.3392386

Pittaway, L. (2021). Spaces for entrepreneurship education: a new campus arms race?. In C. H. Matthews, E. W. Liguori (Eds.), *Annals of Entrepreneurship Education and Pedagogy–2021*, (pp. 44–62). Edward Elgar Publishing. https://doi.org/10.4337/9781789904468.00011

Robinson, T. J., Fischer, L., Wiley, D., & Hilton, J. (2014). The impact of open textbooks on secondary science learning outcomes. *Educational Researcher, 43*(7), 341–351. https://doi.org/10.3102/0013189X14550275

Silton, R. (2012). More than just a grade. *Observer,* 25(2). http://www.psychologicalscience.org/index.php/publications/observer/2012/february-12/more-than-just-a-grade.html

Sindik, A. & Graybeal, G.M. (2017). Media entrepreneurship programs: Emerging isomorphic patterns. *International Journal on Media Management, 19*(1), 55–76. https://doi.org/10.1080/14241277.2017.1279617

Wiley, D. (2013, October 21). What is open pedagogy? *Improving learning: Eclectic, pragmatic, enthusiastic.* https://opencontent.org/blog/archives/2975

Indulkar, P. (2022) Regional global report: Southern African countries present risky terrain. *Toxic Avenger, November 2022.* https://yoursosteam.wordpress.com/regional-global-report-southern-african-countries-present-risky-terrain/

Author Bios
Michelle Barrett Ferrier, Media Innovation Collaboratory
Michelle Barrett Ferrier, Ph.D., is executive director of the Media Innovation Collaboratory, an incubator for media, communication and technology solutions. Dr. Ferrier is the immediate past president of the International Association of Women in Radio & Television International and founder of TrollBusters, an educational service for journalists experiencing digital harms.

Geoffrey Graybeal, University of South Carolina
Dr. Geoffrey Graybeal is a Clinical Associate Professor in the Darla Moore School of Business at the University of South Carolina. Dr. Graybeal is the former Undergraduate Curriculum Program Director of the Entrepreneurship and Innovation Institute in the Robinson College of Business at Georgia State University.

6

Free is Good: Designing and Implementing a Composition 1 Template Course with Help from an Affordable Learning Georgia (ALG) Grant

Jeanne Law, Kennesaw State University
Tamara Powell, Kennesaw State University

Abstract

A multi-disciplinary team comprising veteran and early career instructors—composition and rhetoric specialists as well as literature professors—instructional designers, and students was awarded a grant from Affordable Learning Georgia to create a template 50% hybrid course. This course was developed to share with last minute hires assigned to teach hybrid versions of Composition 1. At our institution we define hybrid in three ways, with each definition referencing a week: 50% means the class meets face-to-face one day and online one day; 33% means the class meets face-to-face two days and online one day; 66% means the class meets face-to-face one day and online for what would be two class sessions. The team chose to use a low-cost textbook in the creation of the course and also integrated various other research-based elements that were shown to support student success. After analyzing the data regarding the success of the template, the team found that when using the template, limited-term and part-time colleagues had lower drop, fail, withdrawal, and incomplete rates. Sixteen percent more students passed the course.

Keywords: learning analytics, English composition, hybrid courses, open education, student success, template/master courses

Suggested citation: Law, J., & Powell, T. (2024). Free is good: Designing and implementing a Composition 1 template course with help from an Affordable Learning Georgia grant. In T. Tijerina (Ed.), *Pedagogy opened: innovative theory and practice* (pp. 156-183). University of North Georgia Press. https://alg.manifoldapp.org/read/pedagogy-opened-v1-a6/.

Introduction

This project begins, as all projects must, with a story. For years, the faculty in the English department at Kennesaw State University (KSU) has been widely opposed to providing template courses, also known as master courses or prebuilt courses, for faculty to teach from. The argument has been that faculty teach better when they teach their own courses and that providing template courses interferes with academic freedom and disrespects our colleagues' expertise, whether they be newly hired or veteran. We see the validity in this argument, and in an ideal world there would be no template courses, as all faculty would have the time, resources, support, and motivation to build their own.

However, at KSU, a change in university policy regarding online and hybrid courses meant that courses could not be taught until they went through an approval process, and that meant that faculty hired at the last minute to teach online or hybrid courses would have to be given pre-built, or template, courses, at least for their first semester teaching. This fact meant that the English department would need to come up with a template.

In addition to the university policy charge, part of the rationale for the Composition 1 template course design was directly related to the department's need to provide high-quality courses that could be implemented for last-minute hires. Given KSU's growth over the past several years, limited-term and part-time colleagues are often hired within the last two weeks before a given semester, giving these colleagues little-to-no time to prepare a high-quality course before they begin to teach. Another advantage to template courses that influenced the project is the Department's need in leveraging a course design that is aligned to the first-year composition (FYC) program's instructional guidelines (Appendix). Also, the FYC program relies heavily on hybrid courses to minimize the space issues with finding a classroom on campus. The template course we designed and taught in our pilot filled all of these needs.

Faculty who taught the Composition 1 template course in Fall 2022 represent a wide range of experience with teaching FYC. In fact, 80% had never taught a hybrid course before. Additionally, four faculty were new to KSU, while three were returning. These demographics presented a challenging but motivational opportunity regarding professional development and training for both KSU's learning management platform, Desire2Learn (D2L), and the Achieve learning system, which accompanies the low-cost *Everyday Writer* textbook used for the pilot version of this course.

Composition 1 (ENGL 1101 at our institution) is a ubiquitous course on college campuses. The learning outcomes for the course we created, which are likely similar to the learning outcomes for most Composition 1 courses, are as follows:

1. Practice writing in situations where print and/or electronic texts are used, examining why and how people choose to write using different technologies.
2. Interpret the explicit and implicit arguments of multiple styles of writing from diverse perspectives.
3. Practice social aspects of the writing process by critiquing your own work and the work of your colleagues.
4. Analyze how style, audience, social context, and purpose shape your writing in electronic and print spaces.
5. Craft diverse types of texts to extend your thinking and writerly voice across styles, audiences, and purposes.

Most first year students are required to take Composition 1. At KSU, this fact means that more than 250 sections each semester must be offered, and sometimes English faculty—part timers, limited-term, or graduate students—must step in at the last minute to teach a section. Key questions to ask are (1) how do we support those late hires and help them to offer high quality, 50% hybrid (meeting face-to-face one day a week and online asynchronous one day a week) and 33% hybrid (meeting face-to-face two days a week and online asynchronous one day a week) courses on such short notice? And (2) how do we support our students by making sure all their courses are high quality and have important student success features? This was our challenge, and our solution was to first garner a grant from Affordable Learning Georgia (ALG) to support this project and second, to form a team to design and implement an effective template. We are using the term template to describe this pre-built course shell. In this case, template means completely designed hybrid course with the weekly, asynchronous portions completely built and the face-to-face portions addressed with a facilitator guide document. The facilitator guide document provides various options for conducting the face-to-face sessions, including PowerPoint presentations and classroom activities such as quiz show type games, and helps the instructor to connect the online and face-to-face portions of the course. In this way, the instructor can concentrate on teaching and grading, knowing that there is a support and guide helping both the instructor and students move through the course successfully.

Literature Review

In building this Composition 1 50% hybrid template course, we knew we wanted to integrate research-based student success features into the course. We found research both on how template courses support faculty success and on particular features of courses that support student success. We are defining faculty success as teaching a course effectively and helping students move through the course successfully. We are defining student success as improving outcomes for learning subject matter, progressing through the course, completing the course, passing the course, and moving toward graduation.

Best practices for resource integration include advice from subject matter experts (SMEs) from multiple disciplines. While every master or template course is not automatically superior just by the virtue of being a template course, high quality template courses can ensure a consistent and successful experience for students in online and hybrid courses. As Trammell et al. (2018) notes that

> [A]s the use of contingent or adjunct instructors (part-time instructors, graduate students, and nontenure track appointments) approaches 70%

of classes, it is important that faculty and administrators find a way to ensure this academic rigor is present for adjunct instructors who may not have the expertise or permanency to do so. (p. 164)

Trammell et al.'s mention of permanency brings up another strong point in favor of a template. It seems hardly fair to ask a newly hired part-time faculty member to invest the additional time to build out an individual version of a course for no additional pay.

It was also important for us to identify the features of a high-quality template course. Gaddis (2022) notes that master classes, which we refer to as template courses, help solve the problem of inconsistency, including inconsistent quality, in online courses. Gaddis recommends template courses be designed using "backwards design," "andragogy," and "authentic assessments" (p. 105). Backwards design is a hallmark of successful online course design and practiced by our design team. We also are admirers of Paulo Freire and the importance of respecting the learners' experiences, which is an aspect of andragogy. While some feel that authentic assessment is a challenge in English composition courses, our team would disagree. With assignments such as analyzing the rhetoric of advertisements and evaluating logical claims, we are able to help students see the value in the writing lessons practiced in Composition 1 for life beyond the classroom. The facilitator guides also include information for faculty to share with their classes on the real-world importance of these assignments. The facilitator guides also include discussion prompts that the faculty can use to engage students in discussion and share their own experiences with rhetoric, logic, analysis, and other topics required to successfully write the assigned papers.

In order to build the template course, we started with a low-cost textbook for our 50% hybrid course design. Colvard, Watson, and Park's (2018) well-known work on open educational resources and student success put us on the path to search for a low-cost or no-cost option. While at first we believed the benefits of the data analytics features in the low-cost option made it worth the price, we have since created a no-cost version of our course using *Writing Guide with Handbook* (https://openstax.org/details/books/writing-guide) by Openstax to provide choice to instructors adopting the template. Colvard, Watson, and Park found OER "level the academic playing field" for students (p. 273), especially those who might need extra support in the realm of student success. We also wanted to think outside the box a bit. In Arulkadacham et al. (2021), one of the main findings in their work on student success was the need for self-care resources among online students. Having technological skills, an orientation to the course, an opportunity for student-student contact and student-teacher contact, and resources to support student learning were all named as predictors of success in a course (p. 5). For this reason, the course included an orientation module, links to important campus resources, and frequent reminders to ask the instructor if there were questions. Trammell et al. (2013) further observes "Separating course content and assignments into units or modules allows students to conceptually organize information and complete work in a timely manner" (p. 165). For this reason, the course was organized into weekly modules to assist both faculty and students in managing their time, keeping up with the course, and planning each week.

Given that one of the perceived audiences for this template would be newly hired faculty, we wanted to be conscious of the faculty workload we built into the course. In "Where We Are: Writing Initiatives Designed to Support Well-Being: Facilitating Well-Being in a Pandemic through Writing Course Innovation," Macklin et al. (2022) found that the persons adopting the template course they created (TAs in this case) felt that they were working more than the assigned 20 hours a week. This overwork concerned them, as they wanted to be mindful of the grading load (p. 202), as did we when we created the interactive exercises in lieu of discussion boards. Some feel that "[d]iscussion is an essential dimension of human learning," and discussion boards are essential because, "[w]ithin asynchronous online courses, the discussion board essentially replaces face-to-face interaction in the brick and mortar classroom," (Borgemenke, Hold, & Fish, 2013, p. 19). We agree that that may be true in some cases; however, we tried to balance the importance of discussion with innovative, interactive features in the course in order to lessen the grading load on the instructors teaching with the template.

Our thinking was thus: one of the primary audiences for this course would be late hires. This person may even be hired to teach five sections of this course. Until this template course was created, this new hire could very possibly be given a textbook, access to our learning management system, and a sample syllabus, and maybe a quick explanation of how hybrid courses are defined at our institution. And that was it. No matter how talented this new hire might be, it's very difficult to learn a new institution and whip up a composition course in hybrid format in a short amount of time. The template course, then, serves to assist the new hire in seeing the expectations of faculty teaching Composition 1 and also helps to ensure the students have a consistent and successful experience. Given that this faculty member may be teaching five sections of this course, and there are weekly face-to-face meetings each week, we didn't want to overburden the new faculty member with grading weekly discussions on top of grading papers, rough drafts, and assignments. To this end, our team used interactive presentation software (specifically Genially and Articulate Storyline 360) to deliver interactive, self-graded presentations to students on key topics such as rhetorical strategies, the writing process, and addressing style and audience. These presentations allowed students to get the interaction we wanted them to have (not always possible on discussion board assignments) without the instructor having to grade or monitor the experience. After instructors teach with the template course once, they are encouraged to build their own versions of Composition 1, and they may at that time choose to build back in discussion board assignments that specifically support their teaching goals and methods.

Our First Year Composition team holds Mary-Ann Winkelmes' work with Transparency in Learning and Teaching (TILT) in high regard and also incorporated aspects of TILT-ed practices, including practice activities to support confidence in learning and clear explanations of the rationale behind various assignments (Winkelmes, 2019, p. 19). For this reason, many of the learning materials and subject matter expert videos share not only how an activity will benefit the student in the class but also how these skills will be valuable in the future. In addition, the template course includes practice exercises to help students gauge their own learning, interactive activities to help students stay engaged with the content, guided and interactive presentations to give students individual experiences while engaging with the content, friendly videos from our subject matter experts to explain more complex concepts, clear assignment guidelines with grading rubrics, and navigational guides to support students successfully completing every module.

On a final note, and at a higher level of organization, according to Newell et al. (2021), scaffolding assignments supports student success by helping students to work on one skill at a time that builds up to mastery of more complicated skills (p. 202). The template course included scaffolding activities such as prewriting exercises, rough drafts, and peer reviews to support students as they moved to create the final draft of each assignment. The low-cost textbook we chose for the original version of the course also included learning analytics software and adaptive quizzing features that set individual student learning goals and helped them to achieve them throughout the course.

Study Context and Demographics

KSU teacher-researchers working on the ALG project used a team-based approach and felt that it provided a deeper perspective when building the course. We also had a diverse team in our project, including five seasoned English instructors with backgrounds in both literature and composition and rhetoric, an instructional designer, and two students. The students were not English majors but rather one was majoring in education and the other in environmental science. We designed and implemented a high-quality Composition 1 course to be delivered in a 50% hybrid format (meeting one day a week and online asynchronous one day a week). Through the support provided by our ALG grant, we developed the course as a low-cost (less than $40) alternative to courses with traditional textbooks. At KSU, Composition 1 textbooks can cost upwards of $100. Our course design sought to demonstrate that effective instruction and affordability can be compatible and achieve university student success goals.

University Overview

Kennesaw State University is the third-largest institution of higher education in the state of Georgia. We are known for our strong academic programs and supportive learning environment. KSU offers 180 undergraduate and graduate degree programs across various disciplines, including business, education, engineering, humanities, and social sciences. More than 43,000 students are enrolled at KSU, almost 40% of whom are first-generation students.

The university prides itself on its commitment to student success and offers numerous resources to help students excel academically, including tutoring services, academic advising, and career development programs. Additionally, KSU values experiential learning and offers numerous opportunities for students to gain hands-on experience through internships, cooperative education programs, and research projects. Student success is at the core of KSU's mission, and this commitment begins with first-year courses such as Composition 1.

University Demographics

According to the Fall 2022 enrollment data, the student body at KSU is diverse and includes students from 47 states and 142 countries. The racial and ethnic makeup of the student body is as follows: 46% white, 25% Black/African American, 14% Hispanic/Latinx, 6% Asian, 3% international, and 5% multi-racial. The student body at KSU is 49% female and 51% male.

The university has a student-to-faculty ratio of 20:1 and employs over 1,800 faculty members, 88% of whom hold terminal degrees in their respective fields. KSU is accredited by the Southern Association of Colleges and Schools Commission on Colleges (SACSCOC) and holds numerous programmatic accreditations from specialized accrediting bodies in various fields.

Description of the Project

We have already described the rationale for the project, the theoretical underpinnings, and the motivation and context. But how did it actually proceed? Two English Department faculty wrote the ALG grant to support the project. After being awarded the grant, two seasoned faculty were selected as faculty designers to build each weekly module, including the face-to-face class meeting facilitator's guide, the face-to-face class meeting student preparation guide, and the online course module. ALG requires that all deliverables be publicly available, as they must be truly open. For this reason, we built the weekly modules in SoftChalk so that they could be linked into a D2L section for university faculty and linked to a website to share with the world. SoftChalk served as our project management tool for this project, as we were able to share access to the modules across the team. Another benefit of using SoftChalk is that for the life of the project, any updates or corrections made in the original SoftChalk modules will automatically update to all instances of the course using the links. This means anyone using the linked version of the course will always be using the latest version.

The instructional designer created the interactive, self-graded presentations on topics such as rhetorical analysis, style and audience, and the writing process. The faculty member managing the project inserted these into the SoftChalk modules and created the public-facing website. The student members of the team were also trained in online course accessibility, so they were able to provide a dual role. They were accessibility specialists, and they gave us feedback from a student perspective. We included a part time instructor on the grant to give us feedback on the facilitator guides; specifically, what would make them most helpful to part-time faculty adopting the course to teach. Our faculty member serving as the data analysis expert set up surveys and data collection opportunities. Finally, the faculty designers added syllabi, schedules, assignments, and rubrics into the learning management system and loaded the learning management system versions into zipped files. The zipped files were added to the department website, which made them available to all English department members. To support faculty adopting the templates, the First Year Composition director scheduled training sessions before the semester started.

It must be mentioned that the 50% hybrid runs in two formats: online for the first session and face-to-face for the second session each week (version 1), and the reverse (version 2). Hybrids are scheduled this way so that two classes can occupy the same physical space each week. In order to make the template work for both schedules, the faculty designers created an online "start here" module at the beginning of version 1 that was added into module 1. In version 2, the start here stands alone, so that the same module 1 serves as the online portion. In this way, the online modules serve as the same for version 1 and 2. Or, to put it another way, there was no need for the faculty designers to create two versions of the hybrid course. We simply adjusted the "Start Here" information so that whether a course started face-to-face or online on the first day, all were using the same online and face-to-face modules.

Finally, as mentioned above, a low-cost textbook was used for the initial version of this course. A version using the OpenStax *Writing Guide with Handbook* (https://openstax.org/details/books/writing-guide) was created a year later so that faculty could have a choice whether to adopt a low-cost or no-cost textbook.

Analysis and Discussion

In this section, we will discuss the context of the analysis and present the qualitative and quantitative results of the project.

Context for Course Analysis

In Fall 2022, we launched the Composition 1 template course in 26 sections taught by seven instructors. These instructors represented a wide range of experiences, with four new-to-teaching and three returning instructors from the previous year. The project co-PIs, both tenured professors, also taught the course.

For the qualitative data piece of the study, we surveyed 676 students in these sections, with 119 responding. This yielded a 18% response rate, which we believe to be a significant number to draw conclusions about learning experiences. We surveyed seven instructors who taught using the template course.

Quantitative Data Results

DFWI (drop, fail, withdraw, incomplete) Rates: Because Composition 1 is a gateway course, pass rates are important in terms of retention, progression, and graduation. For the template course pilot, we had 26 sections, resulting in an 18.4% overall DFWI rate. This rate was calculated using final grade submissions in KSU's Banner program and from Institutional Research. We compared our rate to the Fall 2022 overall Composition 1 rate, which was 20.3%. For limited-term and part-time (LT/PT) colleagues, the 2022 rate was 23%. LT/PT colleagues who used the template course had a combined DFWI rate of 17.3%, an improvement from 5.7% versus colleagues who did not. What this means practically is that, when using the template course, LT/PT colleagues had lower DFWI rates. Out of the 624 students taught by LT/PT colleagues, 516 students passed (cumulative 82.7% PASS rate). As we compared DFWI rates, we understood that KSU's first-year writing program, of which Dr. Law is the director, has standardized learning objectives and program guidelines that allow instructors the freedom to customize major assignments within specified assignment types that are consistent and aligned in the curriculum. Knowing that the template courses were also designed with these guidelines and standard learning objectives/assignments in mind, our team felt that the analysis of DFWI data was reliable.

Overall, 18.4% of students, out of a total 676 students affected, dropped, failed, withdrew, or took an incomplete from the template courses during our initial study implementation. This number compares to the overall ENGL 1101 DFWI rate: just shy of 20.3%. While this percentage may seem small, we know that "moving the needle" on pass rates becomes an incremental enterprise when rates dip below 25%. We also know that, at an institution the size of KSU, every percentage point represents hundreds of students who now can progress along their general education pathway towards graduation.

Qualitative Results: Student Learning Experiences

Student success at the course level is a mixed methods initiative, with DFWI rates being key quantitative measures. While quantitative data pointing to retention, progression, and graduation (RPG) is certainly important in considerations of course design and delivery, our team also felt that the qualitative aspects of students' learning experiences were significant as we piloted the course and planned for future modifications. We conducted surveys and obtained feedback through point-of-need tech support during the semester. Foundational to student qualitative data reporting is a transparent, analytical process wherein our team conducted surveys in which we assessed the efficacy of the course design, pacing, and assignment structure through the lens of continuous improvement. All data collection and analysis were intended for course assessment.

Overall, students in the Composition 1 template courses reported positive learning experiences, especially in relation to the technology applications. Of the 119 students who responded to the survey, 80% of them reported that they were able to start the course easily and find course materials quickly. Given the instructor feedback, which indicated a desire for more tech support in this area, students seemed to have no difficulties.

Our team designed the hybrid Composition 1 course to mindfully cultivate connections between online learning content and face-to-face interactions. Some of these pedagogical choices included adaptive quizzing, embedded videos, interactive activities, and student-to-student discussions, all organized to provide previews and snapshots of content delivered in face-to-face class meetings that came after each online module. We intentionally designed each weekly module to feed into the next and all online content to feed in-person learning. This part of the course design was remarkably successful, with only three of 119 students not seeing the connections between the online learning parts of the course and course goals/assignments.

Further key takeaways from our student surveys focused on ease-of-use and engagement with the low-cost textbook and Achieve platform. These results were mixed. Less than half of students navigated to the online textbook with no trouble, even though they could access the other course materials with ease. However, 30% of students felt that the Achieve diagnostics helped them execute a study plan that made them better writers at the end of the course. A textual trend among these students is evidenced in a representative quote:

> Direction—a sense of direction. Something that I've always struggled with writing was I was never taught in a way that I was able to grasp the concept... whether that would be physically in class: video/ live (zoom) lecture/ presentation, online or a mix of. Though I believe it's not just the study plan that determines the student's success—It's a mix of how the professor engages with the students, the material they teach in the in-class portion and how the professor teaches their course material coordinating with the online portion of it and the study guide that has been created.

We also learned that students wanted more practice or ungraded activities. The figure below further shows students' clear preferences for adding more ungraded items to the course design. The course design had many low-stakes graded assignments (weekly) and only three major assignments. Participation was also a graded item throughout the semester. We were intrigued that students wanted more ungraded opportunities to practice their skills.

Students were asked "Would you like to have more of the following in the course?" with answer choices being "Ungraded quizzes to test your knowledge," "Discussions on the discussion board," "Ungraded writing activities to provide practice on writing assignments," "Small group exercises online," "Something else (please share)," and "Nothing else." As Figure 1 shows, out of 119 responses, the majority of students (51%) wanted ungraded quizzes to test their knowledge and ungraded writing activities to provide practice on writing assignments.

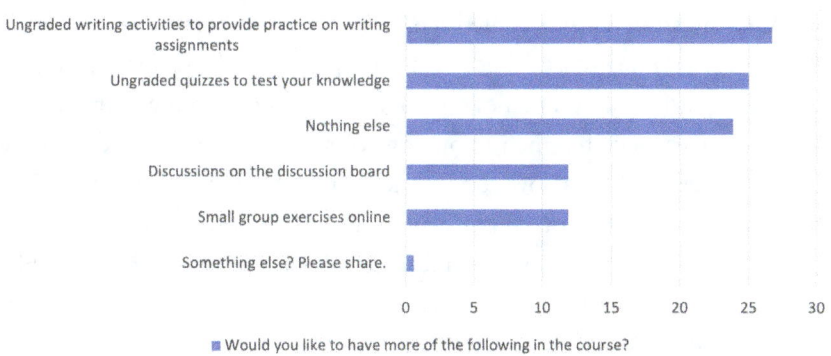

Figure 1: Student Preferences for Ungraded Items

This piece of data is significant for us in terms of course design as we revise going forward.

Open-Ended Student Feedback on OER Course Templates

The survey provided opportunities for open-ended feedback, to which students responded with rich answers, all of which related to how well-designed the OER course was (or was not). Trends in open-ended response to feedback for course materials trended positive, with the most common words used being (1) easy-to-access, (2) good explanations, (3) effective connections, (4) personalized to each student, and (5) effective mapping/ organization. The positive themes reported by students are indicative of what our team's SMEs described as foundations and bellwethers of effective OER course design. Negative feedback tended to include words like (1) device/browser compatibility, (2) better text to speech options, (3) D2L navigation, (4) difficulty accessing Achieve for first-time, and (5) major assignment sequencing. This last item was surprising, but several students mentioned that they would rather have the major assignment re-ordered. Unfortunately, they gave no indication of which assignments. This unanswered data piece gives us an opportunity to re-work the question to see if we can find the answer in the next course iteration. Both positive and negative student responses were framed through the lens of their learning experiences with OER materials and a course designed mindfully using OER resources.

Overall, students appreciated the diagnostics and personalized learning provided by the low-cost Achieve learning platform. This type of learning experience usually accompanies textbooks that range to more than $90.00, and students articulated their knowledge of receiving personalized learning opportunities within a low-cost model. The complete student data set helped our team reflect on what we did well and plan revisions for areas that needed improvement for an enhanced student learning experience, while maintaining a no- or low-cost model.

Possible implications for student learning gleaned from overall positive student responses to low-cost materials and OER course design include the following:

- **Cost savings:** One of the primary benefits of free or low-cost materials is that they make education more accessible and affordable for students. Positive feedback from students on the redesigned course may indicate that they appreciate the cost savings that come with using low-cost materials.
- **Increased engagement:** OER and low-cost materials are often designed to be interactive and engaging, allowing students to participate actively in their own learning. Positive feedback from students on the low-cost materials may suggest that they feel more engaged with the course material and that this engagement is leading to a deeper understanding of the subject matter.

- **Flexibility:** OER and low-cost materials are often available online and can be accessed from anywhere with an internet connection. Positive feedback from students on the low-cost materials may suggest that they appreciate the flexibility that comes with being able to access course materials on their own schedule and from any location.

Overall, positive feedback from students on low-cost materials and OER can indicate that these materials are making education more accessible, engaging, and effective, and that students are benefiting from the use of these resources.

Rationale and Faculty Experiences

Key takeaways from the instructor survey and feedback include technical and administrative support for instructors teaching the course. For example, all instructors found the technical and administrative training at the beginning of the semester to be helpful. One missing piece for future revisions was clear: there was a definite trend in the qualitative survey feedback that let us know that faculty wanted a "Quick Start" Guide and more support during the semester, especially with the Achieve adaptive learning modules. These modules, which were deeply integrated into D2L for students, nevertheless presented challenges for faculty. A few reported a steep learning curve with assigning and sustaining peer review modules. One of the reasons our team went with Achieve for *Everyday Writer* was the diagnostic quizzing that provided each student with a personalized learning plan for the semester. Instructors overwhelmingly appreciated and used this feature. In fact, almost all faculty assigned and used the diagnostics, while only half assigned the study plan.

Although the team surmised that the adaptive learning would be intuitive to navigate, we did not find that to be necessarily so. Instead, intuitiveness had a direct relationship with individual instructors' more advanced technological knowledge. This was a bit of a disappointment because we know that adaptive learning generates deeper student engagement and can have a positive impact on course pass rates as well as depth and breadth of learning. In future, faculty recommended that we provide more up-front training on Achieve, with complementary training during the semester, before major assignments are due.

Further trends we noted from faculty fell into two strands, quoted below:
1. **Favorite/Most-Used Parts:** diagnostic and study plans that allow each student to progress at their own pace with their individualized content; having the course shell on D2L already set up with modules for students. Faculty also liked that the template provided teaching ideas and tools for the face-to-face sessions.
2. **Least favorite:** technical issues with the platform and how it works for students. Faculty also wanted more self-assessments or other engagement materials in the template course—but not things instructors have to grade. Feedback on ungraded assignments matches with students' feedback for more of these types of low-stakes assignments as well.

Overall, both student and instructor feedback, while overwhelmingly positive, also gave the team some areas for improvement for increasing course quality in terms of content engagement, faculty pedagogical needs, and participation in personalized learning goals.

Lessons Learned

Based on the feedback we received from instructors and students who used the template, we believe that we built an effective facilitator guide, with 100% of instructors, not including the two Co-PIs (n=5), agreeing that the guide was helpful. Given that 80% of instructors only rated the guide as somewhat helpful, along with comments indicating it was a bit too general, we learned that instructors really wanted a ready-to-go course that had specific instructions for weekly modules in the facilitator guide. We also learned that instructors were overall happy with the course content in both amount and quality. Based on student feedback (n=119, 18% response rate), we learned that 80% of students found the course easy to navigate. About half of students found the low-cost textbook hard to navigate. All students liked the study plan from the low-cost textbook, but only 30% thought that the grammar diagnostics helped them improve their writing. As a result of student feedback, we decided to keep the low-cost, adaptive learning text in our Composition 1, 50% hybrid revision, but drop it from the 33% hybrid course and our upcoming Composition 2, OER build.

Four Key Project Outcomes

As stated earlier, we built this course with an Affordable Learning Georgia (ALG) course transformation grant. We have received notice that we are also funded to revise the course as part of an ALG continuous improvement grant. As part of this commitment, we have key project outcomes associated with the course design and revision.

Because Composition 1 is a gateway course with DFWI rates that can sometimes be above 30% in hybrid modalities, it is an important contributor to retention, progression, and graduation. Fall 2022 data shows that the Department of English offered 87 sections of 50% hybrid Composition 1, which represents 39% of 222 total Composition 1 sections offered in Fall 2022 semester. Of this enrollment, we created a low-cost template course that was used by instructors in 26 sections of Composition 1, resulting in approximately 676 students using the template. This number is 6 sections less than our grant proposal as a result of last-minute part-time staffing shifts. Approximately 12% of our 5,432 Composition 1 students used the template.

Outcome 1: A key challenge with offering this many hybrid courses that also must be compliant with accessibility laws is that part-time faculty hired at the last minute may have no training in creating successful courses and no access to the D2L learning management system until a week into the semester. The Low-Cost Composition 1 Hybrid Design project alleviated that pain point.

Outcome 2: Our project also answered a university mandate with innovative learning science techniques. In summer of 2021, KSU's Curriculum and Academic Innovation in Academic Affairs mandated a review process by which all online and hybrid courses would meet federal standards for accessibility and engagement. In the Radow College of Humanities and Social Sciences, 1000-level courses were mandated to meet standards before Fall 2022. In this situation, hiring part timers at the last minute with no template (formerly known as master) course available was no longer possible. The Low-Cost Composition 1 Hybrid Design Project team designed a high-quality hybrid Composition 1 template course with low-cost materials, copious student success features, and data-gathering capability. The course met federal guidelines for accessibility and

engagement. The course was designed to be "shovel ready" for new hires with features to make it easy to teach successfully:
- a facilitator guide with lecture and reminder guides for face-to-face days, and
- an online module with engaging and interactive online activities that minimize time consuming discussion board grading but provide opportunities for students to interact with the content, especially threshold concepts, with relevant and instant feedback.

Outcome 3: This course was made available in D2L but was also made available outside D2L to share globally. We created materials using SoftChalk and Articulate so that they are functional inside or outside of D2L. They will be hosted on ALG's instance of Manifold, OpenALG, as well. The team presented the course at the Open EDUCA Berlin (OEB) conference; based on that experience, the course is also available now using OpenStax's *Writing Guide with Handbook* (https://openstax.org/details/books/writing-guide).

Outcome 4: DFWI Rates: As mentioned before, Composition 1 is a gateway course, and pass rates are important in terms of retention, progression, and graduation. In the pilot, 26 sections of hybrid Composition 1 used the template. At the end of the semester, in the template courses, there was an overall 18.4% DFWI rate. In this study, 526 students in the courses using the template achieved passing grades, for a cumulative 82.7% pass rate.

Sustainability and the Path Forward

The Department of English plans to offer this course to late-hire colleagues each semester. All course content created in this project aligns to the program guidelines and learning outcomes for First-Year Composition at KSU. The course will be reviewed and updated every year per these guidelines. Our goal was to build a template course that is easy to maintain and only requires minor updates each semester to accommodate broken links and software updates. For this reason, topics and readings were chosen not only to accommodate a wide audience but also to be suitable for a long period of time.

In order to remain in compliance with requirements with regard to hybrid course quality, the department will maintain a template Composition

1 to support the hiring of part timers. For this reason, this project will be used and kept current for the foreseeable future. More course sections will be added as the need for additional sections grows. Also, it is important to note that this template is not limited to use by part timers. Full time faculty who may be assigned hybrid Composition 1 courses have used this template, as well. In fact, an additional student success feature of this project became clear early in the pilot when a new hire was not able to teach just a week after the semester started. Because the template was being used, two senior professors were able to step into the open courses and continue the course without the students experiencing much disruption at all.

Conclusions and Future Work

Our data and pilot suggest a robust beginning to our open educational resources (OER) pedagogical approach. Indeed, as we move forward, our team has considered the integration of resources that expand our reach to multiple student audiences and contexts, including units and modules that feature diverse resources on human rights, experiences of underrepresented groups, and localized civil rights histories. Members of the team have also been included on other ALG grants, including a transformation grant awarded to the Georgia Gwinnett College, whose team is building a Composition 1 template focused on Latinx readings and assignments.

Going forward, KSU faculty, instructional designers, and student researchers will continue to revise and reimagine OER resources in ways that innovate pedagogical strategies and increase student success.

References

Arulkadacham, L., McKenzie, S., Aziz, Z., Chung, J., Dyer, K., Holt, C., Garivaldis, F., & Mundy, M. (2021). General and unique predictors of student success in online courses: A systematic review and focus group . *Journal of University Teaching & Learning Practice*, *18*(8), 1–22. https://doi.org/10.53761/1.18.8.7.

Borgemenke, A., Hold, W. C., & Fish, W. W. (2013). Universal course shell template design and implementation to enhance student outcomes in online coursework . *Quarterly Review of Distance Education*, *14*(1), 17–23. https://eric.ed.gov/?id=EJ1144785

Colvard, N. B., Watson, C. E., & Park, H. (2018). The impact of open educational resources on various student success metrics. *International Journal of Teaching and Learning in Higher Education, 30*(2), 262–76. https://eric.ed.gov/?id=EJ1184998

Gaddis, M. (2022). The master course design process explained using General College Botany as a case study. *Journal of the Scholarship of Teaching & Learning, 22*(3), 105–19. https://doi.org/10.14434/josotl.v22i3.32353

Macklin, T., shepherd, d., Van Slyke, M., & Estrem, H. (2022) Where we are: Writing initiatives designed to support well-being: Facilitating well-being in a pandemic through writing course innovation. *Composition Studies, 50*(2), 201–04. https://compositionstudiesjournal.files.wordpress.com/2022/11/macklin-shepherd-vanslyke-estrem.pdf

Newell, J. R., Bartlett, S., Mixson-Brookshire, D., Moore, J., Powell, T., Lee, S., Tijerina, T., Milam, B., Snider, L., & Cochran, J. (2021). Time-efficient techniques for improving student and instructor success in online courses. *International Journal on Advances in Intelligent Systems, 14*(3), 193-207. http://www.iariajournals.org/intelligent_systems/intsys_v14_n12_2021_paged.pdf

Trammell, B. A., Morgan, R. K., Davies, W., Petrunich-Rutherford, M. L., & Herold, D. S. (2018). Creating an online course shell: Strategies to mitigate frustration and increase student success across multiple campuses. *Scholarship of Teaching and Learning in Psychology, 4*(3), 164–80. https://doi.org/10.1037/stl0000109

Winkelmes, M. (2019). Why it works: Understanding the concepts behind transparent teaching and learning. In M. Winkelmes, A. Boye, & S. Tapp (Eds.), *Transparent design in higher education teaching and leadership: A guide to implementing the transparency framework institution-wide to improve learning and retention*, (pp. 17-35). Routledge.

Acknowledgements

Special thanks to Affordable Learning Georgia for supporting this program. Access the current version of the 50% Hybrid course on SoftChalk (https://kennesaw.softchalkcloud.com/lesson/serve/CBXvL94OYaw2To/html). Access the current version of the 33% Hybrid course on SoftChalk (https://kennesaw.softchalkcloud.com/lesson/serve/iu0TeNOCKY8PEv/html)

Author Bios
Jeanne Law, Kennesaw State University
Jeanne Law is a Professor of English and the Director of Composition at Kennesaw State University. She is an early adopter and researcher on ethical uses of generative artificial intelligence in college writing courses, and she is passionate about cultivating innovative approaches to open educational resources, especially in general education programs. She is also a historiographic researcher who seeks to create connections between pivotal human rights moments of the past and present cultural moments through a feminist rhetorical lens.

Tamara Powell, Kennesaw State University
Dr. Tamara Powell earned her PhD from Bowling Green State University in Ohio and is an English professor at Kennesaw State University. Her research includes open educational resources and teaching strategies to support success in underserved populations.

Appendix: FYC Program Pathways: Alignment and Consistency for 1101 and 1102

Overview

The following major assignments for ENGL 1101 and 1102 will help generate consistent language and engender alignment across the FYC program at KSU. In creating these assignment structures, FYC faculty working groups have considered multiple stakeholders, including students, colleagues, and administration (in this case USG) – in that order. Moreover, the working groups created these assignment sequences in consultation with FYC faculty at KSU and after careful consideration of faculty syllabi and best practices comparator and aspirational institutions. Adopting these frameworks in our classrooms will ensure that students have consistent and transferrable learning experiences in FYC, that our colleagues have creative license to innovate in their classes, and that administration has necessary metrics against which we can map student learning.

For our work, we delineate differences between **types** of assignment and actual assignments themselves. The **type** of assignment should be overarching and not include specific instructions or rubrics. For example, an "analysis" (see 1101 section below) is a "type" or "genre" of writing. An instructor's assignment that aligns to that type might be framed as a multimodal text, may be an essay that asks a student to consider how an author approaches purpose/audience/style/context, or it may even be a deep dive into a social issue that has been written about across publication contexts. Whatever the assignment looks like in form and function, as long as it meets the criteria to be considered an analysis, then it is aligned appropriately.

As we develop a programmatic future that aligns with trends in the field of FYC, comparator and aspirational institutions, and USG expectations, it's important to remember that this is a "living document." Program growth requires that we retain flexibility to revise this document as trends in the field change, as we situate ourselves uniquely within the USG, and as we consider KSU as a model for embracing best practice trends in the field. **For now, these assignment types continue to be in-place for AY 2022-2023.**

Guiding Principles for Use of These Assignments in the Classroom

1. We will have a genre/type-based assignment sequence in FYC going forward so that our students, faculty, and other stakeholders can expect consistency of learning as well as local, sustainable, and measurable data that shows student success.
2. We will have a syllabus style/template that gives faculty the freedom to determine percentages for major assignments, the actual assignments they can align to the required types for each gateway course, their texts of choice selected from the current FYC approved list, and scaffolding/pacing of their course.
3. These are major assignment types only; three (3) major assignments per course[1].
4. Low-stakes and scaffolded work, as well as day-to-day lesson plans are left up to individual instructors.
5. Assignments aligned with these types need not be traditional papers (though they very well may be). While writing will be an important component of any major assignment, the final product may take the form of alternative media or be multimodal in accordance with the instructor's course structure and pedagogy.

Brief Overview of Course Assignments

Every section of our FYC courses will align with the relevant major assignment sequences below. More details on each are provided in the following section. Sample assignments and syllabi from colleagues, TILTed resources, and examples of rubrics are located in the FYC D2L portal. **Please note: Effective Summer 2022, the first two assignment types for ENGL 1102 can be assigned in the order below or reverse order, depending on an instructor's pedagogical strategies.**

ENGL 1101
1. Narrative/Reflective Assignment
2. Analysis Assignment
3. Argument Assignment

---

1 This is a minimum number of assignments. Faculty may choose to offer more on their own.

ENGL 1102
1. Research Review/Annotated Bibliography
2. "First Look" Research-based Assignment
3. Research Project

Detailed Overview of Course Structures, Learning Outcomes, and Assignment Descriptions

ENGL 1101
English 1101 Course Description

English 1101 focuses on skills required for effective writing in a variety of contexts, with emphasis on exposition, analysis, and argumentation. Also includes introductory use of a variety of research skills.

English 1101 Course Outcomes

Upon completion of English 1101, students will be able to . . .
1. Practice writing in situations where print and/or electronic texts are used, examining why and how people choose to write using different technologies.
2. Interpret the explicit and implicit arguments of multiple styles of writing from diverse perspectives.
3. Practice the social aspects of the writing process by critiquing your own work and the work of your colleagues.
4. Analyze how style, audience, social context, and purpose shape your writing in electronic and print spaces.
5. Craft diverse types of texts to extend your thinking and writerly voice across styles, audiences, and purposes.

Major Aligned Assignments
1. **Narrative/Reflective Assignment:** a narrative assignment asks students to write through a *story* or a *history* (or both). This could take the form of a reflection. Chronology is a synonym here as well. Sample assignments include but are not limited to:
    a. Personal narrative
    b. Collage/multi-genre narrative

c. Literacy narrative/digital literacy narrative
   d. "This I Believe" assignment
   e. Transition narrative (into college or another important transition)
   f. Family history
   g. History of a profession or work narrative
   h. Reflective portfolio cover letter
2. **Analysis Assignment:** an analysis assignment asks students to break some object of study into its component parts and examine those parts carefully to come to a better understanding of the whole. Sample assignments include but are not limited to:
   a. Rhetorical analysis
   b. Genre analysis/comparative genre analysis
   c. Audience analysis/kairotic analysis/rhetorical situation analysis
   d. Stakeholder analysis
   e. Text in context analysis
   f. Pattern + interpretation
   g. Conceptual lens/interpretive lens analysis
3. **Argument Assignment:** an argument assignment includes persuasion as an explicit goal. Persuasion can be broadly conceived; this assignment need not involve taking a stand on a controversial issue (though it may). Sample assignments include but are not limited to:
   a. Persuasive assignment
   b. A specific argument method: Rogerian, Toulmin, etc
   c. Causal argument
   d. Definition argument
   e. Op-ed (or another "public" argumentative genre)
   f. Joining the conversation or they say/I say essay

ENGL 1102
English 1102 Course Description

English 1102 focuses on developing writing skills beyond the levels of proficiency required by ENGL 1101. Emphasizes interpretation and evaluation and advanced research methods.

English 1102 Course Outcomes

Upon completion of English 1102, students will be able to . . .
1. Locate print and digital sources that represent multiple perspectives.
2. Analyze sources by critically reading, annotating, engaging, comparing, and drawing implications.
3. Practice working through the writing process, including brainstorming, drafting, peer review, revision, and publication.
4. Compose a rhetorically-situated, researched text that enters an ongoing conversation, integrating relevant sources.

Major Aligned Assignments[2]

1. **Research Review:** in this assignment type, students present key insights gathered from the research they have been conducting as they work towards developing their research project's thesis. In producing a research review, students use databases and other university (and other) resources to find research materials; assess the quality of that research in relation to a larger, ongoing research project; and demonstrate appropriate academic documentation style. Sample assignments include but are not limited to:
    a. Literature Review
    b. Annotated Bibliography
    c. Journal of notes/ note cards (submitted for review)
2. **"First Look" Research-based Assignment:** students present their projects' topic, preliminary research, tentative thesis and/or potential argumentative points at an intermediate stage of the research-project process for feedback from peers and/or the instructor. Sample assignments include but are not limited to:
    a. Outline
    b. Précis
    c. Proposal
    d. Rough Draft (submitted for a grade)
3. **Research Project:** the research project represents the culmination of the recursive practices of the course. Students will present a

---

2 Please note: ENGL 1102 is not a literature-based course. We do not teach literary research in this course. Also note: effective Summer 2022, assignments 1 and 2 may be taught in reverse order.

polished product of their work that illustrates the development of the project from the aforementioned stages. Consequently, the project should include a properly-documented, carefully-developed argument that makes use of research. Sample assignments include but are not limited to:

a. Research Paper
b. Researched Essay
c. Multimedia Project
d. "Ted Talk"

7

Breaking the Textbook Barrier: Autoethnographic Reflections on Open Educational Resources and Equity in Higher Education

Daniel J. Bartholomay, Texas A&M University – Corpus Christi
Bailey Otter, Texas A&M University – Corpus Christi

Abstract

This paper critically examines the escalating expenses of textbooks, which pose a formidable barrier to education for low-income students. In response, the study explores the potential of open educational resources (OER) as a remedy for achieving educational equity. Employing autoethnography and drawing from the sociological lens of conflict theory, the authors reveal how and why the use of OER and zero-cost course materials are beneficial for both college students and professors. The paper underscores the urgent need to address rising textbook costs by advocating for the adoption of OER, which could substantially enhance access and success rates for low-income students. Incorporating in-depth, reflective accounts from a professor and a student with first-hand experience with OER, the study argues for widespread implementation of OER in higher education, illuminating their role in promoting social justice and diminishing inequalities within the system. The paper concludes by suggesting how colleges and universities may support the implementation of OER as an accessible, zero-cost alternative to traditional textbooks, thus advancing inclusivity and equity in higher education.

Keywords: open educational resources, OER, textbook, justice, equity, education

Suggested citation: Bartholomay, D. J., & Otter, B. (2024). Breaking the textbook barrier: Autoethnographic reflections on open educational resources and equity in higher education. In T. Tijerina (Ed.), *Pedagogy opened: Innovative theory and practice* (pp. 184-205). University of North Georgia Press. https://alg.manifoldapp.org/read/pedagogy-opened-v1-a7/.

The increasing cost of college tuition is a widely acknowledged issue in the United States, however, the surging costs of textbooks is a topic that has garnered attention only in recent years. According to the U.S. Bureau of Labor Statistics (2023), textbook costs have risen by 148% since 2001, more than doubling the rate of inflation of 65%. In addition to being financially burdensome, high textbook costs have been found to negatively affect students' academic performance, delay degree completion, and worsen mental health (Appedu et al., 2021; Jenkins et al., 2020). Textbook-related challenges are further exacerbated for low-income and Pell-eligible students, who are disproportionately students of color (Wimberly et al., 2020). As a result, the issue of textbook costs can be presented as a social problem that perpetuates systemic economic and racial disparities, creating obstacles that impede marginalized communities' access to education.

Social justice within educational settings demands the equitable distribution of learning materials to all students (Jenkins et al., 2020). This includes replacing textbooks with zero-cost course materials, including open educational resources (OER). OER refer to educational, research, and teaching materials that are available in any format and medium and are either in the public domain or subject to copyright but released under an open license. This license enables others to access, adapt, reuse, repurpose, and redistribute these materials at no cost (UNESCO, 2023).

Although an expanding body of research presents convincing empirical evidence of the benefits of OER, we believe that the literature on OER is lacking in-depth, thickly descriptive holistic accounts on how and why OER benefit both students and professors as people. We collaboratively write this persuasive, autoethnographic essay as a professor (Daniel) and a student (Bailey) who have both professional and personal connections to OER. Aware of their positive educational outcomes for low-income students, Daniel has exclusively used zero-cost course materials and OER in his college courses since 2017. In addition to eliminating financial barriers to education for his students, Daniel has also encountered unforeseen pedagogical advantages stemming directly from incorporating OER into his courses. Bailey was first introduced to OER when she took Daniel's Introduction to Sociology course in 2022. As a low-income, first-generation college student, the financial savings Bailey experienced from courses that used OER significantly affected her quality of life. Applying the sociological perspective of conflict theory, we share our stories in this paper to argue that OER should be more widely adopted in colleges and universities to address power imbalances in higher education that disproportionately disadvantage low-income, working-class students.

Benefits of OER Usage

When used instead of traditional textbooks, OER offer various advantages to students. The most prominent of these is that OER are a zero-cost alternative. The burden of paying for textbooks and other class materials can have a significant impact on a student's financial well-being, leading to stress, anxiety, and even dropping out of college (Nusbaum et al., 2020). The average college student in the United States spends between $600 and $1,200 on textbooks and supplies per year, but expenses differ depending on various factors (Florida Virtual Campus, 2022; Gallant, 2022; Senack, 2014). High textbook costs can lead to students not purchasing required textbooks, avoiding courses with high material costs, getting poor grades, and withdrawing from courses (Florida Virtual Campus, 2022). The use of OER has the potential to address these issues and make higher education more affordable and accessible for all students. According to a study conducted at the University of Georgia, students have saved over $8.2 million since the inception of their OER initiative in 2013, which has resulted in increased retention and completion rates, particularly for Pell-eligible students (Colvard, Watson, & Park, 2018).

One of the primary benefits of OER is their potential to enhance universal access to educational resources. Contributing to Universal Design for Learning (Reale, et al., 2022), OER make educational materials freely accessible online, eliminating financial barriers to education and granting opportunities for learners who may not have otherwise accessed traditional educational resources. This can have a particularly significant effect on marginalized communities, such as low-income students and those from underrepresented backgrounds. OER also offer learners opportunities to interact with a broader range of viewpoints and ideas, supporting diversity and inclusivity in higher education. Furthermore, OER can be a tool for empowerment and self-determination for marginalized students, providing them with the tools to create their own learning experiences, explore their own interests, and gain the skills and knowledge necessary to succeed both within and outside of their academic journey.

In this regard, OER can foster students' intrinsic motivations to learn. Guay et al. (2008) found that students who are intrinsically motivated have higher levels of engagement, better academic performance, and a greater sense of purpose in their learning. Providing a pathway for them to find intrinsic motivation through OER will make marginalized students more likely to stay in school, complete their degree, and succeed in their careers (Ladson-Billings, 2006; Warschauer & Matuchniak, 2010). Furthermore, intrinsic motivation can provide a sense of personal fulfillment that can lead to greater levels of social and economic mobility (Cerasoli et al., 2014). Finally, OER are consistently regarded positively by both faculty and students, who assess them as either equivalent to or superior to traditional textbooks (Fischer et al., 2015; Hilton, 2016; Jhangiani et al., 2018). For these reasons, we contend that OER hold the promise to inspire deeper student learning and academic success, disrupt the poverty cycle, and open up avenues for improved social and economic prospects among underprivileged student groups.

OER and Conflict Theory

Originating from the ideas of Karl Marx (1849/1902), conflict theory serves as a sociological framework for comprehending social inequalities and power imbalances among different groups in society. According to this perspective, addressing most inequalities requires a fairer distribution of scarce resources among all groups, ensuring that people, regardless of their class, race, gender, or other identities, have the necessary means to participate as productive members of society.

From the conflict theory standpoint, OER can act as a tool for social change by redistributing educational resources in a manner that makes educational achievement equally accessible to everyone, not just those with high socio-economic status. By replacing cost-prohibitive educational materials, OER has the potential to promote equity in higher education, thereby creating a more balanced and just learning environment. This redistribution of educational resources provide a way to resist existing power structures within higher education and challenge the privileges enjoyed by those benefiting from the current structuring of education.

This equitable distribution of educational materials leads to increased completion rates of college, which creates opportunities for those who might not otherwise have them. Additionally, a rising number of students in higher education are in or near poverty. The percentage of dependent undergraduate students in or near poverty increased from 12% in 1996 to 20% in 2016, while the percentage of independent undergraduate students in or near poverty increased from 29% to 42% during the same timeframe (Fry & Cilluffo, 2019). The same study found that the amount of nonwhite undergraduate students has increased from 29% in 1996 to 47% in 2016. This demonstrates that higher education is no longer an institution dominated by wealthy white men and there is a need for change within the landscape of educational resources to reflect this shift. To adapt to the changing needs of students in higher education, institutions should make a concerted effort to integrate OER into the classroom setting. The emergence of marginalized groups in higher education has amplified the demand for low-cost or no-cost learning materials, a need that OER can meet. By embracing OER, higher education institutions can actively promote social justice and advance diversity, equity, and inclusion initiatives.

Methodology

We have opted to utilize autoethnography to detail our own experiences surrounding OER. Autoethnography is a research approach that allows authors to recount their personal experiences as a way of understanding greater cultural experiences (Ellis et al., 2011). Autoethnography allows the authors of a paper to become the subject of their own research, a unique and valuable dimension that distinguishes this method from other qualitative approaches (Belbase et al., 2008). While subjectivity is often critiqued in scholarship, the unfiltered reflexivity provided through autoethnographic research provides thickly descriptive data that can be lost when data is collected and analyzed at the aggregate level. We agree that the authenticity and situated way of knowing inherent in autoethnographic work make this method transformative (Custer, 2014).

By applying autoethnography to sociology, this writing style encourages a comprehensive utilization of C. Wright Mills' (1959) concept of the sociological imagination, which examines the interplay between individual experiences and societal structures. In essence, the sociological imagination explores how individuals and society mutually influence each other. When they use autoethnographic approaches in their work, authors are prompted to deeply examine how their personal experiences and seemingly individual choices are both influenced and constrained by larger social forces.

Consider instructors who wish to adopt OER for their courses. Their choices are inevitably shaped by cultural and institutional factors. Some universities might mandate all instructors teaching the same course to use the same textbook. Additionally, instructors with heavier teaching loads might prefer digital textbooks with auto-graded assignments to ease their workload. Others might select a textbook authored by a colleague to promote a healthy work environment.

Similarly, the decisions made by students regarding how, where, and when to purchase textbooks are influenced by various external factors. While used and discounted textbook options might be available online, for example, students purchasing books with financial aid may be required to buy them at full price from campus bookstores. In summary, using autoethnography within sociology helps illuminate the intricate interplay between personal experiences and larger social contexts. It allows for a deeper understanding of how both instructors and students are influenced by broader societal structures when it comes to textbook choices in academia.

Applying a sociological imagination within a conflict theory framework, we both individually wrote a detailed reflection regarding our extensive experiences using OER. Daniel's viewpoint is primarily shaped by the literature surrounding the benefits of OER and his experience as a professor utilizing OER methods, whereas Bailey's knowledge of OER was primarily shaped by her experiences as a student within classrooms that both use and do not use OER. Both perspectives offer unique and vital viewpoints to the discussion surrounding OER usage within higher education, as instructors considering the implementation of OER should know what the process of utilizing OER entails for them, along with how OER have an impact on the lived experiences of the students they are teaching.

Though autoethnography is a somewhat contentious approach to research, there are many benefits to autoethnographic methods. By completing a detailed reflection of their own experiences, authors of ethnographic research allow for their audience to gain an extremely in-depth and personal understanding of the subject, therefore conveying research in a perspective centered around the human experience, which is not able to be achieved through other methods. Autoethnography also encourages authors to be emotionally invested and influential within research, rather than encouraging them to hide from their personal beliefs (Ellis et al., 2011).

However, due to the limited scope of experiences autoethnographic inquiry allows, we encourage future researchers addressing the topics of OER to complete larger-scale interview projects including a diverse demographic of students throughout multiple institutions. We also encourage researchers to focus on differential perspectives of faculty members on OER across disciplines. Additionally, since research surrounding OER usage is relatively new, longitudinal studies surrounding the implementation of OER and its effects on students and faculty members would provide a unique viewpoint.

A Professor's Perspective on OER

Daniel, who was a first-generation college student and worked 20 to 40 hours per week during his college years, recalls the stress he experienced at the start of every new semester when shopping for textbooks. Rarely able to afford new copies of texts from the university bookstore, Daniel would search the internet for used books, older editions, or rental options. Even with options at reduced costs, Daniel would often have to pick up extra shifts bartending and waiting tables to be able to afford this additional college expense at the start of every new term.

When he began teaching his own courses as a graduate student in 2015, Daniel found it problematic to ask his students to pay upwards of $100 for a book that some of them would not even open. He knew firsthand how the hundreds of dollars students spent on textbooks every semester added up and negatively affected their abilities to make it through college. However, as a new instructor of record, Daniel did not know what other choice he had. Textbook publishers' sales representatives would visit Daniel's office and present him with supposedly "affordable" options, such as digital "inclusive access" textbook models. Nevertheless, Daniel discovered (and still perceives) "inclusive access"—also known as automatic textbook billing—as a predatory tactic, since students are charged automatically (and often without their realizing it) for the slightly discounted materials unless they actively opt out.

With no alternative in sight, Daniel did what many new instructors do and adopted the same textbook that his former professor used for the course. Daniel assured himself that if his senior colleagues had used the text, it was surely an acceptable choice. While well written and informative, a new copy of the text cost $80. Daniel knew his students could find more affordable used and rental options online; however, the university Daniel was at had a policy that instructors were only allowed to direct students to the university bookstore for their course materials. Working in the precarious position of a graduate student instructor, Daniel did not want to risk his job, even though he knew his students could easily save $50 or more by purchasing the book's previous edition online, which barely differed from the more expensive newest edition.

It did not take long for students to express their grievances regarding the price of the textbook. Daniel immediately felt guilty. As a graduate student himself, he knew the frustrations and hardship of paying hundreds of dollars a semester on course materials. He was situated in a position of power as an instructor of record with the autonomy to choose a more affordable option, but he had failed to do so. He did not intend to adopt an expensive text for his first course, but with limited time and resources of his own to spend reviewing alternative textbook options, what was he to do? The irony of the situation was not lost upon him—he was a sociologist specializing in the study of inequalities while simultaneously contributing to inequalities in education.

To relieve the financial burden he imposed upon his students, Daniel took various measures to assist students in obtaining the required textbook. He guaranteed that the library had a copy accessible for check out, and he even lent his personal copy to a student who couldn't afford to purchase one. Daniel observed that individuals from underrepresented communities were the least likely to buy the book, and some students expressed apprehension about their academic performance due to their inability to purchase the text. The educational barriers resulting from high textbook costs concerned Daniel, so he was determined to take action to address this issue.

Over the next few semesters as graduate student instructor, Daniel carved out pockets of time for researching more affordable textbook options, resulting in his discovery of OER. He has exclusively used OER and supplemental zero-cost course materials since 2017. The switch to zero-cost course materials has benefited Daniel's students in many ways, particularly now that he works at a Hispanic Serving Institution. Many of his students come from low-income backgrounds and would not be able to afford expensive textbooks. Daniel thinks using OER is a tool of redistributive justice in education that levels the playing field and ensures that all of his students have access to the same educational resources, regardless of their financial circumstances.

Daniel has identified several pedagogical advantages of using OER. One significant benefit is that OER are readily available to all his students from the very beginning of the semester, eliminating any instructional time lost while waiting for students to obtain their textbooks. Additionally, he no longer needs to constantly monitor the bookstore's stock levels or grapple with the ethical implications of scanning copyrighted material for his course website. The hassle of handling emails from students experiencing difficulties or delays in getting the required text is also a thing of the past. By adopting OER, Daniel can redirect all the time he saves toward his students and their learning.

Daniel has also found that OER are often more up-to-date and relevant than traditional textbooks. OER are created by experts in the field who are passionate about sharing their knowledge with others, and they are often updated and improved as new research and ideas emerge. Daniel also finds that OER tend to do a better job than most traditional textbooks in providing representation for underserved communities. When seeing themselves and their experiences represented in their education reminds students that they belong and inspires them to move forward.

The equity and diversity promoted through OER inspired Daniel to further explore ways to foster inclusivity in his classroom. Since students were not purchasing course materials, Daniel felt more freedom to collaborate with his students to discuss how each course would be designed and what content would be covered. In some of his courses, Daniel asks students to help create the syllabus. During the first week of class, Daniel and his students collaboratively discuss the topics they would like to cover, how they would like to utilize their class time, and what kinds of assignments they would like to complete. After these discussions, Daniel finds and assigns OER and other zero-cost materials that address the course topics and learning outcomes that were agreed upon.

Adopting OER proved to be a catalyst for Daniel to embrace this collaborative and student-centered pedagogical approach. Without the constraints of a rigid chapter-by-chapter structure found in traditional textbooks, Daniel felt more empowered to meet his students at their individual learning levels and address their specific academic needs. This cooperative approach led to an increased level of student engagement and investment in the course, as they actively participated in choosing the materials they wanted to study and co-piloted the direction of the class. The positive feedback received from student evaluations further supports the success of this collaborative teaching approach in the courses designed together with the students:

> I like the fact that the coursework was almost entirely student dependent. There was little lecturing, but rather, mostly group discussions around what was presented to us. It made for a more active and engaging learning environment, and one where I, as someone with ADHD, could more easily learn compared to just sitting and listening to a lecture for an hour where I will easily get distracted and lose focus.

> There is no one who fosters a better learning environment than you! Our class was a safe space to discuss difficult sociological issues despite the

many different backgrounds without hostility. That's not an easy thing to accomplish given the subject matter of our class. It is so refreshing to have a professor that cares as much as you do. You care not only about our education but about us as students. Seeing how people's worldviews changed was awe inspiring.

In sum, Daniel feels his decision to switch to zero-cost course materials, including OER, has been a game-changer for his students. From Fall 2019 to Spring 2023, Daniel has taught 1,189 students at his current university. Using the estimate that materials for any given course cost students, on average, $100 (Gallant 2022), Daniel's students have saved roughly $118,900. By eliminating the textbook cost barrier to education and by subsequently promoting further inclusive pedagogical practices, he is helping to ensure that all his students have an equal opportunity to succeed, which in turn combats inequality and promotes a more just and equitable society.

A Student's Perspective on OER

As a queer, first-generation, and low-income student, taking classes with professors who utilize OER has alleviated much of the stress from Bailey's college experience. During her first two semesters of college, Bailey was working 30 hours a week and taking 19 credits a semester. All the money she earned went either to groceries or into her educational pursuits. Despite being on a Pell Grant, Bailey had to spend around $400 each semester for textbooks or digital learning material for her courses. With her minimum wage job paying only $7.25 an hour, nearly 100 hours of her work each school year went towards obtaining course material that was essential to pass her classes. That was 100 hours of pay that could have gone to groceries, healthcare, or transportation, among other things to enrich her quality of life. Instead, Bailey resorted to a grocery list filled with cheap and processed foods, never thought about going to the doctor when she was sick and used the remainder of her paychecks to get transportation to and from her place of employment.

However, the past year of her educational journey has been vastly different. Since enrolling in her sociology classes, most of Bailey's professors have primarily utilized OER with the occasional use of low-cost textbooks. Bailey has seen a significant increase in her quality of life and in her motivation and passion to learn. This academic year, Bailey has saved roughly $800 on learning materials. These savings have allowed her to purchase fresh food rather than frozen items and access her needed healthcare and medicine. Additionally, Bailey was able to get a job that was less demanding so that she could invest her time into research, an essential aspect of getting into graduate schools.

Furthermore, Bailey has found that, when professors utilize OER, the material is more likely to be relevant to the coursework, resulting in greater student engagement with the material. Rather than professors giving generic textbook readings that somewhat correlate to the class material, when instructors utilize OER, they can choose from a wide variety of material that connects to and enriches the material being covered in class. Bailey has noticed a dramatic change in class participation within courses that utilize OER versus those who are centered around traditional textbook readings. She and her peers connect on a deeper level to the diverse range of biographies being told through OER rather than simply reviewing generic material that comes from often-dated textbook readings. She recalls many times when her peers would state that it was the first time they felt seen within courses or that they were able to understand fully what was being taught.

Additionally, like many other college students, Bailey came from an extremely small town, filled with conservative and limited views that severely limited her scope of the world. Within her Introduction to Sociology course—the first time she was introduced to OER in college—she was able to see a diverse range of stories being represented that allowed her to critically examine different narratives than the few she was exposed to in her small town. Through the implementation of OER within her Sociology of Sexuality course, she learned about the rich history of the LGBTQ+ community. As a result, she was able to feel more connected to and at peace with her place in the community.

However, Bailey recognizes that her positive experience with OER is also affected by her privilege as a white person with easy access to technology. Being a student at a Hispanic Serving Institution (HSI) made up of 57.37% students of color (Levitz, 2018), Bailey has been in classes with many individuals who did not have access to the internet or personal computers. This created complications with their usage of OER, and some of Bailey's peers voiced anxiety regarding their performance in the courses. However, instructors discussed these issues with students and started to bring several physical copies of the OER to every class for students to take home if needed.

Overall, Bailey finds herself more empowered and excited to learn in classes that utilize OER. OER alleviate the stress of affording textbooks, are more tailored to classes, are more user-friendly for people with learning disabilities, and create opportunities for representation for marginalized students. Bailey strongly encourages educators to consider switching to OER rather than continuing to use traditional textbooks, as OER are powerful tools for students with marginalized identities. Through OER, Bailey has found herself consistently succeeding in a college setting without the additional burden of financial stress. While she recognizes there are challenges for OER usage for some students, Bailey believes that professors will be able to collaborate with students to find solutions to problems that may arise, whereas issues with affording traditional textbooks cannot be solved as easily.

OER Limitations and Considerations for Future Research

OER can be a significant tool in reducing inequities in higher education, yet several barriers may deter instructors and students from adopting, adapting, and accessing OER. One of the biggest limitations relating to justice in higher education is lack of access to technology for underserved populations. It is important to acknowledge that, though they are not forced to be online, OER usage is primarily done through digital mediums. As a result, OER still largely require the use of the internet and technology for their access, an often taken-for-granted privilege within the digital age. It might be difficult for some low-income and marginalized populations to obtain access to OER. As a result, advocacy for greater access to technology and the internet is a crucial step to consider when discussing the implementation of OER. It is also noteworthy that some students may prefer traditional hardcopy textbooks to digital OER. In fact, a recent survey found that over 80% of students wanted to have the option to purchase print versions of their textbooks at a reduced cost (Florida Virtual Campus, 2022).

OER have emerged as a promising solution to reduce the financial burden on students and promote equity in education (Bartholomay, 2022). However, it is important to recognize that the adoption, adaptation, and creation of OER can be a time-consuming and labor-intensive process for faculty (Epley Sanders et al., 2022). Faculty members who opt to use OER may require additional training on pedagogical techniques and technology, as well as specialized instruction on the various types of copyrights and licensing restrictions that determine how OER can be used and adapted (Jhangiani et al., 2016; Lantrip & Ray 2021). OER can have specific requirements, such as attribution or the ability to modify and adapt the content. Understanding the intricacies of OER licensing typically involves instruction from librarians or open education experts. Unfortunately, the responsibility of seeking out these training and informational resources often falls on individual faculty members since institutional support for OER is not universally available (Belikov & Bodily, 2016).

Few universities have established clear guidelines for how OER adoption and creation can contribute to faculty promotion and tenure (but see the [model](https://www.doers3.org/tenure-and-promotion.html)) proposed by the Driving OER Sustainability for Student Success [DOERS3] collaborative). Failing to provide clear procedures on how the adoption, adaptation, and creation of OER will contribute to faculty promotion and tenure can discourage faculty from pursuing this work. Further, faculty who persist in utilizing and creating OER at institutions with unclear promotion and tenure policies may not receive adequate credit for their labor. While instructors who choose to use OER may be helping their students save money and promoting equity for marginalized students, they may also be sacrificing valuable time and effort that could be dedicated to other activities, such as research and scholarship, which are more explicitly linked to promotion and tenure. Therefore, it is essential that universities recognize the time and labor costs associated with OER adoption and creation and provide adequate support and incentives for faculty who choose to engage in these activities.

For example, the library at Daniel's university has a strong commitment to supporting professional development for faculty who are interested in using OER. The library secured funding and created a stipend program to compensate faculty for engaging with OER. The program accepted applications from faculty with varied levels of experience with OER, from beginners to experts. Faculty admitted into the program had a variety of projects they could choose from to engage with OER, from reviewing an OER in the instructor's field, to adopting an OER for their course, to adapting a preexisting OER, to creating their own OER. The stipends faculty received varied in size to reflect the amount of time and effort each project required. At the end of the academic year, the program participants were invited to an OER showcase wherein several participants shared the OER projects they completed throughout the year. Providing paid professional development opportunities such as these underscores the value of OER in the culture of higher education. We encourage OER advocates at colleges and universities to pursue internal and external funding opportunities to develop similar programming.

Conclusion

Justice-based solutions are imperative to enrich the experience of students and, overall, contribute to the evolution of higher education. Institutions of higher education should make every effort to expand their usage of OER to alleviate financial stress from their students, create a more robust learning environment, and level the playing field of higher education. The potential for OER to aid and encourage marginalized student communities to pursue paths of higher education without added financial stress is extremely powerful within our society, as education is a direct pathway to an improved socioeconomic status. Additionally, we encourage future researchers to expand the limited discourse surrounding OER as tools for educational justice.

Empirical data is critical in highlighting the challenges that students face and the benefits that OER can provide, but it is important not to lose sight of the human impact of these issues. Conflict theory posits that resources must be distributed more equitably to combat inequality. In the case of higher education, adopting and promoting the use of OER can be seen as an act of social justice, promoting education as a right for all, rather than a privilege for those who can afford it. While they may need to sacrifice their own time and energy to adapt, adopt, or create OER for their courses, professors should keep in mind the impact OER can have on their students. By sharing our personal stories as a professor and a college student who have experienced the transformative effects of OER, we hope to inspire other educators to follow suit. By doing so, they can reduce the financial burden on students and contribute to a more equitable and inclusive learning environment for everyone.

References

Appedu, S., Elmquist, M., Wertzberger, J., & Birch, S. (2021). Inequitable impacts of textbook costs at a small, private college: Results from a textbook survey at Gettysburg College. *Open Praxis, 13*(1), 69–87. https://doi.org/10.5944/openpraxis.13.1.1147

Bartholomay, D. J. (2022). A time to adapt, not "return to normal": Lessons in compassion and accessibility from teaching during COVID-19. *Teaching Sociology, 50*(1), 62–72. https://doi.org/10.1177/0092055X211053376

Ma, J., Baum, S., Pender, M., & Libassi, C. J. (2019). Trends in college pricing 2019. *College Board.* https://research.collegeboard.org/media/pdf/trends-college-pricing-2019-full-report.pdf

Belikov, O. M., & Bodily, R. (2016). Incentives and barriers to OER adoption: A qualitative analysis of faculty perceptions. *Open Praxis, 8*(3), 235–246. https://doi.org/10.5944/openpraxis.8.3.308

Caswell, T., Henson, S., Jensen, M., & Wiley, D. (2008). Open educational resources: Enabling universal education. *International Review of Research in Open and Distributed Learning, 9*(1), 1–11. https://files.eric.ed.gov/fulltext/ED500517.pdf

Cerasoli, C. P., Nicklin, J. M., & Ford, M. T. (2014). Intrinsic motivation and extrinsic incentives jointly predict performance: A 40-year meta-analysis. *Psychological bulletin, 140*(4), 980–1008. https://psycnet.apa.org/doi/10.1037/a0035661

Collins, R. (1971). Functional and conflict theories of educational stratification. *American Sociological Review, 36*(6), 1002–1019. https://

doi.org/10.2307/2093761

Colvard, N. B., Watson, C. E., & Park, H. (2018). The impact of open educational resources on various student success metrics. *International Journal of Teaching and Learning in Higher Education*, *30*(2), 262–276. https://files.eric.ed.gov/fulltext/EJ1184998.pdf

Custer, D. (2014). Autoethnography as a transformative research method. *The Qualitative Report*, *19*(37), 1–13. https://doi.org/10.46743/2160-3715/2014.1011

D'Antoni, S. (2009). Open Educational Resources: the way forward. *UNESCO*. https://unesdoc.unesco.org/ark:/48223/pf0000157987

D'Antoni, S. (2009). Open educational resources: Reviewing initiatives and issues. *Open Learning: The Journal of Open, Distance and e-Learning*, *24*(1), 3–10. https://doi.org/10.1080/02680510802625443

Ellis, C., Adams, T. E., & Bochner, A. P. (2011). Autoethnography: An overview. *Historical Social Research/Historische Sozialforschung*, *36*(4), 273–290. https://www.jstor.org/stable/23032294

Epley Sanders, J., Zoccolillo, A., Bartholomay, D., & Marquez, A. (2022). An interdisciplinary case study of cost concerns and practicalities for open educational resources at a Hispanic-serving institution in Texas. *Journal of Interactive Technology and Pedagogy*, *21*. https://cuny.manifoldapp.org/read/an-interdisciplinary-case-study-of-cost-concerns-and-practicalities-for-open-educational-resources-at-a-hispanic-serving-institution-in-texas/section/cc074226-c6bb-4107-93ac-3cfb27cb69bf

Fischer, L., Hilton, J., Robinson, T. J., & Wiley, D. A. (2015). A multi-institutional study of the impact of open textbook adoption on the learning outcomes of post-secondary students. *Journal of Computing in Higher Education*, *27*, 159–172. https://doi.org/10.1007/s12528-015-9101-x

Florida Virtual Campus. (2022). *Student textbook and instructional materials survey: Results and findings*. https://assets.website-files.com/646e59f2d76c6e8c0c5223de/64de6132148ed7739bc186e4_FLVC%20Textbook%20Survey%20Report%20-%202022.pdf

Friesen, N. (2009). Open educational resources: New possibilities for change and sustainability. *International Review of Research in Open and Distributed Learning*, *10*(5). https://doi.org/10.19173/irrodl.

v10i5.664.

Fry, R., & Cilluffo, A. (2019). A rising share of undergraduates are from poor families, especially at less selective colleges. *Pew Research Center.* Retrieved from https://www.pewresearch.org/social-trends/2019/05/22/a-rising-share-of-undergraduates-are-from-poor-families-especially-at-less-selective-colleges/

Gallant, J. (2022). Calculating and reporting student savings. In A.K. Elder, S. Buck, J. Gallant, M. Seiferle-Valencia, & A. Ashok (Eds.), *The OER Starter Kit for Program Managers* (pp. 292–297). Rebus Community. https://press.rebus.community/oerstarterkitpm/chapter/chapter-22-calculating-and-reporting-student-savings-2/

Guay, F., Ratelle, C. F., & Chanal, J. (2008). Optimal learning in optimal contexts: The role of self-determination in education. *Canadian Psychology/Psychologie canadienne, 49*(3), 233. https://doi.org/10.1037/a0012758

Hilton, J. (2016). Open educational resources and college textbook choices: A review of research on efficacy and perceptions. *Educational Technology Research and Development, 64,* 573–590. https://doi.org/10.1007/s11423-016-9434-9

Hylén, J. (2020). Open educational resources: Opportunities and challenges. Retrieved from https://www.oecd.org/education/ceri/37351085.pdf

Jenkins, J. J., Sánchez, L. A., Schraedley, M. A., Hannans, J., Navick, N., & Young, J. (2020). Textbook broke: Textbook affordability as a social justice issue. *Journal of Interactive Media in Education, 1*(3), 1–13. https://doi.org/10.5334/jime.549

Jhangiani, R. S., Dastur, F. N., Le Grand, R., & Penner, K. (2018). As good or better than commercial textbooks: Students' perceptions and outcomes from using open digital and open print textbooks. *Canadian Journal for the Scholarship of Teaching and Learning, 9*(1). https://doi.org/10.5206/cjsotl-rcacea.2018.1.5

Ladson-Billings, G. (2006). From the achievement gap to the education debt: Understanding achievement in US schools. *Educational Researcher, 35*(7), 3–12. https://www.jstor.org/stable/3876731

Lantrip, J., & Ray, J. (2021). Faculty perceptions and usage of OER at Oregon Community Colleges. *Community College Journal of Research* and *Practice*, *45*(12), 896–910. https://doi.org/10.1080/10668926.2020.1838967

Levitz, R. N. (2018). Student satisfaction inventory. *Texas A&M University-Corpus Christi*. Retrieved from https://www.tamucc.edu/president/assets/documents/noel-levitz-student-satisfaction-report-2018.pdf

Marx, K. (1902). *Wage-labor and capital*. (L. Sanial, Ed. & H. E. Lothrop, Trans.). New York Labor News Company. (Original work published 1849)

Mills, C. W. (1959). *The sociological imagination*. Oxford University Press.

Nusbaum, A. T., Cuttler, C., & Swindell, S. (2020, January). Open educational resources as a tool for educational equity: Evidence from an introductory psychology class. In *Frontiers in Education, 4*, Article 152. https://doi.org/10.3389/feduc.2019.00152

Ochieng, V. O., & Gyasi, R. M. (2021). Open educational resources and social justice: Potentials and implications for research productivity in higher educational institutions. *E-Learning and Digital Media*, *18*(2), 105–124. https://doi.org/10.1177/2042753021989467

Richter, T., & McPherson, M. (2012). Open educational resources: Education for the world? *Distance Education*, *33*(2), 201–219. https://doi.org/10.1080/01587919.2012.692068

Reale, J., O'Brien, E., Ceallaigh, T. Ó., & Connolly, C. (2022). A third space: Infusing open educational resources (OER) with Universal Design for Learning (UDL). In L. Daniela (Ed.), *Inclusive Digital Education* (pp. 13–25). Springer International Publishing. https://doi.org/10.1007/978-3-031-14775-3_2

Smith, M. S., & Casserly, C. M. (2006). The promise of open educational resources. *Change: The Magazine of Higher Learning*, *38*(5), 8–17. https://doi.org/10.3200/CHNG.38.5.8-17

Warschauer, M., & Matuchniak, T. (2010). New technology and digital worlds: Analyzing evidence of equity in access, use, and outcomes. *Review of Research in Education*, *34*(1), 179–225. https://doi.org/10.3102/0091732X09349791

Weller, M. (2014). *The battle for open: How openness won and why it doesn't feel like victory*. Ubiquity Press.

Wiley, D., Bliss, T. J., & McEwen, M. (2014). Open educational resources:

A review of the literature. In J. Spector, M. Merrill, J. Elen, & M. Bishop (Eds.), *Handbook of research on educational communications and technology* (pp. 781–789). Springer Publishing. https://doi.org/10.1007/978-1-4614-3185-5_63

Wimberley, L., Cheney, E., & Ding, Y. (2020). Equitable student success via library support for textbooks. *Reference Services Review, 48*(3), 373–383. https://doi.org/10.1108/RSR-03-2020-0024

UNESCO. (2023). *Open Educational Resources.* Retrieved from https://www.unesco.org/en/communication-information/open-solutions/open-educational-resources

U.S. Bureau of Labor Statistics. (2023, March 7). College textbooks in U.S. city average, all urban consumers, not seasonally adjusted. BLS Data Viewer. Retrieved from https://beta.bls.gov/dataViewer/view/timeseries/UR0000SSEA011;jsessionid=E0590C296662931F2303454531D8F0F5

Author Bios
Daniel J. Bartholomay, Texas A&M University – Corpus Christi
    Daniel J. Bartholomay is an Assistant Professor of Sociology and Co-Coordinator of Women's, Gender, and Sexuality Studies at Texas A&M University-Corpus Christi. He received his Ph.D. in Sociology from the University of Wisconsin-Milwaukee. In addition to researching social inequalities and health disparities within the LGBT+ community, Bartholomay also studies pedagogical methods that promote equity and justice in higher education.

Bailey Otter, Texas A&M University – Corpus Christi
    Bailey Otter is an undergraduate Sociology student at Texas A&M University – Corpus Christi. She is a McNair Scholar and member of the 2023 cohort of the American Sociology Association's Honors Program. Bailey's research draws upon the sociologies of gender, health, family, and embodiment to understand how nonbinary individuals navigate and experience a binarily gendered society.

8

Practicing What We Preach: Doing Open Pedagogy in a Book About Open Pedagogy

Tiffani Tijerina, Texas Tech University and Kennesaw State University

In a meeting with the advisory board for this first volume of *Pedagogy Opened: Innovative Theory and Practice*, members of the board suggested working with students to design our cover page. I loved the idea—we all did! So, we turned it into our own open pedagogy project. I knew that my department at Kennesaw State University had an undergraduate major in interactive design, so I reached out to find out who was teaching our visual design course. I was excited to learn that my friend, colleague, and fellow Texas Tech University alumna Dr. Leslie Hankey was teaching the course in the following semester. I reached out to her, she agreed that it was a good opportunity for her students, and we hammered out some details. In this section I want to share how this project worked, followed by a display of all submitted designs for the cover of *Pedagogy Opened: Innovative Theory and Practice*.

Matching Our Needs to the Course Requirements

One of the important things to keep in mind when designing an open pedagogy assignment is that it has to fit the course needs and the course design. So, the first thing Leslie and I did was identify where the project could fit in the course and whether it *was* a good fit. She sent me her second course project, which would normally ask students to design a poster influenced by the Bauhaus school of art and design, which aligned with the content they studied in class during that time. We both agreed that our cover design project was a good fit for this, so she re-designed the assignment so that students were designing our front and back covers instead of a poster. To provide a bit of context on the design style, "[t]he Bauhaus movement championed a geometric, abstract style featuring little sentiment or emotion and no historical nods, and its aesthetic continues to influence architects, designers, and artists" (History, 2018).

Once we identified a good spot for the project in her course, Leslie set me up to present on the project to her classes, where I gave them all of the information they needed on the book and our requirements, which I'll summarize in the following section. A key piece to making these kinds of project work, though, is to separate the assignment and grading aspect from the publication aspect. Leslie gave her students their assignment requirements, and I gave them our project requirements. The two pieces worked together, but I never saw students grades on the assignment, and students were not required to submit their work to us for publication—it was entirely their decision to make, and we did our best to make sure they were able to make a fully informed decision.

Project Requirements, as Given to Students

In this section, I'll provide an outline of the information given to the students about the publication side of this project. All of the following information was provided in a live presentation and in a slideshow given to students for review—they were also offered the opportunity to ask questions and to email me if they needed anything.

About the Book/the Team

Edited collection: seven author teams/seven papers related to open pedagogy

Types of papers:
- Research – research studies with results and discussion
- Practice – practical strategies and applications
- Autoethnography – reflections on personal experience

Team: editor (me), University of North Georgia Press, five advisory board members, seven author teams, and student designers (you!)

Format: free e-book and at-cost print

Definitions

Open Pedagogy – teaching and learning practices and environments that promote equity, collaboration, and innovation and invite students to create and share knowledge with future publics, often in association with the use of open educational resources (OER).

Open Educational Resources – educational materials that are freely available under an open license that allows the user to retain, reuse, revise, remix, and redistribute the work and any derivative works, typically through the use of Creative Commons licensing or the public domain.

Sample Titles from the Work

- "Creating learning spaces for social justice projects: Applying the values of Critical Digital Pedagogy and Open Pedagogy"
- "Open Pedagogy assignments in theatre and history courses to promote constructionist learning and digital skills"
- "Breaking the textbook barrier: Autoethnographic reflections on open educational resources and equity in higher education"

About the Project

You will design a front and back cover for the book, following design standards from Dr. Hankey and your course content.

Design submission: *if you want to be considered for publication,* you will email your design to me (more on that later).

Design selection: the editor (me) and the UNG Press will select one cover for the book. All others submitted for consideration will have *front covers* published within the book on a dedicated series of pages. So, it's a guaranteed publishing opportunity!

Project Requirements
Front and back covers, no spine.

Dimensions: 6" by 9" plus a 0.25" bleed on all sides (each)

Outsourced images must carry a Creative Commons Attribution 4.0 International license (CC BY) *or* exist in the public domain (no copyright). Suggested repository for openly licensed images: unsplash.com

Front covers need title and editor lines:
- Title – *Pedagogy Opened: Innovative Theory and Practice*
- Editor line – Edited by Tiffani Tijerina

Back covers should complement front cover and include the book description:

> Open pedagogy is teaching and learning practices and environments that promote equity, collaboration, and innovation and invite students to create and share knowledge with future publics, often in association with the use of open educational resources (OER).
>
> *Pedagogy Opened: Innovative Theory and Practice* seeks to advance the study of open and innovative pedagogy through the belief that their impact and reach are increased by research on and analysis of the theory and practice of open pedagogy across the disciplines and via multiple modalities.
>
> In this first volume of *Pedagogy Opened*, seven author teams explore and share their work with open pedagogy in a variety of ways, including through research, practice, and autoethnographic reflection.

Copyright for the Project
You are not required to submit your design for consideration, and your instructor will grade your work separately.

If you do choose to submit your design to Pedagogy Opened, by doing so you are also agreeing to a Creative Commons Attribution 4.0 International license, which is explained below.

Submission Guidelines

You are not required to submit your design for consideration/publication. Assignment grading will be done independent of publication submission, by your professor.

To submit for consideration/publication, send your design to pedagogyopened@gmail.com and copy Dr. Hankey. Include the following in your email:
1. Your design exported to .jpg
2. Any fonts used in the design
3. Sources for any images used, including links (even if they are public domain)
4. Your preferred publishing name

Open Licensing

Because we are publishing content about open pedagogy and open educational resources, *Pedagogy Opened* will carry an open license itself.

"Open" licensing means that you keep your copyright ownership, but you are giving up-front permissions for users to use your work openly with attribution to you.

Typically, this means that users can retain (keep copies of the work), reuse (use the work), revise (change the work), remix (combine the work with other open works), and redistribute (publish any derivative works based on your work) as long as the user attributes back to you and your original work.

Creative Commons Attribution 4.0 International

Creative Commons makes open licensing easy.

Pedagogy Opened will carry a Creative Commons Attribution 4.0 International license. This license has no additional restrictions of use beyond basic attribution.

Your designs, if you submit them to us for consideration and publication, will carry the same license, with you retaining your copyright. So if someone comes in and uses your design, they will have to attribute back to you (the designer), your design (the original work), and *Pedagogy Opened* (original publication).

References

History. (2018, August 21). Bauhaus. *The History Channel*. Retrieved December 16, 2023 from https://www.history.com/topics/art-history/bauhaus

Cover Design Submissions

Without further ado, the following are all cover designs submitted to *Pedagogy Opened: Innovative Theory and Practice* for consideration. All students consented to publication of their work and name, and all designs are licensed under a Creative Commons Attribution 4.0 International license.

Practicing What We Preach | 211

Logan B. Cooper

Eileen Dong

Riya George

Madelyn Grimes

Aysha Hardizi

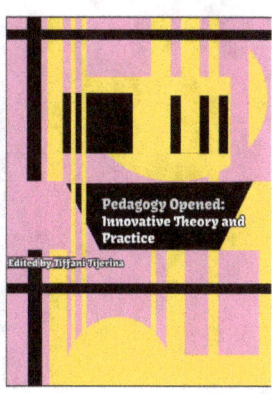
Sha'mari Hightower

Isatou Kijera

Hazel Kim

Savannah Kramer

Katherine Lanham

Hayoung Lee

Mekhyle Lee

Alison Leigh

Elle Nuckolls

Max Ray

Scott Rzasa

Joy Weatherly

Matthew Williams

Reagan Yost

www.ingramcontent.com/pod-product-compliance
Lightning Source LLC
Chambersburg PA
CBHW070803230426
43665CB00017B/2465